T0327698

RESEARCH IN MARITIME HISTORY
NO. 28

NEW DIRECTIONS IN MEDITERRANEAN MARITIME HISTORY

Edited by
Gelina Harlaftis and Carmel Vassallo

International Maritime Economic History Association

St. John's, Newfoundland
2004

ISSN 1188-3928
ISBN 0-9730073-8-9

Research in Maritime History is available free of charge to members of the International Maritime Economic History Association. The price to others is US$15 per copy, plus $3.50 postage and handling.

Back issues of *Research in Maritime History* are available:

No. 1 (1991)   David M. Williams and Andrew P. White (comps.), *A Select Bibliography of British and Irish University Theses about Maritime History, 1792-1990*

No. 2 (1992)   Lewis R. Fischer (ed.), *From Wheel House to Counting House: Essays in Maritime Business History in Honour of Professor Peter Neville Davies*

No. 3 (1992)   Lewis R. Fischer and Walter Minchinton (eds.), *People of the Northern Seas*

No. 4 (1993)   Simon Ville (ed.), *Shipbuilding in the United Kingdom in the Nineteenth Century: A Regional Approach*

No. 5 (1993)   Peter N. Davies (ed.), *The Diary of John Holt*

No. 6 (1994)   Simon P. Ville and David M. Williams (eds.), *Management, Finance and Industrial Relations in Maritime Industries: Essays in International Maritime and Business History*

No. 7 (1994)   Lewis R. Fischer (ed.), *The Market for Seamen in the Age of Sail*

No. 8 (1995)   Gordon Read and Michael Stammers (comps.), *Guide to the Records of Merseyside Maritime Museum, Volume 1*

No. 9 (1995)   Frank Broeze (ed.), *Maritime History at the Crossroads: A Critical Review of Recent Historiography*

No. 10 (1996)   Nancy Redmayne Ross (ed.), *The Diary of a Maritimer, 1816-1901: The Life and Times of Joseph Salter*

No. 11 (1997)   Faye Margaret Kert, *Prize and Prejudice: Privateering and Naval Prize in Atlantic Canada in the War of 1812*

No. 12 (1997)   Malcolm Tull, *A Community Enterprise: The History of the Port of Fremantle, 1897 to 1997*

No. 13 (1997)   Paul C. van Royen, Jaap R. Bruijn and Jan Lucassen, *"Those Emblems of Hell"? European Sailors and the Maritime Labour Market, 1570-1870*

No. 14 (1998)   David J. Starkey and Gelina Harlaftis (eds.), *Global Markets: The Internationalization of The Sea Transport Industries Since 1850*

No. 15 (1998)   Olaf Uwe Janzen (ed.), *Merchant Organization and Maritime Trade in the North Atlantic, 1660-1815*

No. 16 (1999)   Lewis R. Fischer and Adrian Jarvis (eds.), *Harbours and Havens: Essays in Port History in Honour of Gordon Jackson*

No. 17 (1999)   Dawn Littler, *Guide to the Records of Merseyside Maritime Museum, Volume 2*

No. 18 (2000)   Lars U. Scholl (comp.), *Merchants and Mariners: Selected Maritime Writings of David M. Williams*

No. 19 (2000)   Peter N. Davies, *The Trade Makers: Elder Dempster in West Africa, 1852-1972, 1973-1989*

No. 20 (2001)   Anthony B. Dickinson and Chesley W. Sanger, *Norwegian Whaling in Newfoundland: The Aquaforte Station and the Ellefsen Family, 1902-1908*

No. 21 (2001)   Poul Holm, Tim D. Smith and David J. Starkey (eds.), *The Exploited Seas: New Directions for Marine Environmental History*

No. 22 (2002)   Gordon Boyce and Richard Gorski (eds.), *Resources and Infrastructures in the Maritime Economy, 1500-2000*

No. 23 (2002)   Frank Broeze, *The Globalisation of the Oceans: Containerisation from the 1950s to the Present*

No. 24 (2003)   Robin Craig, *British Tramp Shipping, 1750-1914*

No. 25 (2003)   James Reveley, *Registering Interest: Waterfront Labour Relations in New Zealand, 1953 to 2000*

No. 26 (2003)   Adrian Jarvis, *In Troubled Times: The Port of Liverpool, 1905-1938*

No. 27 (2004)   Lars U. Scholl and Merja-Liisa Hinkkanen (comps.), *Sail and Steam: Selected Maritime Writings of Yrjö Kaukiainen*

Research in Maritime History would like to thank Memorial University of Newfoundland for its generous financial assistance in support of this volume.

Table of Contents

ABOUT THE EDITORS

GELINA HARLAFTIS <zeles@otenet.gr> is President of the International Maritime Economic History Association and Associate Professor in the Department of History at the Ionian University in Corfu, Greece. She has published extensively on Greek maritime history in the nineteenth and twentieth centuries, including *History of Greek-owned Shipping* (London, 1996), a book that was honoured with the Runciman Award in 1997. She has taught at universities in Canada and Britain.

CARMEL VASSALLO <carmel.vassallo@um.edu.mt> is Coordinator of the Mediterranean Maritime History Network. He lectures at the Mediterranean Institute of the University of Malta. His recent work includes the editing of a special issue of the *Journal of Mediterranean Studies* (XII, No. 2 [2002]) on "Themes in Maritime History." His research interests centre on the history of trade and trade networks in the Mediterranean, and he is currently preparing a *Directory of Mediterranean Maritime Historians* to facilitate contacts between researchers.

CONTRIBUTORS

MARINA ALFONSO MOLA <malfonso@geo.uned.es> is Professor of Early Modern History at the Universidad Nacional de Educación a Distancia in Madrid, Spain. Her doctoral thesis was awarded Spain's National Sea Award in 1998. Her recent publications on the maritime economy include "The Spanish Colonial Fleet (1492-1828)," in Horst Pietschmann (ed.), *Atlantic History. History of the Atlantic System, 1580-1830* (Göttingen, 2002). She is currently preparing a book on the *Flota Colonial Española durante la época del Libre Comercio (1778-1828)* and has taught at a number of European and American universities.

FLAVIO BONIN <flavio.bonin@pommuz-pi.si> is Director of the Sergej Masera Maritime Museum in Piran, Slovenia. His recent publications include "Proizvodnja soli v piranskih solinah od 16. do druge polovice 18. stoletja" ("Salt Production in Piran's Salt Plants from the Sixteenth Century to the Second Half of the Eighteenth Century"), *Annales*, XI (2001).

JOHN CHIRCOP <john.chircop@um.edu.mt> is a lecturer in social and economic history in the Department of History at the University of Malta. His recent publications include "The Hidden Sea Complex: A Hidden Dimension in Mediterranean Maritime History," in Gordon Boyce and Richard Gorski (eds.), *Resources and Infrastructures in the Maritime Economy, 1500-2000* (St. John's, 2002). His main research interest is the economic history of the central Mediterranean during the nineteenth and early twentieth centuries.

MICHELA D'ANGELO <mdangelo@unime.it> is Professor of History in the Faculty of Political Sciences at the University of Messina. Her research interests centre on English trade and merchants in the Mediterranean, especially Sicily, Malta and Leghorn, in the early modern era. Her recent publications include "In the 'English' Mediterranean (1511-1815)," *Journal of Mediterranean Studies*, XII, No. 2 (2002); and "I Sanderson," in L. Caminiti, M. D'Angelo and L. Hyerace (eds.), *Villa Pace dai Sanderson ai Bosurgi all'Università* (Messina, 2003).

RUTHY GERTWAGEN <ruger@mofet.macam98.ac.il> is a specialist in Medieval and early modern history and underwater archaeology at the University of Haifa and the Tel-Hai Academic College. Her research interests and publications focus on the Venetian maritime empire, naval warfare, maritime trade and Mediterraean ports and ships.

XAVIER LABAT SAINT VINCENT <Xavier.Labat-Saint-Vincent@paris4.sorbonne.fr> is a researcher at the Institut de Recherches sur les Civilisations de l'Occident Moderne at the University of Paris IV-Sorbonne. His research has focussed particularly on Malta, but more generally he is interested in the Mediterranean in the early modern era. He is currently involved in the creation of a database of ship entries in Marseilles in the eighteenth century based on port sanitation records.

CARLOS MARTÍNEZ SHAW <cmshaw@geo.uned.es> is Professor of History at the Universidad Nacional de Educación a Distancia in Madrid, Spain. His recent publications on maritime history include "Bourbon Reformism and Spanish Colonial Trade, 1717-1778," in Horst Pietschmann (ed.), *Atlantic History. History of the Atlantic System, 1580-1830* (Göttingen, 2002). He is currently conducting research on the Real Compañía Marítima de Pesca between 1789 and 1804. He has taught at the Ecole des Hautes Etudes in Paris and at universities in Europe and America.

EYÜP ÖZVEREN <ozveren@metu.edu.tr> is a Professor in the Department of Economics at the Middle East Technical University in Ankara. His research interests include Mediterranean history and the history of economic thought. His most recent publications include "Ottoman Economic Thought and Economic Policy in Transition: Re-Thinking the Nineteenth Century," in M. Psalidopoulos and Maria-Eugenia Almeia Mata (eds.), *Economic Thought and Policy in Less-Developed Europe: The 19th Century* (London, 2002).

GERASSIMOS PAGRATIS <pagratisg@yahoo.com> is a lecturer in Maritime History in the Department of Shipping, Trade and Transport at the University of the Aegean in Greece. His most recent publication is "Greek Commercial Shipping from the Fifteenth to the Seventeenth Century: Literature Review and Research Perspectives," *Journal of Mediterranean Studies*, XII, No. 2 (2002). His current research centres on commerce and shipping in the Ionian during the Napoleonic wars.

M. ELISABETTA TONIZZI <etonizzi@tin.it> is a specialist in Contemporary History in the Department for European Research of the University of Genoa, and she also teaches Contemporary History and the History of Political Parties in the Faculty of Political Science. She has studied the industrial and maritime economy of Genoa in the nineteenth and twentieth centuries, with particular reference to the port, and the links between higher technical education and industrial development, with particular reference to the Higher Institute of Marine Engineering, founded in Genoa in 1870. Her recent publications include *Merci, strutture e lavoro nel porto di Genova tra '800 e '900* (Milano, 2000).

ONUR YILDIRIM <onuryil@metu.edu.tr> is an Assistant Professor in the Department of Economics of the Middle East Technical University in Ankara. His research interests include Ottoman social and economic history and contemporary Turkish-Greek relations. His most recent publications include "Ottoman Guilds as a Setting for Inter-Religious Conflict: The Case of Silk-Thread Spinners' Guild in Istanbul," *International Review of Social History*, XLVII, No. 3 (December 2002).

v

Preface

Mediterranean maritime history has been underrepresented in the publications and congresses of the International Maritime Economic History Association (IMEHA) during the 1990s. In August 2000, during the Third International Congress of Maritime History in Esbjerg, Denmark, and the Nineteenth Congress of Historical Sciences in Oslo, Norway, a number of discussions were held about the need to widen the base of support for the IMEHA in the Mediterranean. An informal meeting attended by Ruthy Gertwagen (Israel), Molly Greene (USA), Gelina Harlaftis (Greece), Ernesto López (Spain), Elisabetta Tonizzi (Italy) and Carmel Vassallo (Malta) agreed to establish a Mediterranean Maritime History Network (MMHN) to promote the objectives of the IMEHA in the region. An action committee was established and a draft document explaining the Network's purpose was circulated; as the months went by the number of people expressing interest in the MMHN increased. It was at that point that the "founders" decided to organize a first meeting. After an abortive attempt to hold it in Tunisia to facilitate attendance by historians from the southern shores of the Mediterranean, Malta was chosen as the site for an initial conference.

The MMHN Malta conference in April 2002, which brought together more than thirty researchers from Britain, France, Germany, Greece, Israel, Italy, Spain, Tunisia and Malta, was particularly useful as a meeting place for researchers from the French- and English-speaking worlds. Indeed, with the benefit of hindsight, it is clear that the meeting turned into an informal, regional pre-conference for the Fourth International Congress of Maritime History, which was held in Corfu in 2004. A special issue of the *Journal of Mediterranean Studies* (XII, No. 2 [2002]) emerged from the Malta conference, containing papers by Alain Blondy, Salvatore Bottari, Sadok Boubaker, Michela D'Angelo, Michel Fonteney, Thomas Freller, Henry Frendo, Ruthy Gertwagen, Simon Mercieca, Gerassimos Pagratis and Daniel Panzac, and the scholars gathered there decided to prepare a Directory of Mediterranean Maritime Historians to facilitate exchanges between scholars.

To a considerable extent, the present volume of *Research in Maritime History* is the culmination of the measures taken after the decision in Esbjerg in 2000 to organize and give more prominence to the Mediterranean and its maritime historians. The selection of articles in this volume has a clear bias towards the early modern period, reflecting both the shadow cast by past grandeur and our range of contacts, but the contemporary era is present in a couple of the papers. There are contributions from Spain, France, Italy, Malta, Slovenia, Greece, Turkey and Israel, and this range should permit some insight into the maritime history being written in these countries to readers who would not ordinarily have access to such material, either because of the language barrier or because of the difficulties of securing non-English publications. Regrettably, efforts to garner contributions from other nations around the Mediterranean in an attempt to be as inclusive as possible were unsuccessful. It is particularly disappointing in this regard not to have been able to secure any contributions from the Arab-speaking countries, despite considerable efforts in this direction. In Corfu this past June, at what was the largest gathering of maritime historians ever held, more than one-third of the papers were from Mediterranean historians. At some stage in the future, we hope to publish another volume of Mediterranean maritime history that will fill in some of the lacunae that are evident in this one.

Our thanks go, first and foremost, to the contributors to this volume. Editing their work has enabled us to understand just how the histories of the various nations which presently face the Mediterranean are interrelated. We would also like to thank Professor Lewis (Skip) Fischer of Memorial University in Canada for his invitation to prepare this latest addition to *Research in Maritime History*.

Maritime History since Braudel

Gelina Harlaftis and Carmel Vassallo

L'histoire maritime est un clé de l'histoire générale.
Jean Meuvret, 1962

Most, or at least much, of Mediterranean history could be said to be maritime history, or the history of the relationship of the many peoples who live on its shores with their ancient sea. Almost sixty years after Fernand Braudel wrote *La Méditerranée*, research on Mediterranean history touches on most of the disciplines he had recourse to in his analysis of *production et circulation* in the sixteenth-century Mediterranean – economics, sociology, politics, geography, demography and technology. But it is perhaps due to the tremendous impact that his unrivalled masterpiece has had on the writing and practice of history that no one has yet attempted to produce such a grand synthesis for the centuries that followed, which while seeking to give a broad overview also provided detailed and incisive insights on production and circulation in the Mediterranean. It may also be that there is never likely to be a single, complete history of "The Mediterranean."[1]

On the eve of the "Age of Exploration," the Mediterranean seemed like the centre of the world to many of its inhabitants, but during the course of the sixteenth, seventeenth and eighteenth centuries it came to be dwarfed by the "discovery" of lands across the infinitely larger Atlantic, Indian and Pacific oceans.[2] During these centuries European powers were absorbed with extending their control over these far-off dominions, and the Mediterranean slipped out of the limelight. But it was destined to recover much of its former prominence and to re-establish itself at the centre of the world's sea routes as a consequence of two major developments – the advent of the industrial revolu-

---

[1]See the review by Cheryl Ward of Peregrine Horden and Nicholas Purcell, *The Corrupting Sea: A Study of Mediterranean History* (Oxford, 2000), *International Journal of Maritime History*, XIII, No. 1 (June 2001), 231.

[2]The focus of this publication is clearly the Mediterranean, but as a quick perusal of the contents will show, it is centred on the northern shore of the sea. In other words, it is essentially a European history. The Eurocentric nature of much of history in general and of Mediterranean maritime history in particular is an important issue, but a discussion of this matter is beyond the scope of this collection.

tion, and the ensuing technological innovations of the steamship and the telegraph, and the opening of the Suez Canal in the nineteenth century. As a consequence of Suez, and the eventual replacement of coal by oil as the principal
source of fuel for ships in the following century, the Mediterranean became
Europe's shortest route to and from the East and to this day remains one of the
busiest sea-lanes in the world.[3]

La Mediterranée may also be held partly responsible for the post-
Second World War birth of maritime history as a sub-discipline of history in
its own right. Braudel's oeuvre stemmed from his concern with the continuous
movement of people, goods and ships across the Mediterranean as he attempted to discover the structure and mechanisms that move the process of
history. His conception of the history of the sea went well beyond the description of great naval battles and swashbuckling pirates, exciting though those
may be. Great naval engagements like Lepanto or the defeat of the Spanish
Armada, or popular heroes like Don Juan of Austria or Sir Francis Drake,
may loom large in national histories, but present-day maritime history does not
deal only with the great, the well known or the successful. Those who currently study the history of the sea tend to focus instead on the millions of
anonymous mariners, port-related workers and entrepreneurs on the high seas
and ashore; countless cargoes ranging from alcohol to zinc but consisting
mainly of food products like grain, salt and fish; exotic and tropical products
like spices, sugar and bananas; raw materials like cotton, coal and iron ore;
and forced and voluntary passengers like slaves, convicts and migrants. It is
the "total history" of the *Annales* School that inspired the emergence of maritime history as a sub-discipline and which stressed an interdisciplinary approach to the past that made history the main axis for a synthesis of all the
social sciences.[4]

The Emergence of Maritime History

Maritime history emerged almost simultaneously in France and England in the
1950s. We can distinguish two periods. The first, during which the French-
speaking world in general and the *Annales* School in particular were pre-
eminent, started in the mid-1950s and continued into the 1970s. During this
period, research conducted almost exclusively by European scholars centred on
the fifteenth to the eighteenth centuries. In the second period, starting in the

---

[3]On a normal day about 2000 vessels of over one hundred tons are sailing in
the Mediterranean. This constitutes about thirty percent of world merchant shipping.
See European Environment Agency, *Community, State and Pressures of the Marine and
Coastal Mediterranean Environment* (Copenhagen, 1999).

[4]Richard J. Evans, *In Defense of History* (New York, 1999), 33. See also
Eric Hobsbawm, *On History* (London, 1997).

1970s, the centre of gravity shifted to English-speaking historians. Since then, research interest has centred mostly on economic and social history in the period from the end of the eighteenth century to the present day and has increasingly attracted historians from all over the world. Let us now look at some of these developments in detail.

The emergence of maritime history as a branch of the discipline of history may be dated to the establishment of the Commission d'Histoire Maritime within the framework of the Comité International des Sciences Historiques in the early 1960s.[5] This event had been preceded in the previous five years by a series of annual Colloques d'Histoire Maritime organized by the so-called Groupe de Travail d'Histoire Maritime, an organization dominated by historians associated with the French *Annales* School.

In addition to Fernand Braudel, these gatherings brought together renowned scholars of the calibre of the Frenchmen Charles Carriere, Pierre Chaunu, Frederic Mauro, Yves Renouard, and Pierre Vilar; Italians such as Ruggiero Romano, Alberto Tenenti and Carmelo Trasselli; Spaniards like Alvaro Castillo and Emili Giralt Raventos; Greeks, including Helen Antoniadou-Bibicou: Germans such as Hermann Kellenbenz, Dutchmen like M.I.J. Brugmans; Portuguese, including Virginia Rau; Yugoslavs, such as Jorjo Tadic; Belgians, especially Charles Verlinden; Danes like Astrid Friis; and many others, including first-class academics from the English-speaking world like John Hopkins University's Frederic Lane, Eleanora Carus Wilson of the London School of Economics, and Cambridge University's Michael Postan.

During the course of the various colloquia that took place during the 1950s prior to the establishment of the Maritime History Commission, the themes pertaining to maritime history and the archival sources suitable for their study were discussed and identified. The surviving documentation included port authority and customs archives; records of tolls paid by ships passing through certain straits, such as the renowned Danish Sound; ship registers; crew lists; shipyard records; the documentation of Admiralty and other maritime courts; consular reports; notarial deeds; and so on – the list is endless. Apart from official archives, researchers have also used the private records of merchants involved in maritime trade, including the business archives of large merchant companies like the Dutch or English East India Company. As Michel Mollat, the first President of the International Commission of Maritime History, put it in 1962, "[t]he uniquely international character of the European maritime economy undoubtedly reflects the production and circulation of goods

---

[5]Michel Mollat, *et al.* (eds.), *Les Sources de l'Histoire Maritime en Europe, du Moyen Age au XVIIIe siècle* (Paris, 1962), 473-474. The decision was in fact taken at the Lisbon meeting of the Groupe de Travail d'Histoire Maritime in September 1960. At the Congress of the Comité International des Sciences Historiques in Stockholm the previous month, the group decided that its work went considerably beyond the scope of the Commission d'Histoire Economique, within which it had been grouped.

of the world economy."[6] From that it was but a short step to declaring that "Maritime history is a key to general history," as did Jean Meuvret, Head of the Ecole Pratique des Hautes Etudes (VIe section), in the same period.[7]

On the other side of the Channel, developments in the discipline of history were running parallel to those in France with *Annales*, the University of Paris and the French *Histoire Economique et Sociale* maintaining an open dialogue with practitioners of British economic and social history. Albeit on a more modest level, Britain followed the same path as France, creating a space for maritime history within the context of the boom in economic history that was taking place at the London School of Economics and at Cambridge University. Scholars from both universities had participated in the meetings of the Groupe de Travail d'Histoire Maritime in the 1950s. According to Eric Hobsbawm, the succession to the chair of economic history at Cambridge University of the LSE's Michael Postan, a cosmopolitan endowed with considerable knowledge, was of pivotal importance for the strengthening of the relations between the French *Annales* School and English economic and social history.[8]

Ralph Davis, a graduate of the London School of Economics, wrote his classic *The Rise of British Shipping Industry* at about the same time. Published in 1962, it came to constitute a model for subsequent British maritime economic history. Another impetus for British maritime history came from Liverpool, at a time when it was still considered the largest port for British shipping after London. Francis Hyde of the University of Liverpool, in fact, opened up new horizons with his *Blue Funnel. A History of Alfred Holt and Company of Liverpool, 1865-1914*. At a time when business history, and even business administration, were regarded as too "practical" to be considered worthy of academic attention at British universities, Hyde wrote a history of this major British shipping company based on its business archives in accordance with the most rigorous academic standards, and thus started what would subsequently be referred to as the "Liverpool School."

Needless to say, British interest in maritime history preceded the 1950s. The tremendous importance of shipping for the British Empire and its colonies had created a "naval" history tradition of considerable importance in Britain. The Hakluyt Society was founded as early as 1845, while the Society for Nautical Research, which publishes *Mariner's Mirror,* was established in 1910. The popular appeal of the history of the sea has meant that there has been a proliferation of amateur historians, nautical museums and associations in the principal ports of the British Isles which has extolled a naval history

---

[6]*Ibid.*, x.

[7]Cited in *ibid*.

[8]Hobsbawm, *On History*, 179.

narrowly conceived to mean the glorious feats of heroic admirals, their stead-fast ships and epic naval encounters. While it undoubtedly is the most "popu-lar" facet of naval history among the general public, it has meant that Anglo-Saxon and other maritime economic historians have found it hard to escape from the antiquarian image and to find acceptance among professional practi-tioners of other, more established, branches of history.

Meanwhile, at an international level, the newly-established Commis-sion d'Histoire Maritime went on to organize a series of academic meetings covering a wide range of themes. The 1960s and 1970s were very important in the process of securing recognition from many of Europe's foremost historians for maritime history as a separate sub-discipline of history. The 1970s were particularly fruitful. Within the framework of the International Commission for Historical Sciences' five-yearly congresses, the Commission Internationale d'Histoire Maritime flourished. There was a mushrooming of the range of sub-jects covered, with particularly popular topics attracting dozens of contribu-tors. Such was the case with the sessions on "*Course et Piraterie*" held at the highly successful and well-attended San Francisco Congress in 1975, where forty papers were presented, of which thirty were in French.

In the English-speaking world, the 1970s were decisive. The arrival of Robin Craig at University College London to teach economic and social history was a significant event in the promotion and supervision of research in maritime history. A graduate of the LSE and a friend of Ralph Davis, he brought with him a wealth of experience acquired during his fifteen-year stint working in shipping in the City. Craig may have been a late starter as far as the academic profession was concerned, but he was to influence the develop-ment of maritime history in a decisive manner in a number of ways.

First of all, he knew shipping from within and as a consequence was knowledgeable about both the existence and the means of accessing the in-credible wealth of documentation concerning the many facets of shipbuilding, shipping and related activities available in state and private archives. He was thus ideally placed to guide a generation of young researchers towards new fields of study while pointing towards appropriate archival sources. His role as mentor to a generation of up-and-coming scholars has proved to be a seminal factor in the "take-off" of maritime history during the last quarter of a century.

A second factor which has made Robin Craig's contribution to the de-velopment of maritime history so important was his role as editor of *Maritime History*, an academic journal focused exclusively on the economic and social history of merchant shipping – a radical departure from traditional naval his-tory. Publication started in 1971 but ceased in 1977 when the publisher re-sponsible for it and a number of other journals ran into financial difficulties.

Last, but not least, Craig not only "discovered" but also helped to save a voluminous collection of crew lists of the British fleet. Stashed away and taking up valuable space in the repositories of the main British state archives, the Public Record Office, they were threatened with destruction when the PRO proposed to keep samples and destroy the rest. Rescued as a consequence of a joint Anglo-Canadian initiative, they were finally deposited at Memorial University of Newfoundland in 1971, coinciding with the establishment at the latter of a Maritime History Archive. The path to internationalization beyond European waters was truly under way.

The crew lists of a British fleet that accounted for at least fifty percent of world shipping after the mid-nineteenth century were in fact the agreements and accounts of crews from 1863 to 1939, a corpus of documentation that covers miles of shelving and constitutes a unique source for the study of seamen, ships, cargoes, freight rates, sea routes and shipping companies.[9] In 1977 the now famous Atlantic Canada Shipping Project was established to process and conduct research on this veritable treasure trove of information, and during the following decade, a group of historians from Memorial University of Newfoundland organized six international conferences and published an equal number of volumes on the history of the North Atlantic maritime economy. This research project transformed the small city of St. John's, formerly a centre for Atlantic fishing, into a modern-day "Mecca" for maritime economic historians from around the world.[10]

The decade of the 1970s was also marked by the advent in the United States of so-called "cliometrics," a quantitative economic history that uses the mathematical tools of neoclassical economics, particularly econometric models. It was a trend that pushed economic history in America in the direction of "historical economics." The use of the material deposited at Memorial to relate the decreasing cost of sea transport to the extraordinary growth of the world economy in the nineteenth century awakened the interest of American economic historians. Nobel Prize winner Douglas North was but one of those who made their way to St. John's and participated in some of the meetings there.

---

[9]See Lewis R. Fischer and Eric W. Sager, "An Approach to the Quantitative Analysis of British Shipping Records," *Business History*, XXII, No. 2 (July 1980), 135-151.

[10]Six volumes were published by Memorial University of Newfoundland University: Keith Mathews and Gerald Panting (eds.), *Ships and Shipbuilding in the North Atlantic Region* (St. John's, 1978); Lewis R. Fischer and Eric W. Sager (eds.), *The Enterprising Canadians: Entrepreneurs and Economic Development in Eastern Canada, 1820-1914* (St. John's, 1979); David Alexander and Rosemary Ommer (eds.), *Volumes not Values: Canadian Sailing Ships and World Trade* (St. John's, 1979); Rosemary Ommer and Gerald Panting (eds.) *Working Men Who Got Wet* (St. John's, 1980); Lewis R. Fischer and Eric W. Sager (eds.), *Merchant Shipping and Economic Development in Atlantic Canada* (St. John's, 1982); and Lewis R. Fischer and Gerald Panting (eds.) *Change and Adaptation in Maritime History: The North Atlantic Fleets in the Nineteenth Century* (St. John's, 1985).

Freight rates subsequently became a theme of research for a number of years. The influence of cliometrics on maritime history has waned considerably, but although the quantitative approach to shipping statistics may have ceased being an end in itself, it remains an important tool.

In the meantime, the "angry young men" of the 1970s, as Professor Jaap Bruijn referred to them in his inspiring 1996 lecture on maritime history, had started graduating from university departments of economic and social history.[11] Many were influenced by Marxist and neo-Marxist perspectives and put forward a vision of "history from below." Seamen and their wages; maritime labour movements and labour relations on board; maritime and fishing communities; and so on constituted the axis around which the newer strands of maritime historical research evolved. Eric Sager and Gerald Panting's *Maritime Capital* and Sager's *Seafaring Labour* are indicative of the sort of work that started to be published. From this group of Canadian historians there also emerged Lewis R. Fischer, better known as "Skip" to the "crew" of maritime history practitioners. As we shall see later, it was his organizational talents, his leadership qualities and his deep knowledge of and passion for maritime history that have proven to be the *sine qua non* for the continuous growth of maritime history in recent years.

In Britain, another focus of maritime history other than London emerged in the shape of the so-called Liverpool School. There, Peter Davies, a former student of, and successor to, Francis Hyde, published his important work entitled *The Trade Makers*, thus continuing the line of research on maritime business history. From his post in the Department of Economic History of the University of Liverpool during the following quarter of a century, Peter Davies went on to develop fruitful ties with Japanese scholars in the 1980s, as well as collaborating with a research group that was based in what eventually became the Liverpool Maritime Museum. In recent years, port history in Liverpool has continued to prosper under the able stewardship of Robert Lee and Adrian Jarvis.

The "boom" in Maritime History eventually caused other universities, such as Exeter, Glasgow and Leicester, to follow in the footsteps of University College London and the University of Liverpool. At the University of Leicester, for example, Ralph Davis and David Williams must be considered two of the founding fathers of Britain's "new" maritime history, with the second being particularly prominent internationally, both in terms of research and organization.

---

[11]Jaap R. Bruijn, "Reflections on the Recent Past of Maritime History in the Netherlands and Abroad," in Paul C. van Royen, Lewis R. Fischer and David M. Williams (eds.), *Frutta di Mare. Evolution and Revolution in the Maritime World in the 19th and 20th Centuries* (Amsterdam, 1998).

But the development of maritime history has not been limited to France in the 1950s and 1960s, and the United Kingdom and North America since the 1970s. In fact, there have been other important centres of activity. Throughout the second half of the twentieth century, the traditional maritime nations of northern Europe, particularly the Netherlands and the Scandinavian countries, have participated in the activities of the Commission International d'Histoire Maritime. Leiden University's Jaap Bruijn has not only been the author of a great number of publications on the maritime history of the Netherlands and a leading member of all international maritime and economic history commissions, but he has also been an excellent and inspiring teacher and mentor to more than fifty maritime historians, including the late Frank Broeze. The Dane, Hans-Christian Johansen, a keen supporter of maritime history in northern Europe, has been responsible for the programme which since the 1970s has processed electronically the data relating to the thousands of ships which passed through the Sound. Norway, one of the most dynamic maritime nations of the twentieth century could not be left out. Its contribution came in the shape of Helge Nordvik, *alter ego* of Lewis R. Fischer in the field of maritime history for many years. His sudden and premature demise in 1998 left an important gap in the ranks of maritime historians. Atle Thowsen, the current President of the International Commission of Maritime History and an able maritime historian in his own right, has followed in his footsteps.

Entering New Waters

It is probably no coincidence that maritime history has tended more or less to follow the course of European maritime expansion in the early modern period. It first crossed the Atlantic and reached the Americas. In characteristic style, the latter's Northern Hemisphere made it its own and proceeded to consolidate and extend the discipline. But it was again by the hands of Europeans that the "new" maritime history reached the lands to the east at the edge of the Indian and Pacific oceans. Following in the footsteps of his ancestors, whose ships had filled their holds with spices in the East Indies (present-day Indonesia), the ship which bore Frank Broeze charted a course which many a Dutch ship had in the past inadvertently strayed into by not finding the right trade winds, and instead of arriving in Batavia ended up wrecked on the western coast of New Holland (present-day Western Australia). But Broeze's ship arrived safe and sound, and the Dutchman landed at the University of Western Australia in the early 1970s; over the next three decades he proceeded to turn Perth into a major centre of world maritime history.[12]

---

[12]Frank Broeze went on to become a leading figure in maritime history; an inspiring professor and a talented writer, this gifted man unfortunately passed away in 2001 at the age of fifty-four.

The globe was thus finally circumnavigated where the Pacific meets the Indian Ocean; where the Spaniards, Portuguese, Dutch and British had met and established the frontiers of their respective colonial empires. It was only natural that the journal of the Australian Association for Maritime History, established in 1979, should have been called *The Great Circle*. The incorporation of the Pacific into the maritime history confraternity would not have been complete without the participation of that other dynamic and important economic and maritime power of the twentieth century, Japan. This was brought about through the good offices of Britain's Peter Davies and the University of British Columbia's William D. Wray, who established regular channels of communication with Japanese scholars.

The 1980s were years marked by turbulence as the dominance of the International Commission of Maritime History (ICMH) by continental scholars was seriously challenged. At the International Congress of Historical Sciences in Bucharest in 1980, Anglo-Saxon historians comprised a majority at ICMH proceedings for the first time.[13] Since then, well-attended ICMH meetings have continued to take place every five years covering a wide range of themes that have reflected trends in historical research: "Maritime Aspects of Migration" in Stuttgart in 1985; "Maritime Trade and Shipping in Foodstuffs" in Madrid in 1990; and so on. But at the same time that the number of topics multiplied and the chronological period covered lengthened, it also became evident that there was a need for a reassessment of the scope of maritime history. The seeds for such a re-assessment were sown during the session on maritime history, organized as a consequence of an initiative taken by Peter Davies, Keiichiro Nakagawa, Lewis R. Fischer and Helge Nordvik within the context of the Ninth International Economic History Congress held in Berne, Switzerland, in August 1986.

During the course of the discussions on maritime history's place within the wider profession, the forty or so scholars determined that the lack of communication between practitioners was one of the key constraints blocking its development as a sub-discipline of history. As a consequence, the group, led by Lewis R. Fischer and Helge W. Nordvik, agreed to set up a Maritime Economic History Group and to produce a newsletter that would endeavour to overcome the barriers of isolation and to share research findings. The group and its newsletter went from strength to strength – to such an extent that within three years, and in response to requests from many of the more than eight hundred social and economic historians who received the newsletter, it embarked on the much more ambitious project of an academic journal. Fischer and Nordvik, the editors of the *International Journal of Maritime History,* summed up the goals of the new publication in four points: that maritime history be truly international in scope, an aspiration which was reflected in an

---

[13]Bruijn, "Reflections," 14-15.

editorial board composed of sixteen different nationalities drawn from four of
the world's continents; that it encompass the social and economic aspects of
the history of the seas; that it seek to improve the quality of writing in that
field of study; and finally that contributors set their writing on maritime history within the wider historical discourse. Regarding the last point they highlighted the unique role maritime history could play as a link between the various sub-disciplines of history. Over the next couple of years two further projects were initiated; the establishment of the International Maritime Economic
History Association (IMEHA) during the Tenth International Economic History Congress in Leuven, Belgium, at the end of August 1990, and the publication of *Research in Maritime History* (RIMH), a companion monograph series
to the *IJMH*, of which this present volume is the twenty-eighth issue.

The last fifteen years have been highly fruitful and successful for both
the IMEHA and its publications. Since its founding the new Association has
organized its own International Congresses of Maritime History in Liverpool
(1992), Amsterdam (1996), Esbjerg, Denmark (2000) and Corfu, Greece
(2004). At the same time it has also participated in International Economic
History Congresses in Milan (1994), Madrid (1998) and Buenos Aires (2002).

At the regional level, taken here to mean groups of countries, there
have also been initiatives over the last few decades to strengthen maritime history. The Association for the History of the Northern Seas, for example, was
founded in 1974 and organizes conferences every couple of years to bring together those studying the maritime history of the Atlantic and the Baltic, while
occasional conferences, like the 1999 *La storiografia marittima in Italia e in
Spagna in età moderna e contemporanea: Tendenze, orientamenti, linee evolutive,* give countries where maritime history conceived in modern terms is still
relatively under-developed the opportunity to take stock.

The practice of maritime history at the national and local levels is the
domain of many large and small organizations. These obviously start with the
activities of the various national commissions of the ICMH but also include
other groups. These range from the National Maritime Museum in the United
Kingdom, with its state-of-the-art, on-line *Journal of Maritime Research* and
Port and its maritime information website; via conferences such as the annual
New Researchers in Maritime History Conference organised by the British
Commission for Maritime History; to the Friends of the Maritime Museum of
Malta, whose periodic seminars provide the principal outlet for the airing of
maritime history research conducted mostly by enthusiastic amateurs.

Whither Maritime History?

The establishment of maritime history as a distinct sub-discipline of history in
the latter half of the twentieth century converged with the international trend in
historiography towards specialization. Eric Hobsbawm has written that "[a]ll

historians are more expert (or to put it another way, more ignorant) in some fields than in others."[14] Indeed, he continues that "[o]n grounds of convenience or technical necessity, historians will tend to specialize...However, basically all history aspires to what the French call 'total history.'"[15] As a consequence of current trends in historiography, history has tended to forge closer links with the social sciences, and in an analogous fashion maritime history has become more integrated into the mainstream of history.[16]

A quarter of a century ago, Frank Broeze set out the broad guidelines of the wide conception of maritime history which has informed much of the current of renewal which has swept this area of studies in the latter decades of the twentieth century and the early years of the twenty-first. In his seminal 1989 article in *The Great Circle*, he proposed six categories which *grosso modo* sum up humanity's relationship with the sea: 1) The use of the resources of the sea and what lies beneath it, including fishing and related activities, and the economic and social life of the communities dependent upon these activities. 2) The sea as a means of communication for the carriage of people and goods, and the structures associated with this phenomenon such as ports, and the communities within which they are lodged. This category is the broadest in maritime history and includes seaborne trade; shipping in all its facets, as well as ancillary institutions such as insurance, finance and registers; navigation; sea-related labour; island and port communities; and so on. 3) The sea as a medium for the projection of power. This means naval power, strategy and technology; government policies relating to the control of the sea and its resources; as well as commerce-raiding, corsairing and piracy. 4) The use of the sea for scientific purposes via oceanography, climatology, and the like, as well as government policies regarding marine science and technology viewed from an historical perspective. 5) The sea as a space for leisure. This refers, first and foremost, to the Mediterranean's premier economic activity, tourism. The sea and the coast were conceived as a regenerative environment and a focus for recreation in general and the practice of aquatic sports in particular. 6) Last but not least, the sea is a source of inspiration in culture and ideology; this includes, for example, the role of the sea in literature and the visual arts and the presence of the sea in a nation's self-image.

---

[14]Eric Hobsbawm, *The Age of Revolution. Europe 1789-1848* (London, 1962), 12.

[15]Hobsbawm, *On History*, 109.

[16]See David M. Williams, "The Progress of Maritime History, 1953-1993," *Journal of Transport History*, XIV, No. 2 (September 1993), 126-141.

Six years after setting out these six categories, Broeze edited a collection of bibliographical essays to which this present volume may, in part, be considered a modest successor. In the introduction he wrote that:

> [i]t is a sign of the advancement and maturity of maritime history that at this stage in its development, a number of critical assessments are being undertaken. Assuming that, as in human life, the future is built on an understanding of the past, the sheer amount, diversity and increasing sophistication of recent work invite, even necessitate, a consideration of what has been achieved and where one should go from here.[17]

Any discipline that does not regenerate and expand is doomed to extinction. Maritime history has certainly undergone a process of regeneration in the last couple of decades, at least regardinng those whose medium of international communication is English. Academic positions are not abundant, but posts have been created, and maritime history is being taught in many more European institutions of higher education than was the case fifteen years ago. In Britain, new centres have joined Liverpool and Leicester in the study of maritime history. These include the University of Hull, with its Maritime Historical Studies Centre established by David Starkey, and the University of Greenwich, with its Maritime Institute set up by Sarah Palmer.[18] At the University of Cambridge, Geoffrey Scammell has produced valuable work in this field.[19] In Denmark, Poul Holm has done a marvellous job at the University of Southern Denmark's Institute of Maritime History. In Greece, in the last fourteen years posts and courses on maritime history have been created at three universities: the University of Piraeus; the University of the Aegean on the island of Chios; and the Ionian University on the island of Corfu. In Germany, maritime history is officially recognized and has been taught in Hamburg by

---

[17]See Frank Broeze, "Introduction," in Broeze (ed.), *Maritime History at the Crossroads: A Critical Review of Recent Historiography* (St. John's, 1995), xvi, for bibliographies on the maritime histories of Australia, Canada, China, Denmark, Germany, Greece, Latin America, India, the Netherlands, the Ottoman Empire, the US and maritime labour.

[18]Sarah Palmer is in fact one of an increasing number of women involved in maritime history, a welcome phenomenon which is reflected in the number of women on the *IJMH* and *RIMH* editorial board and the fact that nearly half the contributors to this volume are women. Other developments in this field include the Women and the Sea network in Britain, coordinated by Jo Stanley.

[19]See, for example, G.V. Scammell, *The World Encompassed. The First European Maritime Empires, c. 800-1650* (London, 1987).

Lars Scholl, while Heide Gerstenberger and Ulrich Welke have undertaken extensive research in modern shipping at the University of Bremen. In the Netherlands, there is a long-established maritime history tradition, as we have seen, and Professor Jaap Bruijn continues at the forefront of maritime history teaching and research. In Norway, students of the late Helge Nordvik, such as Stig Tenold and Berit Johnsen, continue to teach and research in the field of maritime history, while Norwegian historians such as Atle Thowsen and Bjørn Basberg have established themselves in the fields of naval history, merchant shipping and whaling. In Finland, Yrjö Kaukiainen is foremost among a sizeable group of historians who have made Finnish maritime history internationally known. In Canada, Memorial University has for the last fifteen years continued to act as a veritable beacon, sending out information through its publications and generally acting as a promoter of new initiatives. The situation in the US has improved somewhat, according to a recent report.[20] But publications and teaching of the calibre of the Harvard scholars Robert Greenhalgh Albion and J.H. Parry are not easily matched.[21] In Australia, the passing of Frank Broeze has left a huge gap, but even in death Broeze has continued to serve as a source of inspiration, with the establishment of the annual Frank Broeze Lecture in History. Maritime History courses are also given at a number of Australian universities by people such as Ken McPherson, Malcom Tull, Graydon Henning, James Reveley and Simon Ville.

Maritime History in the Mediterranean

The maritime historiography of Mediterranean countries has tended to be somewhat introspective and patchy in its pursuits in the last few decades, and what there is tends to be skewed towards the power-projection facet of the discipline. The premier example of this is, of course, France, which has found the *Annales* a hard act to follow. It is clear that France no longer enjoys the

---

[20]John B. Hattendorf, "L'histoire maritime et son enseignement à l'étranger: Les Etats-Unis," *Chronique d'histoire maritime*, No. 50 (mars 2003), 19-22.

[21]Both were professors of Oceanic History and Affairs at Harvard University. Robert Greenhalgh Albion (comp.), *Naval and Maritime History: An Annotated Bibliography* (4th ed., Mystic, CT, 1972,) remains a highly informative and unique work. It was substantially updated by Benjamin W. Labaree, *A Supplement 1971-1986 to Robert G. Albion's Naval and Maritime History: An Annotated Bibliography* (Mystic, CT, 1988). J.H. Parry was a prolific writer whose works were still being reprinted long after his untimely death in 1982. These include classics such as *The Age of Reconnaissance* (Cleveland, 1963); *The Spanish Seaborne Empire* (London, 1966); *Trade and Dominion: The European Oversea Empires in the Eighteenth Century* (London, 1971); *The Discovery of the Sea* (New York, 1974); *The Discovery of South America* (New York, 1979); and so on.

pre-eminence which historians such as Braudel gave it, and it also seems to have had some difficulty adjusting to the process of internationalization which has swept maritime history.

Maritime history in France has an excellent vehicle in the shape of the Société Française d'Histoire Maritime's *Chronique d'histoire maritime.* A quarterly publication, it carries articles on a range of topics, albeit leaning heavily towards naval matters, as well as information reflecting considerable activity at the local level. France's present-day Société Française d'Histoire Maritime represents the union of the Comité de Documentation Historique de la Marine, established more than fifty years ago, and the Commission Française d'Histoire Maritime, set up in 1979. Excluding a series of short articles over the last year informing on the condition of maritime history in a number of countries, French maritime history, as reflected in the *Chronique,* is loath to venture beyond traditional, well-trodden paths, and yet France has excellent maritime historians such as Michel Fonteney, Daniel Panzac, M. Vergé-Franchesci, Christiane Villain-Gandossi, and many others whose contribution is sorely needed if maritime history is to be truly international. Silvia Marzagalli and John Barzman are very welcome exceptions to this general French absence from world maritime history forums.

The situation in other Mediterranean countries is variable but tends to consist mostly of individual academics who may be considered, and who often consider themselves, maritime historians, but who work in conditions of relative isolation. Representative of such academics are most of the contributors to this volume but also include Jesús M. Valdaliso from Spain and Tomasso Fanfani from Italy.

In Italy, maritime history has been traditionally considered an integral part of economic history, and prominent historians like Alberto Tenenti, Ugo Tucci and Carlo Cipolla have published extensively on subjects closely related to maritime history. In more recent years, the University of Bari's Antonio di Vittorio has been an important focus for the study of maritime economic history, and he has organized a number of conferences focusing on this area.[22] Italy's Salvatore Bono, founder and president of the Société Internationale des Historiens de la Méditerranée, is in a class of his own. Albeit not a maritime historian *per se,* Bono has written extensively on slavery, corsairing, the Maghreb and the Mediterranean in general for over half a century, and has probably done more than anyone else to strengthen ties between historians of the Mediterranean. His twenty-page newsletter, published at irregular intervals every seven to eight months, is a veritable gold mine of information, reporting on conferences and announcing forthcoming ones, and reviewing books. Though aimed at the general historian of the Mediterranean, there is always

---

[22]See Michela D'Angelo's and Elisabetta Tonizzi's contribution in this volume.

much that is of interest to the maritime historian. Its first issue in 1997 was published entirely in French but nowadays carries articles and reviews in several of the languages currently in use in the Mediterranean. In its latest issue of January 2004 (Issue 11), it carried news and reviews in French, Italian, Spanish and English, and not necessarily in that order of importance. Indeed, for the very first time, its lead article was in English. It is a move not unlike that of traditionally Francophone Mediterranean countries that have taken note of changing linguistic patterns in the international community and have gradually adapted their educational systems to accommodate themselves to the increasing importance of English.

Spain's historiography, long dominated by foreign Hispanists, has undergone a remarkable resurgence since the advent of democracy. The Socialist government's investment in education and archives, and numerous conferences and publications, have rendered fertile a previously arid landscape. The early modern period has harvested a particularly rich crop, with associations like the Centre D'Estudios d'Història Moderna "Pierre Vilar" being especially active in the field of economic history. Under the dynamic leadership of Carlos Martínez Shaw, it was instrumental in the formation of a whole generation of historians.[23] A considerable amount of this work centred on the maritime economy, but relatively little of it is known beyond Spain's borders.

In Greece, the fall of the dictatorship in 1974 was accompanied by an upsurge in historical publications which, along with the return from exile of a number of prominent scholars educated mainly in France, gave a great boost to the development of the country's economic and social history. In fact, the mid-1970s are regarded as the beginning of what has been called the "new" Greek historiography. The first generation of economic historians was educated in the 1960s and started publishing in the 1970s. Particular importance was given to the diaspora of merchant communities and the role of shipping as the main link between this populace dispersed around the world and the small Greek state. New areas of research, archival material and interpretations thus became part of the new trend in Greek historiography. Spyros Asdrachas, Vassilis Panayotopoulos, Filippos Iliou, George Dertilis, George Leontaritis, Vassilis Kremmydas and others triggered the processes that produced a new generation of economic historians. Researchers were financed and publications on economic history sponsored by the Historical Archives or Research Foundations of the National Bank of Greece, the Commercial Bank of Greece, the Hellenic Bank for Industrial Development (now the Foundation of the Bank of Piraeus) and

---

[23]See Carlos Martinéz Shaw (ed.), *Historia moderna. Historia en construcción* (2 vols., Lleida, 1990), which brought together work by over fifty historians who had been associated with the Centre.

the Institute of Neohellenic Research at the National Research Centre.[24] In the 1980s Costis Varfis, a former naval officer based at the War Museum, set up the Greek Commission of Maritime History of the International Commission of Maritime History. Mostly focused on naval history, the Greek Commission was essentially a one-man operation and has, in fact, been dormant since Varfis' death. Maritime history in Greece is not organized within a particular group but forms an integral part of the whole development of Greek historical studies, and is presently taught in at least three universities in the country, as mentioned above.

The tiny Maltese archipelago, situated spatially and culturally between both the western and eastern basins of the Mediterranean, and the northern and southern shores of the Sea, has had its maritime history dominated by its role as a naval station of two powerful empires, the Hapsburg and the British, as John Chircop demonstrates in his contribution to this volume. But Braudel and the *Annales* have had an impact here as well, especially by the hand of the island's leading early modern historian, Victor Mallia-Milanes. The gradual opening up to other facets of maritime history in recent years, especially the history of Malta's trading networks, has also been aided by access to remarkably rich archival sources and the presence on the island of organizations such as the International Maritime Law Institute of the International Maritime Organization and the International Ocean Institute. The University of Malta recently hosted the Mediterranean Maritime History Network's first conference and has given increasing prominence to maritime history in its *Journal of Mediterranean Studies*.

The situation in the countries on the southern shore of the Mediterranean is very complex.[25] The Muslim southern shore is comprised of very different realities, a fact often forgotten by those who would place Morocco, Algeria, Tunisia, Libya, Egypt, Lebanon and Syria in the same basket, and it is not easy to know what is happening.[26] Arabic is spoken and read by hundreds

---

[24]See Gelina Harlaftis, "The Maritime Historiography of Greece since 1975," in Broeze (ed.), *Maritime History at the Crossroads*.

[25]These few comments on the historiography, maritime or otherwise, of the Mediterranean's southern shore are limited to the countries about which we have been able to secure some information, namely Morocco, Algeria and Tunisia.

[26]It is worthwhile to note that these different realities have, if anything, been reinforced since independence. Euro-Med meetings have over the years highlighted the fact that economic, cultural and other contacts between Arab countries are negligible compared to the relationships which each has nurtured with European nations across the water. Indeed, relations between them have often verged on the edge of open war. Over the last thirty years the proportion of intraregional trade in the Maghreb and the Middle East, for example, has remained unchanged at around six percent. See Gonzalo Escribano and Josep María Jordán, "Sub-regional Integration in the Southern Shore of the

of millions of people in the world, but it is not an "international" language within easy reach of outsiders, while the way ideas are presented in Arabic does not fit neatly into the Western scheme of things. It must also be recognized that our Eurocentric world view often impedes understanding.[27] The manner in which "Western" history is traditionally divided is also a major problem and is often rejected by Arabic and other scholars, as are many of the topics considered worthy of study. It is perfectly understandable, for example, that present-day Algeria is more interested in the study of its struggle for independence than in France's *outre mer* interpretation of its colonial dominion over the same country.

The French language has provided a bridge of sorts between the northern and southern shores, and leading historians tend to publish in French, but the Arabization of higher education in countries like Morocco will probably reduce contacts. In other places, like Tunisia, for example, there is both a considerable demand for more translations into French of English language works, produced locally to reduce costs, and the increasing use of English, with the establishment of secondary schools with English as the language of instruction.[28] At the other end of the spectrum, civil war and economic difficulties have reduced Algerian scholarly publications, in any language, to a trickle. What is unequivocal is the increase in the number of universities and students in all the Arab countries of the southern shore, in line with rapid population growth.

As far as can be ascertained, maritime history does not loom large in research or on publication agendas in the Maghreb, at least as far as the early modern era is concerned.[29] It may be that the sea has overwhelmingly negative connotations for peoples of Semitic origin, as Semitic languages specialist Martin Zammit has suggested in a paper on the sea from a Semitic perspective

---

Mediterranean and the Euro-Mediterranean Free Trade Area," *Cuadernos del Centro Español de Relaciones Internacionales*, Nos. 5-6 (July 1999), 107.

[27]See footnote 2 above.

[28]Tunisia is an exception. The second *Arab Human Development Report* (2003) highlighted the importance of translation in the dissemination of information in the world but noted that in 1980-1985 the Arab world translated less than one book per million people compared to Hungary's 519 per million and Spain's 920.

[29]Mercedes García-Arenal, "Una década de historiografía Magrebí sobre los siglos modernos," in *Diez años de historiografía modernista* (Barcelona, 1997), 173-184, *passim*.

appropriately entitled "The Depths of Darkness in a Vast Deep Ocean."[30] Ruthy Gertwagen, in her contribution on maritime history in Israel in this volume, highlights that some scholars do, indeed, view the relationship of Jews with the sea as being somewhat ambiguous. As regards the Arab World, on the other hand, it may be that the presence of colonial masters, whose navy and merchant marine probably monopolized maritime connections with both the metropolis and other nations, was not the best environment in which a modern maritime tradition beyond coastal waters could emerge, although one would have to see what presence, if any, colonials had on French, Italian and other vessels.

In the early modern era the fleets of the North African Regencies of Tripoli, Tunis and Algiers had an important role to play as an auxiliary naval force of the Ottoman Navy, as Özveren and Yildirim point out in their paper on the Ottoman Empire in this volume. Peter Earle, Michel Fontenay and many others have described the "lesser war" of corsairing in some detail.[31] The important and prolific scholar Daniel Panzac has recently recounted the last years of the Barbary Corsairs and the lesser-known flourishing of Maghrebi merchant shipping in the early years of the nineteenth century, not long before North Africa succumbed to European empire builders.[32]

One of the difficulties confronted by historians of North Africa is the paucity of local archival documentation, a drawback which is only partly alleviated by recourse to Ottoman archives. The bibliography that does exist on the maritime history of the southern shore of the Mediterranean has often had to rely on primary sources available in Europe. Much, if not most, of what exists has been written by Europeans, but there is an increasing number of contributions from scholars such as Moulay Belhamissi, Abd El Hadi Ben Mansour, Sadok Boubaker, Tahar Mansouri, Abdeljelil Temimi and others who may not perceive themselves as maritime historians but who do periodically write maritime history. One particularly notable focus of activity has been the University of Sfax in Tunisia, where Abdelhamid Fehri of the department of history has been responsible for a number of maritime history initiatives. These have included two conferences in the past five years entitled *L'homme et la mer* and *Les îles méditerranéennes des relais civilisationnels à*

---

[30]Martin R. Zammit, "The Depths of Darkness in a Vast Deep Ocean: The Sea from a Semitic Perspective," in *L'Homme et la Mer* (Sfax, 2001), 203-234.

[31]See Xavier Labat Saint Vincent's article in this volume.

[32]Daniel Panzac, *La course barbaresque. La fin d'une épopée, 1800-1820* (Paris, 1999).

travers l'histoire, in 1999 and 2002, respectively.[33] Both were marked by the impeccable hospitality which we have come to associate with Abdelhamid Fehri, and both provided excellent opportunities to meet Maghrebi scholars. The 2002 conference, in particular, was marked by the presence of academics from Algeria and Morocco as well.[34] Another important initiative with which Fehri is currently involved is the setting up of a museum devoted to the maritime heritage of the island of Kerkenna. It is to men and women like Abdelhamid Fehri that we must look for the beginnings of a maritime history of the southern shore.

In recognition of the linguistic pluralism of the Mediterranean, the Fourth Congress of Maritime History held in Corfu in June 2004 used both English and French as official conference languages. In this very old sea of many nations and ethnicities, many languages and many religions, communication is no straightforward matter. Some of the excellent pieces found in this volume were originally submitted in Spanish or French, and we have translated them in an attempt to reach out beyond our Mediterranean. Ideally, of course, we would like to see even more languages being used at congresses and conferences, but the cost of providing interpretation in the many languages used in the Mediterranean would probably be prohibitive.

The essays in this volume indicate the extent to which the maritime history of one country is found in the history of the others, and how much research in maritime history means research across national boundaries. Our goal is to try to understand better the multi-cultural and multi-ethnic environment in which we live in an effort to "accomplish the old-established goal of 'total' history on the vast expanses of the sea, and the ports and harbours that are to be found on its fringes."[35]

---

[33]The proceedings of the first were published in 2001 as *L'homme et la mer*, while the proceedings of the second are in press.

[34]Khadija Mansouri of the University of Oran; Bouba Majjani and Youssef Abich of the University of Constantine; Mohamed Razouk of the University of Casablanca; and Ibrahim Elkadri Boutchich and Ahmed El Mahmoudi of the University of Mèknes.

[35]See Marina Alfonso Mola and Carlos Martínez Shaw in this volume. The question of whether "total history" is attainable is another matter, as Peter Burke pointed out in his "Introduction" in Burke (ed.), *New Perspectives on Historical Writing* (Cambridge, 1991), but we can still aspire to it.

Maritime Historiography in
Ancien Régime Mediterranean Spain

Marina Alfonso Mola and Carlos Martínez Shaw

Since the study of maritime history is a relatively recent development in Spain, it seems appropriate to look briefly at its meaning. Maritime history encompasses everything that has to do with the sea, and as a consequence it constitutes a meeting point for a number of sub-disciplines. On the one hand it has to do with maritime economic history, which looks at the economic activities related to the sea: maritime commerce, with its mercantile, financial and juridical aspects, and related branches such as corsairing, contraband and shipwrecks; shipbuilding and the materials used in this activity, such as wood, linen, hemp, copper and tar; and fishing or the collection from the sea of mammals, fish, pearls, corral, tortoise shell or sponges, as well as salt, seaweed, amber and so on. On the other hand, it also has to do with recent urban history, as a consequence of its interest in port history, in aspects such as material, sanitary, administrative, fiscal and defence infrastructures. In addition, it is also worth highlighting that while some of the activities carried on in relation to the sea have to do with the urban economy, and only remotely with the rural economy through a number of crops destined for industrial use, another set of activities is carried on outside both town and country: on the high seas themselves.

Maritime history also has a social history facet to it via the study of the actors involved: merchants, in the widest possible sense of the word; entrepreneurs, such as shipowners and victuallers; the many types of mariners; trades to do with dockyards, such as ship carpenters and caulkers; callings to do with ports, such as agents, supercargoes, brokers, pilots, stevedores, dockers, divers, lighthouse keepers and so on; and finally occupations associated with the provision of services to seafarers, such as innkeepers, prostitutes and the like. It is a wide conception which also throws light on aspects of labour history, such as hiring and firing, training, accidents, class struggle and related individuals, including "passengers," be they voluntary, such as migrants, or forced, as in the case of galley rowers, captives and slaves.

In a like manner, maritime history also has an institutional facet in that it examines those organizations related to the sea, such as those engaged in mercantile administration; the Consulates of the Sea, in their triple facets of corporation, professional association and juridical body (and in some instances administrative as well); the Admiralty; the schools of navigation; the organizations entrusted with sanitary supervision, such as sanitation boards and guards and quarantine hospitals; those directly involved in the operations of ports, such as port development authorities, harbour masters and customs officers. Maritime activities also generate legislation relating to chartering, insurance, customs, censuses of mariners, Admiralty jurisdiction, the commissioning of vessels and employment and commercial contracts.

Finally, maritime history has a cultural history facet as well. For a long time this was contained within the framework of the history of discoveries and of scientific expeditions and its handmaidens, cartography and nautical science, but more recently there has been an increasing awareness that the sea gives rise to highly individualistic forms of social and religious behaviour and expressions. At a more sophisticated level, attitudes of seafarers towards life or death, as reflected particularly in such extreme situations as storm or shipwreck, constituted an early phase of the development of the history of *mentalités*.

Resisting the temptation to go upstream and study freshwater fishermen, river boatmen and those who man rafts, one could say that maritime history endeavours to accomplish the long-established goal of "total" history on the vast expanses of the sea, and in the ports and harbours found on its fringes.

The History of the Maritime Economy

Maritime Trade

Setting aside the more traditional sectors of naval warfare and discoveries, the first notable findings of maritime history related to economic history. Indeed, these early findings marked a course which has been followed to the present day, with economic aspects attracting the bulk of those involved in this discipline and giving rise to a disequilibrium in favour of these matters compared to social, institutional and cultural aspects.

For the same reasons, the study of maritime trade developed earliest and most rapidly because it is one of the best known *and* most criticized characteristics of the *Annales* School that it was much more inclined towards exchange than towards production. In maritime history this has meant that considerable attention has been given to maritime routes and relatively little to the economic phenomena taking place in the interior, beyond ports and harbours. Spain, which was initially very much influenced by this approach, has been no exception. In addition, the study of trade has also been influenced by the powerful attractions of overseas commerce, which became the preferred area of study of Spanish and foreign researchers, a position it still retains and which only now is starting to be contested.

Spain's trade with the Americas has been the object of continual attention by researchers; although there are still gaps that need to be filled, we have a fairly clear picture of its structure and evolution through the three centuries of its existence. In this context, and setting aside the presence of Catalan men and vessels on Atlantic routes prior to the establishment of the fleet and galleon systems in 1561-1564, it was not until the eighteenth century that Mediterranean ports were able to establish direct contacts with America.[1] A number of publications have, in fact, centred on the commercial relations between Mediterranean Spain and the latter's overseas territories. These include works by Carlos Martínez Shaw, Josep María Delgado and José María Oliva for Catalonia;[2] Vicent Ribes and Manuel Ardit for Valencia;[3] Carles Manera for Majorca;[4] Carmen Parrón for

---

[1]On the galleons, see E. Otte, "Los comienzos del comercio catalán con América," *Homenaje a Jaime Vicens Vives* (2 vols., Barcelona, 1965), II, 459-480; and C. Martínez Shaw, "Sobre el comerç català amb Amèrica al segle XVI," *Segones Jornades d'Estudis Catalano-Americans* (Barcelona, 1987), 33-39. On direct contacts, see Martínez Shaw, "La respuesta del Mediterráneo al Atlántico. Los puertos mediterráneos y el comercio colonial en el siglo XVIII," *Areas*, X (1986), 150-155; and Martínez Shaw, "Los comportamientos regionales ante el libre comercio," *Manuscrits*, VI (1987), 75-89.

[2]C. Martínez Shaw, *Cataluña en la Carrera de Indias, 1680-1756* (Barcelona, 1981); J.M. Delgado Ribas, "Cataluña y el sistema de Libre Comercio (1778-1818)" (Unpublished PhD thesis, Barcelona, 1981); Delgado Ribas, "Comercio colonial y fraude fiscal en Cataluña, 1778-1808: algunas consideraciones en torno a los registros de Libre Comercio," *Estudios Históricos y Documentos de los Archivos de Protocolos*, VI (1978), 311-326; Delgado Ribas, "Cádiz y Málaga en el comercio colonial posterior a 1778," *Actas del I Congreso de Historia de Andalucía. Andalucía Moderna III* (Córdoba, 1978), 127-139; Delgado Ribas, "El impacto de las crisis coloniales en la economía catalana (1787-1807)," in J. Fontana (ed.), *La economía española al final del Antiguo Régimen. III: Comercio y Colonias* (Madrid, 1983), 97-169; Delgado Ribas, "Política ilustrada, industria española y mercado americano, 1778-1818," *Pedralbes*, III (1983), 253-273; Delgado Ribas, "Els catalans i el lliure comerç," in *El comerç entre Catalunya i Amèrica* (Barcelona, 1986), 83-93; Delgado Ribas, "Libre comercio: mito y realidad," in *Mercado y desarrollo económico en la España contemporánea* (Madrid, 1986), 69-83; Delgado Ribas and J.M. Fradera, *El comerç entre Catalunya i Amèrica, segles XVIII i XIX* (Mataró, 1985); J.M. Oliva Melgar, *Cataluña y el comercio privilegiado con América. La Real Compañía de Comercio de Barcelona a Indias* (Barcelona, 1987); and Oliva Melgar, *Cataluña y el comercio privilegiado con América. La Real Compañía de Comercio de Barcelona a Indias* (Barcelona, 1987).

[3]V. Ribes Iborra, *Los valencianos y América: el comercio valenciano con Indias en el siglo XVIII* (Valencia, 1985); M. Ardit Lucas, "Datos sobre el comercio español con América en el siglo XVIII. Las empresas comerciales de Mariano Canet y Montalbán (1758-1785)," *Estudios dedicados a Juan Peset Aleixandre* (3 vols., Valencia, 1982), I, 157-174; and Ardit Lucas, "Las empresas comerciales de la sociedad 'Viuda de don Mariano Canet e Hijos' y las primeras expediciones directas de Valencia a Veracruz (1786-1805)," *Estudis*, XI (1984), 103-142.

[4]C. Manera Erbina, *Comerç i capital mercantil a Mallorca, 1720-1800* (Palma de Mallorca, 1988). For an earlier period, see J. Pons i Pons, "Els negocis dels mal-

the port of Cartagena;[5] and Aurora Gámez for Malaga.[6] To these we have to add the exhaustive analysis of the figures for *Libre Comercio*, the liberalized trade between Spain and its colonies instituted in the final quarter of the eighteenth century, carried out by John R. Fisher, which has become the standard reference for those working on this period and has made it possible to estimate the shares of the Mediterranean ports in a trade dominated by harbours on Spain's Atlantic coast.[7]

In contrast to the keen interest in the study of colonial trade, there has been relatively little research into maritime commerce conducted with other areas. Nevertheless, studies on Mediterranean trade in the sixteenth and seventeenth centuries became more prominent as a consequence of Fernand Braudel's masterpiece and included pioneering work by Álvaro Castillo and Emilia Salvador based on the archival series of port dues for the city of Valencia.[8] Later, Ricardo Franch gave a good account of Valencia's trade in the eighteenth century.[9] Enrique

---

lorquins a Indies a la segona meitat del segle XVII," in Román Piña Homs (ed.), *Les Illes Balears i Amèrica* (Palma de Mallorca, 1992), 313-318.

[5]C. Parrón Salas, "Cartagena y el Comercio Libre, 1765-1796," *Anales de Historia Contemporánea*, VIII (1990-1991), 215-224.

[6]A. Gámez Amián, *Málaga y el comercio colonial con América (1765-1820)* (Málaga, 1994).

[7]J.R. Fisher, *Commercial Relations between Spain and Spanish America in the Era of Free Trade, 1778-1796* (Liverpool, 1985); Fisher, *Trade, War and Revolution. Exports from Spain to Spanish America, 1797-1820* (Liverpool, 1992); Fisher, *El comercio entre España e Hispanoamérica (1797-1820)* (Madrid, 1993); and Fisher, "Los cambios estructurales en la Carrera de Indias en el periodo borbónico," *Revista de Historia Naval*, XXXXVII (1994), 21-34.

[8]F. Braudel, *La Méditerranée et le monde méditerranéen à l'époque de Philippe II* (París, 1949); A. Castillo Pintado, *Tráfico marítimo y comercio de importación en Valencia a comienzos del siglo XVII* (Madrid, 1967); E. Salvador Esteban, *La economía valenciana en el siglo XVI (Comercio de importación)* (Valencia, 1972); and Salvador Esteban, "Política y comercio en la Valencia del siglo XVII. El tráfico marítimo Génova-Valencia," *II Congresso Internazionale di Studi Storici. Rapporti Genova-Mediterraneo-Atlantico nell'Età Moderna* (Génova, 1985), 131-152.

[9]R. Franch Benavent, *El capital comercial valenciano en el siglo XVIII* (Valencia, 1989).

Giménez López's review of the historiographic production on the region's commerce renders further references unnecessary.[10]

As was to be expected, similar studies were conducted for other regions of Mediterranean Spain. These include works by Josep Fontana, Pierre Vilar and Carlos Martínez Shaw for Catalonia;[11] Andreu Bibiloni for Majorca;[12] Francisco Velasco and Vicente Montojo for Cartagena;[13] and other authors for Malaga.[14] Along similar lines, other publications have centred on the commercial relations

---

[10]E. Giménez López, "Dos décadas de estudios sobre el comercio valenciano en la Edad Moderna," *Revista de Historia Moderna. Anales de la Universidad de Alicante*, VI-VII (1986-1987), 193-206.

[11]J. Fontana Lázaro, "Sobre el comercio exterior de Barcelona en la segunda mitad del siglo XVII," *Estudios de Historia Moderna*, V (1955), 3-23; P. Vilar, *La Catalogne dans l'Espagne moderne* (París, 1962); and C. Martínez Shaw, "Il Mediterraneo nei rapporti economici internazionali catalani (1680-1808)," *Atti del Convegno su Alghero, la Catalogna, il Mediterraneo* (Sassari, 1995), 449-461. See also the summary in J.C. Maixé Altés, "Catalunya i el comerç mediterrani al Set-Cents," *L'Avenç*, CVIII (1987), 10-18; and E. Martín Corrales, "Il commercio della Catalogna con il mondo mediterraneo nel Settecento," *Islam. Storia e Civiltà* (Roma, 1988), 35-51. For some specific ports, see J. Morell Torredamé, *El port de Salou al segle XVIII* (Tarragona, 1986); A. Jordá Fernández, *Poder i comerç a la ciutat de Tarragona, segle XVIII* (Tarragona, 1988); and J. Giménez Blasco, *Mataró en la Catalunya del segle XVII. Un microcosmos en movement* (Mataró, 2001).

[12]A. Bibiloni Amengual, *Mercaders i navegants a Mallorca durant el segle XVII. L'oli com indicador del comerç mallorquí (1650-1720)* (Mallorca, 1992); and Bibloni Amengual, *El comerç exterior de Mallorca. Homes, mercats y productes d'intercanvi (1650-1720)* (Mallorca, 1995).

[13]F. Velasco Hernández, *Comercio y actividad portuaria en Cartagena (1570-1620)* (Cartagena, 1989); Velasco Hernández, *Auge y estancamiento de un enclave mercantil en la periferia. El nuevo resurgir de Cartagena entre 1540 y 1676* (Murcia, 2001); and V. Montojo Montojo, *El Siglo de Oro en Cartagena (1480-1640). Evolución económica y social de una ciudad portuaria en el Sureste español y su comarca* (Murcia, 1993).

[14]J.J. López González, "El comercio y el movimiento portuario de Málaga durante el reinado de Carlos IV," *I Congreso de Historia de Andalucía. Andalucía Moderna, III*, 301-319; and F. Cabrera Pablos, "El comercio portuario malacitano en el siglo XVIII: factores de influencia," *Anuario Jurídico y Económico Escurialense* (1990-1991), 385-404.

between Spanish ports and other parts of the Mediterranean, such as Italy;[15] Malta;[16] or North Africa, with the latter having received particular attention from Eloy Martín Corrales.[17] Other publications, especially those by Bernardo Hernández, have followed the lines set out by Braudel and continued by Joan Reglà in looking at the trade in precious metals.[18] Last but not least, one must

---

[15]V. Vázquez de Prada, "La actividad económica del Levante español en relación con Italia a finales del siglo XVI," *VI Congreso de Historia de la Corona de Aragón* (Madrid, 1959), 901-915.

[16]The various publications by Carmel Vassallo are essential for the trade with Malta, especially *Corsairing to Commerce. Maltese Merchants in XVIII Century Spain* (Malta, 1997); see also the papers by various authors in *Actas del Primer Coloquio Internacional Hispano Maltés de Historia* (Madrid, 1991).

[17]E. Martín Corrales, *Comercio de Cataluña con el Mediterráneo musulmán (siglos XVI-XVIII). El comercio con los "enemigos de la fe"* (Barcelona, 2001). The author had already published parts of his principal work: "El comerç de Catalunya amb els països musulmans al segle XVIII," *L'Avenç*, CVIII (1987), 26-32; "El comercio de Cataluña con Marruecos a finales del siglo XVIII," in *Actas I Congreso Internacional "El Estrecho de Gibraltar"* (3 vols., Madrid, 1988), III, 159-173; "Cereales y capitanes greco-otomanos en la Málaga de fines del siglo XVIII," *Estudis d'Història Econòmica*, II (1989), 87-114; "El comercio de Cataluña con el Levante otomano en el siglo XVIII (1782-1808)," in *VII Jornades d'Estudis Històrics Locals. La Mediterrània. Antropologia i Història* (Mallorca, 1991), 145-160; and "El comerç de Catalunya amb el Nord d'Africa al segle XVI: Una segona exclusió?" *L'Avenç*, XICC (1995), 16-21. Other authors who have written on this topic include A. Alberola Romá and E. Giménez López, "Relaciones entre Alicante y el norte de Africa durante el reinado de Felipe V," *España y el norte de Africa. Bases históricas de una relación fundamental* (Granada, 1987), 407-413; N. Cabrillana Ciezar, "Málaga y el comercio norteafricano (1517-1551)," *Cuadernos de la Biblioteca española de Tetuán*, XVII-XVIII (1978), 215-232; J.B. Vilar, "Relaciones comerciales hispano-argelinas en el periodo 1791-1814," *Hispania*, CXXVII (1974), 435-442; J. Juan Vidal, "El comercio del trigo entre Mallorca y Africa del Norte en los siglos XVI y XVII," *Mayurqa*, XV (1976), 73-92; and Vidal, "El abastecimiento cerealístico mallorquín procedente de la costa norteafricana durante el siglo XVIII," *Les Cahiers de Tunisie*, CIII-CV (1978), 197-215.

[18]B. Hernández, "Barcelona i Catalunya dins la ruta imperial dels metalls preciosos. Les llicències de propi ús concedides per la Generalitat, 1559-1599," in I. Roca and J. Albert (eds.), *La formació del cinturó industrial de Barcelona* (Barcelona, 1997), 23-35. See also J. Reglà, "Los envíos de metales preciosos de España a Italia a través de la Corona de Aragón y sus relaciones con el bandolerismo pirenaico," *Estudios de Historia Moderna*, IV (1954), 191-203; and E. Martín Corrales, "La 'saca' de plata americana desde España hacia el Mediterráneo musulmán, 1492-1830," in A.M. Bernal (ed.), *Dinero, moneda y crédito en la Monarquía Hispánica* (Madrid, 2000), 471-494. Of a more general nature are the works by F. Ruiz Martín, *Los destinos de la plata americana (Siglos*

mention the review of the literature on Spain's Mediterranean trade in the early modern period by Emilia Salvador.[19]

Alternative Forms of Commerce

A number of activities associated with maritime commerce, especially contraband, corsairing and salvage, have recently come to be considered "alternative" forms of trade, with the first two being seen as alternatives to legally registered trade or a means of securing profits through aggression against an enemy's commercial interests, and the third consisting of deriving benefits from the sale of goods salvaged from the sea and converted into trade goods in circuits other than those for which they were originally intended, by individuals and enterprises. With the 1989 *VIII Jornades d'Estudis Històrics Locals*, Gonçal López Nadal took the initiative to convene an international conference on "alternative trade," which considered contraband and corsairing, or privateering, as constituting one conceptual category.[20] Following an opening address by Michel Morineau, the other contributors highlighted the diverse aspects of both contraband and privateering in Spain and elsewhere, emphasizing the latter's role in naval policies and as a means of entry in international trade.[21] The contributors also underlined the

---

XVI y XVIII) (Madrid, 1991); and C.M. Cipolla, *Conquistadores, piratas, mercaderes. La saga de la plata española* (Buenos Aires, 1999).

[19]E. Salvador Esteban, "España y el comercio mediterráneo en la Edad Moderna," *III Reunión Científica de la Asociación Española de Historia Moderna* (2 vols., Las Palmas de Gran Canaria, 1995), II, 13-46. Although covering a shorter time span, see the classic review by H. Lapeyre and R. Carande, "Relaciones comerciales en el Mediterráneo durante el siglo XVI," *VI Congreso de Historia de la Corona de Aragón* (Madrid, 1959), 697-800; and more recently, E. Martín Corrales, "El comercio mediterráneo en la época de Felipe II," *Felipe II y el Mediterráneo* (4 vols., Madrid, 1999), I, 335-356.

[20]The convenor had already published some important contributions on the subject: G. López Nadal, *El corsarisme mallorquí a la Mediterrània occidental 1652-1698: un comerç forçat* (Barcelona, 1986); and "Actividades financieras de los chuetas en la segunda mitad del siglo XVII: armamento en corso y seguros marítimos," in C.A. Longhurst (ed.), *A Face Not Turned to the Wall. Essays on Hispanic Themes for Gareth Alban Davies* (Leeds, 1988), 111-136.

[21]M. Morineau, "La contrabande, la fraude et l'élaboration statistique," *El comerç alternatiu: corsarisme i contraban (ss. XV-XVIII)* (Palma de Mallorca, 1990), 13-26. Papers on contraband were given by A. Bibiloni Amengual, "El contrabando de tabaco en Mallorca durante la segunda mitad del siglo XVIII y su influencia en el litoral mediterráneo peninsular," 317-328; E. Martín Corrales, "El contrabando en el litoral catalán en la primera mitad del siglo XVIII (1720-1759)," 329-345; and A. Picazo i

role of prize ships as objects of trade, particularly as a source of vessels for the colonial fleet.[22]

Interest in "alternative" trade was not limited to the aforementioned conference and, in fact, has been characterized by other contributions. Worthy of mention are the efforts by Andreu Bibiloni to assess the structural nature of contraband or smuggling, as well as the work of other researchers who have shown that together with neutral flags and corsairing, which in any event was never a lucrative business for Spanish shipowners, contraband became commonplace in wartime, in addition to being the most lucrative form of business.[23]

Muntaner, "Contraban i epidèmies a Mallorca a finals de l'antic règim," 347-352. Papers on corsairing in the Mediterranean were given by S. Boubaker, "Les majorquins à Tunis au XVIIème siecle," 163-173; C. Martínez Shaw, "Un mal negocio: el corso catalán durante la guerra de las 13 colonias," 189-199; A. Marí Puig, "Cors i comerç a Menorca. La comercialització de les preses (1778-1781)," 201-216; and G. López Nadal, "El corsarismo en las estructuras mercantiles: las fronteras del convencionalismo," 267-276. M. Fontenay had previously made a valuable contribution on corsairing in the Mediterranean in "Los fenómenos corsarios en la 'periferización' del Mediterráneo en el siglo XVII," *Areas*, X (1986), 116-121.

[22]M. Alfonso Mola, "La procedencia de los barcos en la Carrera de Indias. El corso de la Armada (1778-1802)," in *El comerç alternatiu*, 231-257. For another article by the same author on the same subject, see "Corso y flota de Indias. Los convoyes ingleses apresados en 1780 y 1795," in *Andalucía, América y el Mar* (Sevilla, 1991), 197-223.

[23]A. Bibiloni Amengual, "Comerç de contraban a Mallorca: 1750-1812. El cas del tabac," *Estudis d'Història Econòmica*, I (1988), 65-97; Bilboni Amengual, "Reforma econòmica i 'legalització' del contraban a Mallorca. 1650-1720," *Randa*, XXVI (1990), 85-102; Bilboni Amengual, "Mallorca i les relacions comercials amb els 'enemics:' el contraban (1650-1720)," in *VII Jornades d'Estudis Locals. La Mediterrània: Antropolgia i Història* (Palma de Mallorca, 1989), 217-228; N. Coll y Juliá, "Aspectos negativos del tráfico marítimo en el siglo XV. Actos de piratería y consecuencias para el comercio internacional. Corsarios en las costas de la Corona de Aragón," in *V Congreso de Historia de la Corona de Aragón* (Zaragoza, 1952), 113-139; M. Barrio Gonzalo, "El corso norteafricano y su incidencia en el Principado de Cataluña durante el siglo XVIII," *Annals de l'Institut d'Estudis Gironins*, XXVII (1984), 313-327; J.A. Asensio Bernalte y J. Fábregas Roig, "Incidencias corsarias en las costas catalanas durante el reinado de Carlos III (1759-1788), según la Gazeta de Madrid," *I Congrés d'Història Moderna de Catalunya* (2 vols., Barcelona, 1984), I, 721-729; E. Martín Corrales, "Impulso de la actividad marítima catalana y corsarismo norteafricano (1680-1714)," *XIII Congrés de Història de la Corona d'Aragó* (3 vols., Palma de Mallorca, 1990), III, 185-194; Martín Corrales, "El corsarismo norteafricano y la flota catalana en la Carrera de Indias," *Manuscrits*, X (1992), 375-393; A. Gámez Amián, "Aproximación al contrabando en las costas meridionales durante el siglo XVIII y primera mitad del XIX," *Cuadernos de Ciencias Económicas y Empresariales*, IX-X (1982), 23-41; and Martín Corrales, "El

Financing

As a consequence of maritime trade being the principal focus of research, there have been a number of studies concerning its sources of finance, although these have not been as numerous as one would have expected or desired. The most frequent form of finance was the *prêt a la grosse aventure,* or sea exchange, a common and constant practice in European port cities from Antiquity to the early twentieth century, when it was finally replaced by other forms of credit. It consists in essence of an interest-bearing loan on the vessel or the cargo, and requires repayment of the loan in the event of a successful outcome or non-repayment if the results are unsuccessful. Some studies on the juridical character of the sea exchange have been carried out, at least for the maritime cities of the Crowns of Aragon.[24]

Insurance is not strictly speaking a financial instrument, although it has a close association with the perils at sea. Legal texts tend to view insurance as a hybrid, involving both insurance and a form of credit, which forms an integral part of maritime mercantile capitalism. In any event, the various forms of insurance have received a considerable amount of attention from legal historians.[25] It is nonetheless true that some of the research on insurance has tended to use insurance policies to study other topics which were considered of more interest, such as trade routes, exports or imports, and commercial conditions.[26] Nevertheless, lately there has been a spate of studies that look at insurance as an integral part of

---

contrabando en el litoral catalán durante el reinado de Carlos III," *Pedralbes*, VIII, No. 1 (1988), 485-494.

[24]M.J. Peláez, *Cambios y seguros marítimos en derecho catalán y balear* (Bolonia, 1984).

[25]In addition to the previously-cited work by M.J. Peláez on risk and insurance, see L. García Bravo, *El seguro marítimo. Notas para un capítulo sobre su historia dentro de la del derecho español* (Madrid, 1960); S.M. Coronas, "Los orígenes de la regulación consular burgalesa sobre el seguro marítimo," in *Derecho mercantil castellano. Dos estudios* (León, 1979), 173-224; A. García Sanz, "El seguro marítimo en España en los siglos XV y XVI," *Actas del V Centenario del Consulado de Burgo* (Burgos, 1995), 443-498; and García Sanz, "Estudios sobre los orígenes del derecho marítimo hispano-mediterráneo," *Anuario de Historia del Derecho Español*, XXXIX (1969), 212-316.

[26]Representative of such studies are the works by E. Giralt Raventós, "El comercio marítimo de Barcelona entre 1630 y 1665. Hombres, técnicas y direcciones del tráfico" (Unpublished PhD thesis, Barcelona, 1957); and C. Martínez Shaw, "El comercio marítimo de Barcelona, 1675-1712. Aproximación a partir de las escrituras de seguros," *Estudios Históricos y Documentos de los Archivos de Protocolos*, VI (1978), 287-310.

maritime commerce.[27] Other recent works have focussed on companies specializing in insurance, a phenomenon formerly thought to have been limited to the eighteenth century.[28] Within the context of a more general work on mercantile companies in Catalonia in the seventeenth century, Isabel Lobato has looked at the different forms of insurance cover provided by these companies, including protection against loss of cargo, vessel, charters, life, and freedom by those embarking as passengers.[29]

Shipbuilding

While the commercial system and trade flows have been closely studied over the years, researchers have shown considerably less interest in getting to know about the means of transport used in both coastal waters and on the high seas, including vessels used to ensure regular contact with the Americas. Indeed, we have to accept that despite its evident importance, merchant shipping has always been relegated to a second-class position by historians.

Nevertheless, some researchers have used hitherto untapped archival sources to estimate the size of the Spanish merchant fleet. Abbot Payson Usher, for example, used the figures provided by Tomé Cano to calculate Spain's merchant fleet at the end of the sixteenth century; Ruggiero Romano used French consular reports to calculate the number of Spanish vessels and their tonnage in the 1780s in relation to European fleets; and José Alcalá-Zamora, using information provided by Canga Argüelles, made an estimate, which holds to this day, of the merchant fleet in the early nineteenth century, in addition to looking at the evolution of the sail-powered merchant fleet from the beginning of the early modern period to its replacement by steam in the nineteenth century.[30] In any event,

---

[27]J. Pons i Pons, "El coste del seguro marítimo en Mallorca durante la segunda mitad del siglo XVII," *Estudis d'Història Econòmica*, II (1990), 51-76.

[28]J. Pons i Pons, *Companyies i mercat assegurador a Mallorca (1650-1715)* (Mallorca, 1996); Pons i Pons, "Assegurances i canvis marítims a Mallorca: les companyies, 1660-1680," *Estudis d'Història Econòmica*, II (1988), 43-67; Pons i Pons, "Les companyies en el sistema asseguratiu mallorquí (1660-1680)," *Mayurqa*, XXII (1989), 885-893; C. García Montoro, "Sociedades de seguros marítimos en Málaga en el siglo XIX," in *Homenaje a Carlos Seco* (Madrid, 1989), 261-271; and C. Martínez Shaw, "La compañía de seguros de Salvador Feliu de la Penya (1707-1709)," *II Congreso Internacional "El Estrecho de Gibraltar"* (Madrid, 1995), 405-413.

[29]I. Lobato Franco, *Compañías y negocios en la Cataluña preindustrial* (Sevilla, 1995).

[30]A.P. Usher, "Spanish Ships and Shipping in the Sixteenth and Seventeenth Centuries," in Arthur H. Cole, Arthur L. Dunham and N.S.B. Gras (eds.), *Facts and Factors in Economic History* (1932; reprint, New York, 1967), 189-213; T. Cano, *Arte*

the reason for the lack of studies in this area has to do with the fact that those researchers who have looked at shipbuilding at all have tended to concentrate overwhelmingly on warships, reflecting both the interest in the latter's complex technology and the political and military pride deriving from the Navy's success. A reflection of this lack of interest in the merchant navy is the fact that work on the Mediterranean is practically limited to Josep Maria Delgado's publication on Catalan shipbuilding from the late eighteenth century to the opening decades of the nineteenth.[31]

This lack of publications extends to naval dockyards as well. José Patricio Merino adhered strictly to the methodology of the French school in his pioneering study on the output of the naval yards at Ferrol, Cadiz and Cartagena in the eighteenth century, but few have followed his example.[32] Among those who have are María Teresa Pérez-Crespo, whose descriptive study of Cartagena did not really go beyond José Patricio Merino's excellent contribution more than a decade earlier.[33]

---

para fabricar, fortificar y aparejar naos de guerra y merchants (Sevilla, 1611); R. Romano, "Per una valutazione della Flotta mercantile europea alla fine del secolo XVIII," *Studi in onore di Amintore Fanfani*, V (1962), 573-591; J. Alcalá-Zamora y Queipo de Llano, "Evolución del tonelaje de la flota de vela española," *Estudios del Departamento de Historia Moderna de Zaragoza* (Zaragoza, 1975), 177-224; and J. Canga Argüelles, *Diccionario de Hacienda* (London, 1826-1827).

[31]J.M. Delgado Ribas, "La flota catalana del comercio libre (1778-1804): un caso de acumulación previa" (Unpublished MA thesis, Barcelona), 197, the contents of which are partly reflected in four articles: "Auge y decadencia de la marina colonial catalana," *Boletín Americanista*, XXIX (1979), 31-64; "La industria naviera en Cataluña y el País Vasco: un estudio comparativo (1750-1850)," *I Coloquio Vasco-Catalán de Historia* (1982), 89-107; "La construcció i la indústria navals a Catalunya, 1750-1820," *Recerques*, XIII (1983), 45-64; and "La indústria de la construcció naval catalana (1750-1850). Una visió a llarg termini," *Drassana*, II (1994). On the same topic, see also C. Martínez Shaw, "La procedencia de los capitales en la industria naviera catalana del siglo XVIII: los barcos del comercio atlántico (1744-1752)," *Anuario de Estudios Americanos*, XXX (1973), 471-488; and M. Andreu Vidiella, "La financiación de la industria naval en Barcelona (1745-1760)," *Pedralbes*, I (1981), 267-293.

[32]J.P. Merino Navarro, *La Armada española en el siglo XVIII* (Madrid, 1981); and Merino Navarro, "Técnica y arsenales en España y Francia hacia 1800," *Investigaciones Históricas*, II (1980), 167-191.

[33]M.T. Pérez-Crespo Muñoz, *El arsenal de Cartagena en el siglo XVIII* (Madrid, 1992); and J.P. Merino Navarro, "Cartagena: el arsenal ilustrado del Mediterráneo español," *Áreas*, I (1981), 40-52.

It still remains to refer to the shipbuilding enterprise itself to complete this review of the complex world of the vessel. It is practically uncharted territory where we only encounter the magnificent study by Pierre Vilar on the Catalan *barca* which touches on three sectors: the actual construction, in which merchant capital awards the commission to the *mestre d'aixai*, or shipwright; the shipping enterprise itself in the form of *parçoners*, shareholders possessing one or more one-sixteenth shares called *setzens*; and the merchant enterprise, often in the hands of the shipowner, who is entrusted with the *commenda*.[34]

Fishing

Fishing is another important sector in the maritime economy which has failed to attract the attention it deserves. Enlightenment reformers shed light on its problems and advanced possible solutions but still left it to the side as they concentrated on improvements in agriculture, industry and trade.[35] This is also reflected in the lack of studies on fishing which has made it the Cinderella of early modern Spanish economic history. Still, this desolate landscape is not completely arid, as is shown by a recent review of the literature which centres on the eighteenth century, although it must be noted that noteworthy publications referring to the period prior to the eighteenth century which transcend purely local issues are practically non-existent.[36] One of the studies relating to eighteenth-century fishing is a first attempt to quantify the human and material resources involved in fishing in the eighteenth century in the various regions of Spain.[37]

Studies have also been undertaken on the various coastal regions of Spain. The case of Catalonia, for example, has been researched by Roberto Fernández and Carlos Martínez Shaw and by Jordi Lleonart and Josep Maria

---

[34]Vilar, *La Catalogne*, III.

[35]C. Martínez Shaw, "La pesca en los economistas españoles del siglo XVIII," *Actas del VII Congreso Internacional de Historia de América* (Zaragoza, 1998), 1675-1690.

[36]C. Martínez Shaw, "La pesca española en el siglo XVIII. Una panorámica," in G. Doneddu and M. Gangemi (eds.), *La pesca nel Mediterraneo Occidentale (secc. XVI-XVIII)* (Bari, 2000), 39-60. In the same volume, see also Martín Corrales, "La pesca española en el Maghreb (ss. XVI-XVIII)," 9-38.

[37]R. Fernández Díaz and C. Martínez Shaw, "La pesca en la España del siglo XVIII. Una aproximación cuantitativa (1758-1765)," *Revista de Historia Económica*, III (1984), 183-201.

Camarasas;[38] Valencia, by Rafael Viruela;[39] and Mediterranean Andalusia by a number of historians from Malaga – Marion Reder, Andrés Sarriá and Manuel Burgos – who have been particularly interested in the conflicts which arose as a result of *bou* fishing techniques introduced by Catalans in southern waters.[40] Historians have also looked into certain forms of fishing which are characteristic of the Mediterranean, such as tunny fishing and the gathering of coral.[41]

---

[38]R. Fernández and C. Martínez Shaw, "Els sistemes de pesca a la Catalunya de l'Antic Règim," *L'Avenç*, XXXIII (1980), 42-53; Fernández and Martínez Shaw, "La pesca en la Cataluña del siglo XVIII. Una panorámica," *Pedralbes*, VIII, No. 1 (1988), 323-338; Fernández and Martínez Shaw, "El despliegue de los bous catalanes en el siglo XVIII," *Congrés "Història Moderna, Història en Construcció"* (Lérida, 1999), I, 61-65; and J. Lleonart and J.M. Camarasa, *La pesca a Catalunya el 1722, segons un manuscrit de Joan Salvador i Riera* (Barcelona, 1987).

[39]R. Viruela Martínez, "Difusió de la pesca del bou en el litoral valencià (segles XVIII i XIX)," *Cuadernos de Geografía*, LIII (1993), 145-161; and Viruela Martínez, "Aproximació a l'activitat pesquera valenciana del segle XVIII," *Estudis*, XXI (1995), 179-200.

[40]M. Reder Gadow, "Conflictos pesqueros catalano-malagueños en la costa marbellí a mediados del siglo XVIII," *Baetica*, XIII (1991), 255-279; A. Sarriá Muñoz, "Las Ordenanzas de Gibraltar relativas a la pesca y las jábegas malagueñas (1697-1711)," *Jábega*, LXVIII (1990), 25-32; M. Burgos Madroñero, "Precisiones en torno a la pesca y a la gente de mar de Málaga en el siglo XVIII," *Isla de Arriarán*, III (1994), 21-43; and Burgos Madroñero, "La pesca de parejas del bou y Málaga (siglos XVIII y XIX)," *Isla de Arriarán*, VIII (1996), 45-63.

[41]On the former, see J.M. Madurell i Marimon, "L'Almadrava de Tossa i la pesca de corall al comtat d'Empúries i a la Selva de Mar," *Annals de l'Institut d'Estudis Gironis*, XXV-II (1981), 1-35; M. Oliver Narbona, *Almadrabas de la costa alicantina* (Alicante, 1982); and C. Martínez Shaw: "La situación jurídica de las almadrabas españolas a fines del Antiguo Régimen," *Hommage au Professeur Didier Ozanam* (in press). A number of seminal articles referring to the Catalan coral business include L. Camos y Cabruja, "Referencias documentales en torno al tráfico del coral en Barcelona en el siglo XV," *Boletín de la Real Academia de Buenas Letras de Barcelona*, XIX (1946), 145-204; S. Raurich Ferriol, *La pesca del coral en las costas de África. Reseña histórica* (Madrid, 1944); and V. Palacio Atard, "La frustrada Compañía del Coral a fines del siglo XVIII," *Jahrbuch für Geschichte von Staat, Wirstchaft und Gesellschaft Lateinamerikas*, IV (1967), 543-556. More recent works include J.M. Grau and R. Puig, *El corall a la costa de l'Empordà (Begur, segles XVIII-XIX)* (Barcelona, 1993); E. Martín Corrales, "L'activitat dels corallers catalans en el litoral africà al segle XIX. Algèria, Marroc i Cap Verd," *Drassana*, II (1994), 18-23; and Martín Corrales, "Los coraleros catalanes en el litoral argelino en el siglo XVIII," in C. Martínez Shaw (ed.), *El Derecho y el Mar en la España moderna* (Granada, 1996), 427-456.

Port Infrastructure

Situated on the threshold between land and sea, ports and harbours are centres for a range of economic activities (trade, navigation, fishing, finance, shipbuilding and repair). They are the venues for a very specific society endowed with a singular form of production. They are, at one and same time, a node of communications and a melting pot, and they act as agents for change and modernization, although these themes fall outside the subject at hand.

First of all, one has to keep in mind that port history is essentially a branch of urban history to the extent that ports fall within the spatial boundaries of cities. Port cities belong to two worlds. On the one hand they are a type of city, as are agro towns, industrial towns or capital cities, but at the same time the port is an autonomous entity with a particular infrastructure which includes fortifications; warehouses; reception centres, such as inns, hostels and brothels; and port works, sanitary and customs authorities. The study of ports is a long-established pursuit in the historiography of France and even more so in Britain. In Spain, on the other hand, interest in port installations and their relationship with urban life is a recent phenomenon, even though partial studies, especially centring on defensive works, have been produced by geographers, engineers and architects. Historians, on the other hand, started publishing in earnest only in the 1980s, with their work centring increasingly in the 1990s on the contemporary period. This reflected a general tendency within economic history, as well as the requirements of the port authorities which sponsored the studies. Nevertheless, it is also a fact that port cities did not set about overcoming infrastructural deficiencies through the construction of stone quays, breakwaters and seawalls, and the introduction of cranes, jibs and dredgers, until well into the nineteenth century, even though they had already played a role in the opening of the littoral to the market and the extension of the latter to the national level. The economies of port cities and their hinterlands eventually grew at an exceptional pace within the context of the industrial revolution and the onset of capitalism.[42]

Although publications offering an overall picture of Spanish ports in the *Ancien Régime* are few and far between, we can cite the contributions by a number of historians to the collective work sponsored by the Centro de Estudios Históricos de Obras Públicas y Urbanismo (CEHOPU), as well as a number of publications by Agustín Guimerá, including two series centring on Spanish port systems starting with the first international conference on the subject held in Madrid in October 1995.[43]

---

[42]C. Martínez Shaw, "La ciudad y el mar. La ciudad marítima y sus funciones en el Antiguo Régimen," *Manuscrits*, XV (1997), 257-278.

[43]CEHOPU, *Puertos españoles en la Historia* (Madrid, 1994). A. Guimerá and D. Romero (eds.), *Puertos y Sistemas Portuarios (siglos XVI-XX)* (Madrid, 1998), includes a number of contributions relating to the Spanish Mediterranean: A. Guimerá, "El sistema

Over and above these collective works, some ports have also received individual monographic attention. Particularly noteworthy in this regard are the excellent studies on the port of Malaga by María Teresa López Beltrán, Isabel Rodríguez Alemán and Francisco Cabrera, respectively.[44] To these we must add the studies on Palma, on Barcelona by Joan Alemany and on Tarragona.[45]

Social History

The maritime history associated with the *Annales* School placed more importance to the economic than on the social aspects of history, and when it was concerned with the societal aspects of the world of maritime business, it tended to focus almost exclusively on merchants, hardly touching on shipowners or mariners. In contrast, there is now an increasingly greater preoccupation with the actual economic agents, merchants and non-merchants alike. This also reflects the tendency within history in general to "return to the subject," and within maritime history in particular to centre on the protagonists of economic activities associated with the sea, even before an adequate knowledge of these activities has been achieved.

---

portuariio español (siglos XVI-XX): perspectivas de investigación," 125-141; E. Martín Corrales, "La proyección mediterránea del sistema portuario español: siglos XVI-XVIII," 143-165; D. Romero Muñoz and A. Sáenz Sanz, "La construcción de los puertos: siglos XVI-XIX," 185-212; and F.R. Cabrera Pablos, "El puerto de Málaga en el siglo XVIII. Sus implicaciones urbanísticas," 313-331. J.M. Delgado Barrado and A. Guimerá Ravina (eds.), *Los puertos españoles: historia y futuro (siglos XVI-XX)* (Madrid 2000), includes contributions on the Mediterranean during the *Ancien Regime*: J.L. Casado Soto, "El Estado y los puertos españoles en la Edad Moderna," 13-33; and A. Guimerá Ravina, "Los puertos españoles en la Historia (siglos XVI-XX)," 47-60; it also includes a bibliography and thus makes it unnecessary for us to set out more details here.

[44]M.T. López Beltrán, *El puerto de Málaga en la transición a los tiempos modernos* (Málaga, 1986); I. Rodríguez Alemán, *El puerto de Málaga bajo los Austrias* (Málaga, 1984); F.R. Cabrera Pablos, *El puerto de Málaga a comienzos del siglo XVIII* (Málaga, 1986); Cabrera Pablos, *Puerto de Málaga. De Felipe V a Carlos III* (Málaga, 1994); and Cabrera Pablos and M. Olmedo, *El puerto de Málaga: 30 siglos de vida, 400 años de historia* (Málaga, 1988).

[45]On Palma de Majorca, see F. Sevillano Colom and J. Pou Muntaner, *Historia del puerto de Palma de Mallorca* (Palma de Mallorca, 1974). On Barcelona, see J. Alemany Llovera, *El port de Barcelona. Història i actualitat* (Barcelona, 1994); C. Martínez Shaw, "Les transformations du port de Barcelone au XVIIIe siècle," in *I porti come impresa economica* (Florencia, 1988), 89-101; and J.M. Delgado, "El puerto de Barcelona en la época preindustrial," in A. Carreras, J. Clavera, J.M. Delgado and C. Yáñez, *Economía e Historia del puerto de Barcelona* (Barcelona, 1992), 17-80. On Tarragona, see J. Alemany, J. Blay and S. Roquer, *Puerto de Tarragona. Historia y actualidad* (Barcelona, 1986).

Social history must look at all those who are actors in the world of ports and the sea, be they entrepreneurs, such as merchants, shipowners, naval contractors or fishing vessel owners; workers in the various spheres, such as mariners of all types, fishermen, dock and dockyard workers; and intermediaries, such as civil servants, brokers or agents. Finally, one may also include passengers, especially those who, forcibly or of their own free will, migrated across the seas.

The Merchant Bourgeoisie

From early on, "Spanish" economic history has devoted some of its effort into the study of economic exchanges, an area to which it has given preferential treatment, and to analysing the part played by the economic actors involved. This has also been the case in maritime history, to such an extent that here we can only cite a representative sample of works which have looked at the role of entrepreneurs in Mediterranean maritime trade.

A brief review of the work in this area includes the publications of Ricardo Franch on Valencia;[46] the previously-cited Enrique Giménez on Alicante;[47] Emili Giralt, Joan Carles Maixé, Roberto Fernández and Josep Maria Delgado on Barcelona;[48] and Begoña Villar and Aurora Gámez on Málaga.[49]

The merchant of the *Ancien Régime* was an all-rounder who engaged in a range of deals to do with the sea involving credit, companies, charters, insurance, imports and exports, and so on. The bibliography to date shows few instances of specialization, although it is difficult to determine at this stage whether this is because these types of entrepreneurs appeared at a later stage or whether

---

[46]R. Franch Benavent, *Crecimiento comercial y enriquecimiento burgués en la Valencia del siglo XVIII* (Valencia, 1986).

[47]Giménez López, *Alicante*.

[48]E. Giralt Raventós, "La colonia mercantil francesa de Barcelona a mediados del siglo XVII," *Estudios de Historia Moderna*, VI (1956-1959), 218-278; J.C. Maixé Altés, *Comercio y banca en la Cataluña del siglo XVIII. La compañía Bensi & Merizano de Barcelona (1724-1750)* (La Coruña, 1994); R. Fernández Díaz, "La burguesía barcelonesa en el siglo XVIII: la familia Gloria," in P. Tedde (ed.), *La economía española al final del Antiguo Régimen* (Madrid, 1982), 3-131; Fernández Díaz, "La burguesía barcelonesa en el siglo XVIII" (Unpublished PhD thesis, Lérida, 1987), with a summary of the same in *Areas*, X (1986), 156-158; and J.M. Delgado Ribas, "Els comerciants catalans en la cursa de les Índies durant el segle XVIII," *III Jornades d'Estudis Catalano-Americans* (Barcelona, 1990), 75-87.

[49]B. Villar García, *Los extranjeros en Málaga en el siglo XVIII* (Málaga, 1982); and A. Gámez Amián, *Comercio colonial y burguesía mercantil "malagueña" (1765-1830)* (Málaga, 1992).

they have simply not received attention from researchers. As a consequence, the abundant literature on merchants contrasts with the little information we have on shipowners or operators who formed one side of the ship-chartering equation.

Seafarers and Those in Ancillary Trades

The group most clearly identified with the maritime economy is the seafarers, a term which includes officers, seamen and all others comprising the crew of a vessel, including the cooks and storemen responsible for victualling; the carpenters, caulkers and divers who look after the maintenance of the vessel; the pursers and writers who attend to the administrative chores; and those responsible for the spiritual and physical care of those on board, namely the chaplains and surgeons. Fishing vessels normally have more modest crews, but they may include specialists in the particular type of fishing being undertaken. Those involved in seafaring on the high seas tended to belong to the Confraternity of Saint Elmo, while those involved in fishing tended to belong to the Confraternity of Saint Peter. Apart from seafarers we also ought to consider those engaged in trades related to the sea, such as carpenters, caulkers, sail and rope makers, and others who build and maintain vessels but are based ashore. Lower down the scale we could also include the dockers, porters and boatmen involved in the loading and unloading in ports and who thus supplemented the crew's own efforts.

Publications focussing on seafarers and port-related trades are fairly recent and relate exclusively to Catalonia.[50] We can complete the picture by also referring to those studies which focus on those "other" seafarers – the pirates and corsairs and the oarsmen propelling the galleys in the Mediterranean.[51] Some researchers have also looked at situations of social conflict involving seafarers.[52] The situation is not much better as regards dock or shipyard crafts. Work on these

---

[50]J.M. Delgado, "La navegació catalana d'altura: els mariners de comerç lliure," *L'Avenç*, XXXV (1981), 52-58; and R. Fernández Díaz and C. Martínez Shaw, "La gente de mar en la Cataluña del XVIII," *I Congrés d'Història Moderna de Catalunya* (Barcelona, 1984), I, 553-567.

[51]E. Sola, *Un Mediterráneo de piratas, corsarios, renegados y cautivos*, (Madrid, 1988); and F.J. Guillamón Alvarez and J. Pérez Hervás, "Los forzados de galeras en Cartagena durante el primer tercio del siglo XVIII," *Revista de Historia Naval*, XIX (1987), 63-75.

[52]F. Mas i Marquet, *La revolta dels Joseps. Un conflicte dels pescadors de Lloret al segle XVIII* (Lloret, 1988).

seems to be limited to the contributions by Joaquim Llovet and Josep Maria Delgado on Catalan shipwrights.[53]

The situation regarding port occupations, such as sail and ropemakers, gunsmiths, boatmen, dockers, porters and cart men is characterised by a complete absence of research, excluding Josep Maria Delgado's study of the port of Barcelona.[54] Neither has any work been done on topics such as salaries, with the exception of some research on the singular form of remuneration in the fishing sector.[55]

Institutional History

The study of the institutions related to maritime activities is still at an early stage as far as early modern Spain is concerned, but it is not easy to determine the reasons for this backwardness in view of the long-established traditions and achievements in Spain of both legal and institutional history. In any event, for our purposes we shall look first at the studies on the legislation dealing with maritime matters, such as charters, insurance, duties, exchanges, letters patent for corsairing, censuses of seafarers, licensing, crewing contracts, and so on, as well as naval jurisdiction, and subsequently look at the actual institutions, including the Consulates of the Sea, boards of health and nautical schools.

Legislation

The legislation relating to maritime matters covers a broad spectrum of topics. Allied to this, legislation in the *Ancien Régime* was characterised by dispersion; in other words, it is not to be encountered in a single focussed legal *corpus*. As a consequence, we are confronted with a potentially vast field, many aspects of which have not been studied in any meaningful way. The navy's administrative

---

[53]J. Llovet, *Constructors navals a l'ex-provincia marítima de Mataró* (Madrid, 1971); and J.M. Delgado Ribas, "La construcció naval catalana: els mestres d'aixa," *L'Avenç*, XXXVII (1981), 44-50.

[54]J.M. Delgado Ribas, "La organización de los servicios portuarios en un puerto preindustrial," in Martínez Shaw (ed.), *El Derecho*, 107-146.

[55]J.M. Massip Segarra, "El arte y la parte en la pesca mediterránea noroccidental española (aproximación a una relación laboral poco común)," *Revista de Treball*, IV (1987), 115-130; J.M. García Bartolomé, "El sistema de remuneración a la parte en la pesca: una aproximación desde el enfoque de las ciencias sociales," *Información Comercial Española*, Nos. 653-654 (1988), 97-104; and J.J. Pascual Fernández, "La pesca artesanal y el sistema a la parte," *Jornadas sobre economía y sociología de las comunidades pesqueras* (Madrid, 1989), 547-574.

organization was one of the first topics to be examined in the classical works on the Spanish Navy or more recently in contributions on Admiralty jurisdiction.[56]

The study on the *Libre del Consolat de Mar*, or *Book of the Consulate of the Sea*, which constituted the basis of mercantile relations from the Middle Ages to the end of the early modern period, was the point of departure for work on maritime law.[57] There followed studies on specific aspects of commercial and maritime life in early modern Spain, such as maritime insurance, customs administration, juridical instruments used in commerce, shipbuilding, duties on trade, contraband and shipwrecks.[58] One topic which has received considerable attention from historians is the *Matrícula de Mar*, or List of Seafarers – how it functioned and its consequences on the communities on which it was imposed.[59]

---

[56]Gervasio de Artiñano y Galdácano, *La Arquitectura Naval española (en madera)* (Barcelona, 1920); Cesáreo Fernández Duro, *Disquisiciones náuticas* (6 vols., Madrid, 1876-1881); Cesáreo Fernández Duro, *Armada española, desde la unión de los reinos de Castilla y León* (9 vols., Madrid, 1895-1903); and D. Matamoros Aparicio, "Administración y jurisdicción de Marina en Cataluña (1714-1777)," in Martínez Shaw (ed.), *El Derecho*, 273-297.

[57]See, for example, A. García Sanz, "Estudios sobre los orígenes del derecho marítimo hispano-mediterráneo," *Anuario de Historia del Derecho Español*, XXXIX (1969), 212-316; and S. Hernández Izal, *Els Costums Marítims de Barcelona* (Barcelona, 1986).

[58]On insurance, see J. Pons i Pons, "El pago del seguro marítimo y los conflictos ante el Tribunal Consular," *Pedralbes*, XII (1992), 71-94; and Pons i Pons, "Legislación y práctica del seguro marítimo. Las contradicciones de la segunda mitad del Seiscientos en Mallorca," in Martínez Shaw (ed.), *El Derecho*, 39-58. On customs, see J. Muñoz Pérez, "Mapa aduanero del XVIII español," *Estudios Geográficos*, LXI (1955), 747-798. On business instruments, see J.C. Maixé Altés, "Los instrumentos jurídicos de la circulación mercantil y la actividad económica catalana en el siglo XVIII," in Martínez Shaw (ed.), *El Derecho*, 357-382. On shipbuilding, see M. Mestre Prat de Pàdua, "La construcción naval de guerra en la España del siglo XVIII. El marco legal de los procesos de financiación," in Martínez Shaw (ed.), *El Derecho*, 299-321. On duties, see C. Parrón Salas, "La legislación relativa al almojarifazgo (siglos XV-XVIII)," in Martínez Shaw (ed.), *El Derecho*, 147-171. On contraband, see A. Bibiloni Amengual, "El derecho de contrabando en las relaciones comerciales mallorquinas (1640-1720)," in Martínez Shaw (ed.), *El Derecho*, 31-38. On shipwrecks, see J. de Castro Fresnadillo, "El problema de las competencias en materia de naufragios en la España del Setecientos. Algunos casos conflictivos de jurisdicción," in Martínez Shaw (ed.), *El Derecho*, 323-356.

[59]F.X. de Salas, *Historia de la Matrícula de Mar y examen de varios sistemas de reclutamiento marítimo* (Madrid, 1879); A. O'Dogherty, "La matrícula de mar en el reinado de Carlos III," *Anuario de Estudios Americanos*, IX (1952), 347-370; O. López Miguel and M. Mirabet Cucala, "La institucionalización de la Matrícula de Mar: textos normativos y consecuencias para la gente de mar y maestranza," in Martínez Shaw (ed.),

Institutions

The Consulate of the Sea was an institution which emerged in the late Middle Ages. It was an association charged with the defence of the common interests of the maritime merchant class *vis-à-vis* political power, but it was also a tribunal entrusted with the administration of justice in matters of trade and the sea. In addition, it was responsible for the promotion of commerce in general via the construction, maintenance and improvement of port infrastructure such as wharves, docks and canals; supervision over readying and loading vessels; and the establishment of schools of commerce and navigation.

Positivist Spanish historians had already shown an interest in this topic in the early twentieth century, but it was not until Robert Sidney Smith's 1940 publication that a "modern" treatment of the subject was available.[60] Smith looked at the various aspects of the consulates from their Medieval origins to the end of the seventeenth century. In his wake came other contributors, such as Francisco Bejarano on Málaga; Jaume Carrera Pujal on the *Junta de Comercio*, or Board of Trade, of Barcelona; and Francisco Figueras on Alicante and Román Piña on Palma de Majorca, written due to an initiative of the regional bourgeoisie represented by the respective Chambers of Commerce.[61] All project a positive perception of the Consulates, which they portray as agents of anti-feudal modernity. A

El Derecho, 217-239; and R. Fernández Díaz and C. Martínez Shaw, "Las Revistas de Inspección de la Matrícula de Mar en el siglo XVIII," in Martínez Shaw (ed.), *El Derecho*, 241-271. For specific regions, see J. Llovet, *La matrícula de mar i la província de Marina de Mataró al segle XVIII* (Mataró, 1980); M. Burgos Madroñero, "La Matrícula de Mar en Málaga en los siglos XVIII y XIX," *Hespérides. IX Congreso de Profesores-Investigadores* (El Ejido, Almería, 1990), 271-290; and Burgos Madroñero, "La Matrícula de Mar y la pesca en Andalucía. Siglos XVIII y XIX," *Isla de Arriarán*, II (1993), 13-26.

[60]A. Ruiz y Pablo, *Historia de la Real Junta Particular de Comercio de Barcelona* (Barcelona, 1919); and R.S. Smith, *The Spanish Merchant Guild. A History of the Consulado, 1250-1700* (Durham, NC, 1940).

[61]F. Bejarano, *Historia del Consulado y de la Junta de Comercio de Málaga (1785-1859)* (Madrid, 1947); J. Carrera Pujal, *La Lonja del Mar y los Cuerpos de Comercio de Barcelona* (Barcelona, 1953); F. Figueras Pacheco, *El Consulado Marítimo y Terrestre de Alicante y pueblos del Obispado de Orihuela* (Alicante, 1957); and R. Piña Homs, *El Consolat de Mar, Mallorca 1326-1800* (Palma de Mallorca, 1985). The *Juntas de Comercio* of Valencia and Barcelona have also been studied by P. Molas Ribalta, "València i la Junta de Comerç," *Estudis*, III (1974), 55-111; and Molas Ribalta, *Comerç i estructura social a Catalunya i València als segles XVII i XVIII* (Barcelona, 1977).

good review of the literature was presented by Roberto Fernández at a 1989 conference in Santander.[62]

Health matters were permanent features of port life owing to the continual threat of contagion entering the country via the ports, carried by vessels originating in the Muslim Levant or North Africa. The risk of plague was well known to European port authorities who sought to erect barriers to prevent the much-feared interruption of commercial relations by measures taken to avoid the transmission of infection via individuals, clothing or goods. In eighteenth-century Spain there was an important advance in the extension and centralization of health measures, especially those of a preventive nature. There was a proliferation of measures, including the reorganization and modernization of boards of health, a more rigorous enforcement of clean bills of health for vessels, people and goods, and the creation of a quarantine service, although it would be some time before quarantine hospitals were set up. In this period, Spain depended on the diligence of quarantine authorities in other European ports to control infected vessels or those suspected of infection, and there were instances of ships being admitted to protect commercial interests, despite the health risk. In any event, the terrible impact of the Marseilles plague of 1720 was the catalyst for the renewal of port health measures in eighteenth-century Spain.[63]

The historiography on maritime health in Mediterranean Spain is still in its infancy, although some introductory work has already been published on some of the main themes, which could constitute a point of departure for more detailed studies. One could highlight the research on the reorganization of Spain's health services in the eighteenth century, especially on boards of health and the quarantine service, including quarantine hospitals.[64] In a similar manner, some writers

---

[62]R. Fernández Díaz, "Burguesía y Consulados en el siglo XVIII," in T. Martínez Vara (comp.), *Mercado y desarrollo económico en la España Contemporánea* (Madrid, 1986), 1-39. See also the earlier work by P. Molas Ribalta, "Instituciones administrativas y grupos sociales en la España del siglo XVIII. Las Juntas de Comercio," *Actas de las I Jornadas de Metodología Aplicada a las Ciencias Históricas* (5 vols., Santiago de Compostela, 1975), III, 795-802.

[63]M. Peset and M. Mancebo, "Valencia y la peste de Marsella de 1720," *III Congreso de Historia del País Valenciano* (Valencia, 1976), 567-577; and Peset, *et al.*, "Temores y defensa de España frente a la peste de Marsella de 1720," *Asclepio*, XXIII (1971), 131-139.

[64]E. Rodríguez Ocaña, "La cuestión del lazareto marítimo permanente en la España del siglo XVIII, de Cádiz a Mahón," *Asclepio*, XL (1988), 265-276; Rodríguez Ocaña, "El resguardo de la salud. Organización sanitaria española del siglo XVIII," *Dynamis*, VII-VIII (1987-1988), 145-170; and Rodríguez Ocaña, "Organización sanitaria española en el siglo XVIII: Las Juntas de Sanidad," in J. Fernández and I. González (eds.), *Ciencia, técnica y Estado en la España Ilustrada* (Madrid, 1990), 399-411.

have looked at quarantine facilities in the various ports. Some were by medical historiants.[65] Other, perhaps more systematic, efforts were carried out by Gonçal López Nadal, Eloy Martín Corrales and Josep Maria Cortés Verdaguer.[66]

The last item under this heading relates to the historical studies on professional training, especially in the nautical schools which came into being towards the end of the eighteenth century. Though the literature on this subject is sparse, and we lack any sort of comparative study which might give us an overview, we do have an initial outline of developments in the main Mediterranean ports. Particularly noteworthy are Josep Maria Pons Guri's study on the school for pilots at Arenys de Mar and Roberto Fernández and Elena Sierco's work on the Barcelona Nautical School.[67]

Culture and *Mentalités*

Maritime history has also looked at what the *Annales* school referred to as the level of civilizations. As a consequence, the first steps have already been taken, albeit following imported models, towards a history of maritime culture and of the mind set of human beings associated with the sea.

The more traditional forms of the history of maritime culture are framed within two long-established disciplines, the history of overseas discoveries on the one hand, and the history of science on the other. Nevertheless, the history of

---

[65]See, for example, J.L. Cabrillo Martos, "Una institución sanitaria ilustrada: la Junta de Sanidad de Málaga," *Cuadernos de Historia de la Medicina Española*, XII (1973), 447-466; and S. Gascón Casulla, "El lazareto de Barcelona (1720-1820)" (Unpublished MA thesis, Barcelona, 1987).

[66]G. López Nadal, "La Sanidad marítima menorquina anterior al funcionamiento del Lazareto de Mahón. Introducción a su estudio histórico," in *Menorca en la historia de la sanidad. El doctor Orfila, toxicología y medicina legal. El Lazareto, fundación del Rey Carlos III en Menorca* (Madrid, 1987), 81-108; López Nadal, "Estructuras e instituciones sanitarias en los puertos del levante ibérico entre los siglos XVI y XVIII (una visión de conjunto)," in *I porti*, 65-88; E. Martín Corrales, "Dos obstáculos en las relaciones comerciales entre Cataluña y los países musulmanes en el siglo XVIII: el corso y la peste," in *I Congrés d'Història Moderna de Catalunya* (Barcelona, 1984), 611-617; Martín Corrales, "Sobre sanidad y pesca en la Cataluña del siglo XVIII," *Estudis d'Història Econòmica*, I (1988), 45-64; and J.M. Cortés Verdaguer, "La prevención sanitaria en Mallorca (1718-1756)," *Espacio, Tiempo y Forma*, XIII (2000), 421-456.

[67]J.M. Pons Guri, *Estudi dels Pilots. Ensayo monográfico sobre la real escuela náutica de Arenys de Mar* (Arenys de Mar, 1960); and R. Fernández and E. Sierco, "Enseyament professional i desenvolupament econòmic: L'Escola Nàutica de Barcelona," *Recerques*, XV (1984), 7-30.

discoveries has been so prolific since it became established academically that it would be impossible in the limited space available to give a reasonable account of it. In any event, it is of tangential interest for a publication focussed on the Mediterranean. Within the history of science one would include research referring to cartography, nautical science and the art of navigation. Representative of such work, albeit focussing more on the Atlantic than on the Mediterranean, are the publications by José Luis López Piñero and Manuel Sellés.[68]

Other areas have more recently been opened up for academic research. Thus, the social history of people associated with maritime activity occasionally drifts towards labour relations and the history of conflict on land and sea.[69] By this route we come to identify the particular lifestyle of mariners who have a special culture in all aspects: world view, sociability and forms of expression. The study of this type of lifestyle enables us to get to the history of *mentalités*, as has been done for the maritime world in a series of works mainly by French historians.[70]

In Spain there already exist a number of publications of this type, but they focus on navigation on the high seas and specifically on the Atlantic, as is the case of Pablo Emilio Pérez-Mallaína's pioneering studies on mariners on the Indies route in Hapsburg Spain as it relates to recruitment, work days, culture and attitudes towards death and the beyond.[71]

It is clear that while the histories of overseas discoveries and nautical science are long established in Spain, the history of *mentalités,* as regards life at sea or in communities dependent on the sea, is still in an early phase, although it is clear that it is a very promising field which will soon attract adepts. Such is the case for the world of *ex-votos.*[72] This is also true for studies of religiosity and

---

[68]J.M. López Piñero, *El arte de navegar en la España del Renacimiento* (Barcelona, 1979); and M.A. Sellés, *La navegación astronómica en la España del siglo XVIII* (Madrid, 1990).

[69]M. Rediker, *Between the Devil and the Deep Blue Sea. Merchant Seamen, Pirates, and the Anglo-American Maritime World, 1700-1750* (Cambridge, 1987).

[70]A. Cabantous, *La mer et les hommes. Pêcheurs et matelots dunkerquois de Louis XIV à la Révolution* (Dunkerque, 1980); Cabantous, *Le ciel dans la mer: christianisme et civilisation maritime, XVIe-XIXe siècles* (Paris, 1990); and Cabantous, *Les citoyens du large. Les identités maritimes en France (XVIIe-XIXe siècle)* (París, 1995).

[71]P.E. Pérez-Mallaína Bueno, *Los hombres del Océano. Vida cotidiana de los tripulantes de las flotas de Indias. Siglo XVI* (Sevilla, 1992); and Pérez-Mallaína Bueno, *El Hombre frente al Mar. Naufragios en la Carrera de Indias durante los siglos XVI y XVII* (Sevilla, 1996).

[72]M. Armengou, "Iconografía marinera de tema negrero," *L'Avenç,* LXXV (1984), 48-51.

superstition, rites of passage, the experience of danger and death, oral culture and technical vocabulary.[73]

Conclusion

After navigating the different routes which comprise the complex space which is maritime history, we conclude that in the space of forty years this field of study has gone from being limited almost exclusively to military aspects to research at a university level and with a wider conception of history. In any event, the magnitude and diversity of the latter is such that many areas can be considered a veritable *terra incognita* waiting to be charted by scientific exploration.

Maritime history has the vocation to be a total history in that it contains, and belongs to, economic, social, institutional and cultural history, as well as the history of *mentalités*. It is a history which seeks to turn into reality Braudel's notion of "total history," the inclusive history of Pierre Vilar, within the space it has defined as its own. It is also an amphibious history lying at the juncture of various disciplines, in the sense that it is partly urban history, in contrast to rural history, but at the same time it is a history astride the seemingly immovable littoral and the ever-swirling seas.

---

[73]E. Martín Corrales, "El miedo a las corsarios norteafricanos en la mentalidad colectiva catalana del siglo XVIII," in *El comerç alternatiu*, 217-230.

Trade in the Mediterranean in the Early Modern Era: A Brief Review of the French Literature

Xavier Labat Saint Vincent

No study of commercial exchanges in the Mediterranean in the early modern period can be carried out without an awareness of the geopolitical and military context of the *mare nostrum* and more specifically of the conflicts, tensions, military operations and epidemics which in their own way impacted on commercial relations. As a consequence, before going into detail concerning a specific region, flag or type of goods, it is necessary to become familiar with some of the classic works by authors such as Paul Masson, Charles Carrière, Louis Bergasse and Gaston Rambert, and Robert Paris.[1]

An excellent research tool has just been published by Presses de l'Université de Paris Sorbonne (PUPS). Compiled by Professor Alain Blondy, and appropriately entitled *Bibliographie du monde méditerranéen, relations et échanges (1453-1835)*, it deserves a place on the bookshelves of all those working on the early modern Mediterranean.[2] With a well organized index to authors and subject matter, the various articles and works on a specific topic can be rapidly identified. Drawing on this rich bibliographic source, I propose to set out some of the French-language publications which deal with four main topics: Marseilles and trade in the Mediterranean; corsairing and its effect on trade; relations with the different provinces of the Ottoman empire with particular emphasis on the Barbary Regencies and other parts of the Mediterranean; and the nature of the goods traded. This is clearly not an exhaustive list – that would be beyond the scope of such a short contribution – but it will provide some insight for those not familiar with French-language publications by pointing to the principal works where additional references will be encountered by those who wish to fine tune their search.

---

[1] See Paul Masson, *Histoire du commerce français dans le Levant au XVIIe siècle* (Paris, 1896); Masson, *Histoire du commerce français dans le Levant au XVIIIe siècle* (Paris, 1911); Charles Carrière, *Négociants marseillais au XVIIIe siècle. Contribution à l'étude des économies maritimes* (Marseille, 1973); Louis Bergasse and Gaston Rambert, *Histoire du commerce de Marseille. IV: De 1599 à 1789* (Paris, 1954); and Robert Paris, *Histoire du commerce de Marseille. Vol. V: De 1660 à 1789, le Levant* (Paris, 1957).

[2] (Paris, 2003).

Marseilles

To appreciate the importance of Marseilles it is not only necessary to be familiar with the publications referred to above but also to know where some of the
primary sources may be found. For this, one can use the works of Charles
Carrière and Charles Mourre for information regarding Marseilles, and those
by Philippe Henrat and K.G. Saur for details concerning the archives of Paris.[3]
There are some particularly interesting publications regarding Marseilles, such
as the articles by Louis Dermigny and Paul Buty or the works by Jean-Pierre
Farganel, which are particularly rich in information concerning the workings
of trade in the ports of the Levant, the lifestyle of the protagonists and the role
of the diplomatic and consular personnel stationed in the various provinces of
the Ottoman Empire.[4] On a more general level, Michel Morineau has analysed
the role of the Mediterranean's premier port in the commercial circuits of the
period."[5] In a similar fashion, Carrière and Marcel Courdurié provide a brief
overview of the subject in their "L'espace commercial marseillais aux XVIIe
et XVIIIe siècles."[6]

---

[3]Charles Carrière, *Richesse du passé marseillais. Le port mondial au XVIIIe
siècle* (Marseille, 1979); Carrière, "Les sources provençales de l'économie maritime de
l'époque moderne," in *IVe Colloque d'histoire maritime* (Paris, 1962); Charles Mourre,
La Chambre de Commerce de Marseille à travers ses archives, XVIIe-XVIIIe siècles
(Marseille, 1976); Philippe Henrat, *Inventaire des archives de la Marine, sous série
B7, Vol. V* (Paris 1979); and Conseil international des archives, *Sources de l'histoire du
Proche-Orient et de l'Afrique du Nord dans les archives et bibliothèques françaises* (2
vols., Munich, 1984-1996).

[4]Louis Dermigny, "A propos du port franc de Marseille," *Provence
Historique*, V (1955) and VI (1956); Gilbert Buti, "Marseille au XVIIIe siècle, réseau
d'un port mondial," in *Ville et port, XVIIIe-XXe siècles* (Paris, 1994); Jean-Pierre
Farganel, "Les marchands dans l'Orient méditerranéen aux XVIIe et XVIIIe siècles: la
présence française dans les Echelles du Levant (1650-1750)" (Unpublished thèse
dactylographiée, Université de Paris I, 1992); and Farganel, "Négociants marseillais au
Levant et dirigisme commercial: l'émergence d'une contestation nouvelle de l'autorité
monarchique," *Provence historique* (1996).

[5]Michel Morineau, "Marseiile dans Europe," *Revue d'Histoire Economique et
Sociale*, LXXIV (1968).

[6]Charles Carrière and Marcel Courdurié, "L'espace commercial marseillais
aux XVIIe et XVIIIe siècles," in Pierre Léon (ed.), *Aires et structures du commerce
français au XVIIIe siècle* (Lyon, 1975); and Carrière and Courdurié, "Un sophisme
économique. Marseille s'enrichit en vendant plus qu'elle ne vend. Réflexions sur les
mécanismes commerciaux levantins au XVIIIe siècle," *Histoire, Economie et société*, I
(1984).

Regarding wars and their impact on international trade, a series of articles edited by Michel Vergé-Franceschi are of considerable interest.[7] The financial crises which affected the port and its merchants in 1729 and 1774 are studied by René Squarzoni and François-Xavier Emmanuelli, respectively.[8]

Corsairing

The many facets of corsairing have recently received a considerable amount of attention from French historians. From Christian shores, corsairing was seen as a crusade, a struggle against the centuries-old infidel presence that plagued the Inner Sea. Across the water, on the Muslim side, corsairing was endowed with a similar crusading spirit, this time directed against the Cross and the unbeliever who was to be captured on land or at sea and enslaved. Mistrust and fear long sustained a negative perception of the "other" in this anachronistic struggle whose financial stakes by far outweighed the false rationale put forward to justify it. Among the many excellent contributions in this field one must highlight those by Michel Fontenay. After a thorough exploration of Maltese and French archives, Fontenay has published material which is seminal for an understanding of this activity, especially the recurrent, verging on permanent, hypocrisy on both sides of the Mediterranean that enabled the "heroic" actors involved in this "noble" mission in defence of the "true" faith to enrich themselves.[9] Similarly informative on this topic are the books by René Coulet du Gard, Jacques Heers, Gérard Van Krieken, Ulane Bonnel, Moulay Bel-

---

[7]Michel Vergé-Franceschi (ed.), *Guerre et commerce en Méditerranée, IXe-XXe siècles* (Paris, 1991).

[8]René Squarzoni, "Marseille et l'Europe en 1729-1731. Une crise du commerce et du crédit dans une dépression généralisée," *Cahiers de la Méditerranée* (1976); and François-Xavier Emmanuelli, *La crise marseillaise de 1774 et la chute des courtiers: contribution à l'étude du commerce du Levant et de la banque* (Paris, 1979).

[9]Among his other works, see Michel Fontenay, "Course et piraterie méditerranéennes de la fin du Moyen Age au début du XIXe siècle," in Paul Adam (ed.), *Course et piraterie* (2 vols., Paris, 1975); "Corsaires de la foi ou rentiers du sol? Les Chevaliers de Malte dans le corso méditerranéen," *Revue d'Histoire Moderne et Contemporaine*, XXXV (1988); "La course dans l'économie portuaire méditerranéenne au XVIIe siècle," *Annales Economies, Sociétés, Civilisations*, No. 6 (1988); "Interlope et violence dans l'économie d'échanges: l'exemple des eaux grecques de l'Empire ottoman aux XVIIe et XVIIIe siècle," *El Comerç alternatiu, Corsarism e contraband (ss. XV-XVIII)* (Palma de Majorque, 1990); and "Les derniers feux du corso chrétien à Malte (1679-1798)," in Christiane Villain-Gandossi, Louis Durteste and Salvino Busuttil (eds.), *Méditerranée mer ouverte* (2 vols., Malta, 1997).

hamissi, and articles by Louis Baudoin, Abd El Hadi Ben Mansour, Xavier Labat Saint Vincent, and Jean Mathiex.[10]

The Ottoman Empire

Let us now have a look at the relations between the Christian West and the Ottoman Empire, including the Barbary Regencies. A considerable number of major works were written several decades ago but still retain their usefulness, especially the remarkable work by François Charles-Roux. Still useful as well are older studies by Louis Colomer, Abel Boutin, Paul Giraud and P. Mauroy.[11]

More recently, we can refer to the innovative work done on the eastern basin of the Mediterranean and the importance of French shipping for the domestic trade of the Ottoman Empire by Daniel Panzac.[12] As well, the collec-

---

[10]René Coulet du Gard, *La course et la piraterie en Méditerranée* (Paris, 1980); Jacques Heers, *Les Barbaresques. La course et la guerre en Méditerranée XIVe-XVIe siècles* (Paris, 2001); Gérard Van Krieken, *Corsaires et marchands. Les relations entre Alger et les Pays-Bas, 1604-1830* (Paris, 2002); Ulane Bonnel, *La France, les États-Unis et la guerre de course, 1797-1815* (Paris, 1961); Moulay Belhamissi, *Alger, l'Europe et la guerre secrète (1518-1830)* (Algiers, 1999); Louis Baudoin, "Corsaires seynois et autres de Provence: la guerre de course au XVIIe siècle," *Bulletin de la Société des amis du vieux Toulon*, No. 84 (1963); Abd El Hadi Ben Mansour, "La course algérienne, 1608-1621). Essai d'un bilan," *L'Homme et la mer* (Sfax, 2001); Xavier Labat Saint Vincent, "Course et commerce en Méditerranée au XVIIIe siècle: étude de la présence maritime française à Malte au cours de quatre conflits majeurs," *Les tyrans de la mer: pirates, corsaires et flibustiers* (Paris, 2002); and Jean Mathiex, "Levant, Barbarie et Europe chrétienne. Remarques sur le commerce de course en Méditerranée de la fin du XVIIe siècle au début du XIXe siècle," *Bulletin de la Société d'Histoire Moderne*, No. 5 (1958).

[11]François Charles-Roux, *Les Echelles de Syrie et de Palestine au XVIIIe siècle* (Paris, 1928); Louis Colomer, *Le rôle de Marseille dans les relations politiques et économiques de la France avec les pays d'Orient* (Toulouse, 1929); Abel Boutin, *Les anciennes relations commerciales et diplomatiques de la France avec la Barbarie (1515-1830)* (Paris, 1902); Paul Giraud, *Les origines de l'empire français nord africain. Les Lenché à Marseille et en Barbarie* (Marseille, 1939); and P. Mauroy, *Précis de l'histoire et du commerce de l'Afrique depuis les temps anciens jusqu'aux temps modernes* (Paris, 1852).

[12]For examples of Daniel Panzac's prolific output, see "Activité et diversité d'un grand port ottoman: Smyrne dans la première moitié du XVIIIe siècle," in *Mémorial Ömer Lûfti Barkan* (Paris, 1980); "Affréteurs ottomans et capitaines français à Alexandrie: la caravane maritime en Méditerranée au milieu du XVIIIe siècle," *Revue de l'Occident Musulman et de la Méditerranée* (1982); "L'escale de Chio: un observatoire privilégié de l'activité maritime en mer Egée au XVIIIe siècle," *Histoire,*

tive work edited by Jean-Pierre Filippini; and the studies by Anna Pouradier Duteil-Loizidou (mainly on Cyprus), Traian Stoianovich, Gilles Veinstein, Michel Fontenay and Patrick Boulanger remains worth consulting.[13]

There are many recent and not so recent publications concerning the Barbary Regencies, but one must highlight Edouard Baratier's *Le commerce de Marseille avec l'Afrique du Nord avant 1599.*[14] For Tunisia there is the work by François Arnoulet.[15] Also valuable are Richard Ayoun's studies on the Jews of North Africa; the many excellent contributions by Sadok Boubaker; and the works by M.H. Cherif, Robert Mantran and Ali Zouari.[16] On the French pres-

---

Economie et Société (1985); "Négociants ottomans et capitaines français: la caravane maritime en Crète au XVIIIe siècle," in *L'Empire ottoman, la République de Turquie et la France* (Istanbul, 1986); "Commerce et commerçants des ports du Liban sud et de Palestine (1756-1787)," *Revue du Monde Musulman et de la Méditerranée* (1990); "Négociants ottomans et activités maritimes au Maghreb (1687-1707)," in *Les villes dans l'Empire ottoman: activités et sociétés* (Aix en Provence, 1991); "Le commerce maritime de Tripoli de Barbarie dans la seconde moitié du XVIIIe siècle," *Revue d'Histoire maghrébine* (1993; "Les réseaux d'échanges des ports ottomans, Smyrne, Beyrouth, Alexandrie, Tunis (fin du XVIIIe-début du XXe siècle)," in *Villes et ports, XVIIIe-XXe siècles* (Paris, 1994); and *Commerce et navigation dans l'Empire ottoman au XVIIIe siècle* (Istanbul, 1996).

[13]Jean-Pierre Filippini (ed.), *Dossiers sur le commerce en Méditerranée orientale au XVIIIe siècle* (Paris, 1976); Anna Pouradier Duteil-Loizidou, "La communauté française à Chypre à la fin du XVIIe siècle et au début du XVIIIe siècle," *Chypre et la Méditerranée orientale* (Lyon, 2000); Traian Stoianovich, "Pour un modèle du commerce du Levant. Economie concurrentielle et économie du bazar, 1500-1800," *Bulletin de l'Association Internationale d'Etudes du sud-est européen*, XII, No. 2 (1974); Gilles Veinstein, "Ayan de la région d'Ismir et le commerce du Levant (deuxième moitié du XVIIIe siècle)," *Revue de l'Occident Musulman et de la Méditerranée*, II (1975); Michel Fontenay, "Le commerce des Occidentaux dans les Echelles du Levant vers la fin du XVIIe siècle," in Bartolomé Bennassar and Robert Sauzet (eds.), *Chrétiens et Musulmans à la Renaissance* (Paris, 1998); and Patrick Boulanger, "L'île de Mytilène et le négoce français au XVIIIe siècle," in Daniel Panzac (ed.), *Les villes dans l'Empire ottoman: activités et sociétés* (Aix en Provence, 1991).

[14](Marseille, 1951).

[15]Among others, see François Arnoulet, "Les installations du comptoir corailleur du Cap Negro au XVIIIe siècle," *Revue d'Histoire Maghrébine*, XXV/XXVI (1982).

[16]Richard Ayoun, "Le commerce des Juifs livournais à Tunis à la fin du XVIIe siècle," in *Tunis, cité de la mer* (Tunis, 1999); Ayoun, "Les Juifs d'Algérie, de l'émigration espagnole à la conquête française," *Cahiers des études juives*, No. 2 (1991); Sadok Boubaker, *La Régence de Tunis au XVIIe siècle: ses relations*

ence and influence in Tunisia, the works of H.B. Hassine and Lucette Valensi are useful.[17]

Information on French sources concerning the Regency of Algiers is available in Pascal Even's *Papiers du consulat de France à Alger... (1585-1798)* (Paris, 1988). A more general treatment is provided by the work of Mohammed Amine, Pierre Boyer, Aïcha Guatasse and A. Saadallah.[18] Jean-Claude Zeltner is essential for Tripoli, even though he falls somewhat outside the scope of this essay because he is more concerned with the history of the Regency and trade with its hinterland.[19] Also useful are the previously-mentioned 1993 article by D. Panzac and those by Roger Gaspary and Nora Lafi.[20]

For France's commercial relations with its European neighbours there are a number of very good studies: Mathilde Alonso-Perez on trade between

---

commerciales avec l'Europe méditerranéenne, Marseille et Livourne (Zaghouan, 1987); Boubaker, "La 'Tunisie' et le commerce méditerranéen dans la deuxième moitié du XVIe siècle," in *Felipe II y el Mediterraneo* (Madrid, 1999); M.H. Cherif, "Le beylik, les populations et le commerce maritime dans la Tunisie du XVIIIe siècle," in *Histoire économique et sociale de l'Empire ottoman et de la Turquie (1326-1960)* (Paris, 1995); Robert Mantran, "L'évolution des relations entre la Tunisie et l'Empire ottoman du XVIe au XIXe siècle," *Cahiers de Tunisie*, Nos. 26/27 (1959); and Ali Zouari, *Les relations commerciales entre Sfax et le Levant aux XVIIIe et XIXe siècle* (Sfax, 1990).

[17]H.B. Hassine, "La juridiction consulaire française et ses limites à Tunis au XVIIIe siècle," *Mésogeios*, II (1998); and "Les concessions françaises du corail en Afrique barbaresque," *Mésogeios*, VII (2000); and Lucette Valensi, "Islam et capitalisme: production et commerce des chéchias en Tunisie et en France aux XVIIIe et XIXe siècles," *Revue d'Histoire Moderne et Contemporaine*, XVI (juillet-septembre 1969).

[18]Mohammed Amine, "Conditions et mouvements des échanges de la Régence ottomane d'Alger," *Revue d'Histoire* Maghrébine, Nos. 69/70 (1993); Pierre Boyer, "Marseille et Alger au XVIIe siècle" in Villain-Gandossi, Durteste and Busuttil (eds.), *Méditerranée mer ouverte*; Aïcha Guatasse, "Les commerçants algériens à travers les registres du consulat français (1636-1830)," *Revue d'Histoire Maghrébine*, LXI (1991-1992); and A. Saadallah, "A propos de l'activité militaire et commerciale de la Régence d'Alger au XVIIIe siècle," *Revue d'Histoire Maghrébine*, XXXIII (1984).

[19]Jean-Claude Zeltner, *Tripoli, carrefour de l'Europe et des pays du Tchad, 1500-1797* (Paris, 1992).

[20]Roger Gaspary, "De Tripoli (Libye) de Barbarie à Athènes ou vie privée et commerce à travers la course en Méditerranée," *Marseille*, CXLVIII (1987); and Nora Lafi, "Tripoli de Barbarie: port de mer, port du désert (1795-1835)," in Villain-Gandossi, Durteste and Busuttil (eds.), *Méditerranée mer ouverte*.

France and Spain at the end of the eighteenth century; J. Allemand, René Boudard, G.E. Broche and Charles Carrière on Marseilles' relations with Genoa;
Jean-Pierre Filippini on Marseilles' relationship with Leghorn and the latter's
role in Mediterranean commerce in general; and Patrick Boulanger and J. Tadic on Ragusa.[21] On Malta and its role in the commerce of eighteenth-century
France, there are studies by Xavier Labat Saint Vincent, the Abbot Chaillan,
Jean-Louis Miège and Alain Blondy.[22]

The Goods

Finally, let us look at that which lies at the centre of commerce, the goods that
were traded. There are so many publications on this topic that it would be impossible to make reference to all of them, but those cited cover the essentials

---

[21]Mathilde Alonso-Perez, "Le commerce franco-espagnol en Méditerranée
occidentale (1780-1806)" (Unpublished thèse de Doctorat, Université de Poitiers,
1986); J. Allemand, "Les relations commerciales entre Marseille et Gênes de 1600 à
1789," in *Actes du Ier congrès historique Provence-Ligurie* (Aix-Marseille, 1966);
René Boudard, *Gênes et la France dans la deuxième moitié du XVIIIe siècle (1748-
1797)* (Paris, 1962); Boudard, "Génois et Barbaresques dans la deuxième moitié du
XVIIIe siècle," *Revue d'Histoire diplomatique*, LXXIV (1960); G.E. Broche, *La
République de Gênes et la France pendant la guerre de Succession d'Autriche (1740-
1748)* (Paris, 1935); Charles Carrière, "Notes sur les relations commerciales entre
Gênes et Marseille au XVIIIe siècle," *Actes du Ier congrès historique Provence-
Ligurie*; Jean-Pierre Filippini, "La nation française de Livourne (fin XVIIe-fin XVIIIe
siècles)," in Filippini (ed.), *Dossiers sur le commerce en Méditerranée orientale au
XVIIIe siècle*; Filippini, "Livourne et l'Afrique du Nord au XVIIIe siècle," *Revue
d'Histoire Maghrébine*, VII/VIII (1977); Filippini, "Grandeurs et difficultés d'un port
franc, Livourne (1676-1737)," *Association française des Historiens modernistes* (mars
1978); Filippini, "Les provinces arabes de l'Empire ottoman vues de Livourne au
XVIIIe siècle," *Revue d'Histoire Maghrébine*, XXXI/XXXII (1983); Patrick
Boulanger, "Raguse, une échelle du Levant au XVIIIe siècle," *Balkan*, II (1989) ; and
J. Tadic, "Le commerce en Dalmatie et à Raguse et la décadence économique de
Venise au XVIIIe siècle," in *Aspeti e cause della decadenza economica veneziana nel
secolo XVIII* (Venice, 1961).

[22]Xavier Labat Saint Vincent, "Malte et le commerce français au XVIIIe
siècle" (Unpublished thèse de doctorat dactylographiée, Université de Paris IV-
Sorbonne, 2000); Abbot Chaillan, "Le commerce de Malte avec Marseille et la
France," *Mémoires de l'Institut Historique de Provenc*, XII (1935); Jean-Louis Miège,
"Malte, île entrepôt," in *Iles de la Méditerranée* (Paris, 1984); and Alain Blondy,
*Parfum de Cour, gourmandise de rois: le commerce des oranges entre Malte et la
France au XVIIIe siècle* (Paris, 2002).

and also direct us to other works.[23] With reference to grain there are a number
of works which have come to be considered veritable classics. Such is the case
with the works of Ruggiero Romano; Maurice Aymard's *Venise, Raguse et le
commerce du blé pendant la seconde moitié du XVIe siècle*; and Jean-Louis
Miège's *Les céréales en Méditerranée*, the result of a roundtable organized by
the Marseilles Chamber of Commerce and Industry and the University of
Provence.[24] Other obligatory reading includes works by M. Alexandrescu-
Dersca, Claude Badet, Charles Carrière and Gérard Buty, Jean-Pierre Farganel, José Juan-Vidal and Christiane Veauvy.[25]

Patrick Boulanger's publications are absolutely essential concerning
the olive oil trade. Also useful in this regard is the article by M.T. Mansouri.[26]

---

[23]A representative work is *Commerce de gros, commerce de détail dans les
pays méditerranéens (XVIe-XIXe siècles)* (Nice, 1976).

[24]Ruggiero Romano, *Commerce et prix du blé à Marseille au XVIIIe siècle*
(Paris, 1956). On prices, see Jean Meuvret, "La géographie des prix des céréales et les
anciennes économies européennes: prix méditerranéens, prix continentaux, prix
atlantiques à la fin du XVIIe siècle," *Revista da economia*, IV, No. 2 (1951). See also
Maurice Aymard, *Venise, Raguse et le commerce du blé pendant la seconde moitié du
XVIe siècle* (Paris, 1966); and Jean-Louis Miège, *Les céréales en Méditerranée,
Histoire, Anthropologie, Economie* (Paris, 1993).

[25]M. Alexandrescu-Dersca, "Contribution à l'étude de l'approvisionnement en
blé de Constantinople au XVIIIe siècle," *Studia et acta Orientalia*, I (1962);
Alexandrescu-Dersca, "Quelques données sur le ravitaillement de Constantinople au
XVIe siècle," *Actes du Ier congrès international des études du sud-est européen* (Sofia,
1969); Claude Badet, "La crise de 1709 à Marseille. Les problèmes de ravitaillement
en blé (1709-1710)," in Jean-Louis Miège (ed.), *Les céréales en Méditerranée* (Paris,
1993); Charles Carrière and Gérard Buty, "Un aspect du commerce international du
blé: les échanges de Marseille et l'Andalousie pendant la crise frumentaire de 1753," in
Miège (ed.), *Les céréales en Méditerranée*; Jean-Pierre Farganel, "Aléas du commerce
d'exportation des céréales et relations entre Levantins et Français à Acre et Seyde
(1650-1750)," in Miè (ed.), *Les céréales en Méditerranée*; José Juan-Vidal, "Le
commerce du blé entre Majorque et l'Afrique du Nord aux XVIe et XVIIe siècles,"
Actes du Ier congrès d'histoire et de civilisation du Maghreb (Tunis, 1979); and
Christiane Veauvy, "Structures et significations de l'échange économique en
Méditerranée. L'exemple du blé (Provence/Maghreb, première moitié du XVIIIe
siècle)," *Cahiers de Tunisie*, CLVII/CLVIII (1991).

[26]Patrick Boulanger, *Marseille, marché international de l'huile d'olive. Un
produit et des hommes (1725-1825)* (Marseille, 1996); and M.T. Mansouri, "L'huile et
l'olivier dans le monde méditerranéen, le savoir et le commerce," in Ali Zouari, Riadh
Zhgal and Faouzi Mahfoudh (eds.), *La dynamique économique à Sfax entre le passé et
le présent* (Sfax, 1993).

On cotton and cloth, there is the work of Katsumi Fukasawa, especially his thesis; Charles Carrière's *Le commerce des draps à Marseille au XVIIIe siècle*; and articles by Alain Blondy, Jean-Pierre Farganel, and Maurice Aymard.[27]

This brief review of some of the most important French-language works centring on trade in the Mediterranean in the early modern period will hopefully serve to give some broad directions to those who would work in this field. The researcher unable to carry out a full-scale study of the towering French presence in Mediterranean commerce should find that the reference points which have been provided here should permit him or her some understanding of this vast area of study. In any event, for a rigorous treatment of topics not referred to above, a researcher is bound to draw considerable benefit from dipping into the imposing and recent bibliographical *corpus,* compiled by Alain Blondy, cited at the outset of this essay.[28]

---

[27]Katsumi Fukasawa, *Toilerie et commerce du Levant: d'Alep à Marseille* (Paris, 1987); Charles Carrière, *Le commerce des draps à Marseille au XVIIIe siècle* (Marseille, 1962); Carrière, "La draperie languedocienne dans la seconde moitié du XVIIIe siècle. Contribution à l'étude de la conjoncture Levantine," *Conjoncture économique, structures sociales. Hommage à Ernest Labrousse* (Paris, 1974); Carrière, "La draperie languedocienne d'exportation," in Louis M. Cullen and Paul Butel (eds.), *Négoce et industrie en France et en Irlande aux XVIIIe et XIXe siècles* (Bordeaux, 1980); Carrière and M. Morineau, "Draps du Languedoc et commerce du Levant au XVIIIe siècle," *Revue d'Histoire Economique et Sociale*, XLVI, No. 1 (1968); Alain Blondy, "Mikiel-Anton Vassalli et les réfugiés maltais, principaux agents de la culture du coton en France (1807-1814)," *Journal of Maltese Studies*, Nos. 23/24 (1993); Jean-Pierre Farganel, "Les négociants français et le commerce international du coton: un enjeu économique et politique vu à travers l'exemple des Echelles d'Acre et de Seyde, 1650-1789," in *De la fibre à la fripe...* (Montpellier, 1997); and Maurice Aymard, "Commerce et consommation des draps en Sicile et en Italie méridionale (Xve-XVIIIe siècles)," in Marco Squllanzani (ed.), *Produzione, commercio e consummo dei panni di lana (nei secoli XII-XVII)* (Firenze, 1976).

[28]See note 3.

Recent Maritime Historiography on Italy*

Michela D'Angelo and M. Elisabetta Tonizzi

Part I: The Italian States before Unification

Lights and Shadows

In 1967 Luigi De Rosa noted that maritime history in Italy, particularly relating to economic aspects such as ports, transport, insurance and so on, has never been abundant, even on the Middle Ages, one of the periods most studied by economic historians of the Italian peninsula and islands.[1] Thirty years later not much had changed when Paolo Frascani noted the slow progress in the field and deplored the lack of attention to relevant sources and documents.[2] Even today, maritime history continues to play a secondary role in Italian historiography, while innerable documents on the Italian states during the modern age remain unexplored. Yet in recent decades a number of changes have been progressively shaping maritime history so that it

> does not deal with *res gestae* and distinguished and successful figures, but rather with millions of unknown and insignificant seamen, merchants and shipbuilders; cargoes of salted fish, wheat, timber, and colonial products; and slaves and emigrants: in short, with all the men and merchandise that made up the economies of the lands facing the ocean, as well as with all those who every day wrote and are still writing the history of the sea.[3]

---

*Michela D'Angelo is the author of Part I ("The Italian States before Unification"), and M. Elisabetta Tonizzi is the author of Part II ("Post-Unification Italy").

[1]Luigi De Rosa, "Vent'anni di storiografia economica italiana (1945-1965)," in *La storiografia italiana negli ultimi 20 anni* (2 vols., Milano, 1970), II, 882-883.

[2]Paolo Frascani, "La storia marittima del Mezzogiorno negli studi degli ultimi venti anni," in Antonio Di Vittorio and Carlos Barciela Lopez (eds.), *La storiografia marittima in Italia e in Spagna in età moderna e contemporanea. Tendenze, orientamenti, linee evolutive* (Bari, 2001), 314.

[3]Gelina Harlaftis, "Storia marittima e storia dei porti," *Memoria e Ricerca*, XI (2002), 6.

These topics are, indeed, becoming more popular among the Italian scholars who research maritime activities in the Italian states before Unification (1861). The new topics now emerging are not only due to research by individual scholars but even more important to the inter-disciplinary studies, conferences and workshops which deal with different aspects of maritime history. The conference on Peoples of the Mediterranean Sea, held in Naples in 1980, marked a turning point in the study of various aspects of Mediterranean life in the modern age (ships, seamen, merchants, trade, fishing, etc.).[4] In the same decade, renewed attention was given to both the symbiotic relationship between port and town in the meeting on "Port Cities in the Mediterranean" (Genoa, 1985) and to ports conceived as the core of economic activity at the conference on "Ports as an Economic Enterprise" (Prato, 1987).[5]

Ports in central and southern Italy between the sixteenth and nineteenth centuries were also considered from an innovative perspective due to inter-disciplinary research carried out by historians of architecture and of economics. In the 1990s, under the guidance of Giorgio Simoncini, the ports of the Papal States and of the Kingdoms of Naples and Sicily were examined from the perspective of the development of their economic activities and of the modernization of their infrastructures during the modern age.[6]

New research possibilities also emerged from the conference entitled Italy and the Sea (Viareggio, 1991) which, from a long-term perspective, highlighted the links between shipbuilding, maritime transport and trade.[7] The history of shipbuilding, traditionally a technical subject in naval history, has also been the object of new attention because of inter-disciplinary research.[8]

While these trends in the last two or three decades have given rise to interesting approaches *vis-à-vis* new archival research and analysis, the consensus reached at the conference coordinated by Antonio Di Vittorio on "Trends and Perspectives in Contemporary Maritime Historiography" (Naples,

---

[4]Rosalba Ragosta (ed.), *Le genti del mare Mediterraneo* (Napoli, 1981).

[5]Ennio Poleggi (ed.), *Città portuali del Mediterraneo* (Genova, 1989); and Simonetta Cavaciocchi (ed.), *I porti come impresa economica (sec. XII-XVIII)* (Firenze, 1988).

[6]Giorgio Simoncini (ed.), *Sopra i porti di mare. I: Il trattato di Teofilo Gallaccini e la concezione architettonica dei porti dal Rinascimento alla Restaurazione* (Firenze, 1993); *II: Il Regno di Napoli* (Firenze, 1993); *III: Sicilia e Malta* (Firenze, 1997); and *IV: Lo Stato Pontificio* (Firenze, 1995).

[7]Tommaso Fanfani (ed.), *La penisola italiana e il mare. Costruzioni navali, trasporti e commerci tra XV e XX secolo* (Napoli, 1993).

[8]Arturo Fratta (ed.), *La fabbrica delle navi. Storia della cantieristica nel Mezzogiorno d'Italia* (Napoli, 1990).

1984), which focussed on the period up to the 1980s, was not optimistic. All the contributions specifically devoted to the maritime history of the Italian states in the Medieval and modern ages highlighted common limitations in the many, but often fragmentary, publications produced during the preceding century.[9] This first review was followed by a recent analysis of publications issued in the 1980s and 1990s. At the initiative of Antonio Di Vittorio and Carlos Barciela Lopez, a meeting of Italian and Spanish historians in Bari in 1999 outlined perspectives and progress in maritime history in the two countries. The reports on the Italian states specifically highlighted the fields which remained unexplored while at the same time noting certain innovative aspects.[10]

The papers presented at the last two conferences not only provide an updated bibliography but also can be considered as a sort of *cahier de doléances* of the deficiencies of Italian maritime historiography between the discoveries of the fifteenth and sixteenth centuries and the nineteenth-century introduction of steam navigation. In many respects, the maritime history of the Italian states in the modern age still awaits an interpretation or re-interpretation in line with new trends.

Ports, Trade and Navigation

Early in the modern era, while Tuscan, Lombard, Venetian, Genoese and Neapolitan merchants "were every day weaving their tight web of land and maritime trade from Northern Europe to the Far East," the Italian peninsula was "about to lose its role as the economic engine of the Mediterranean and therefore of the entire West."[11] With the discovery of America and the progressive shift of the main commercial routes towards other seas, a new economic hierarchy took shape among the European powers. Meanwhile, the Spanish viceroyalties of Naples, Sicily and Sardinia, and the other Italian states, were directly or indirectly involved in the conflict between what Fernand Braudel called "the two Mediterraneans" where Spain was confronting the Turkish advance. During the sixteenth century, the Italian ports changed their maritime and commercial functions. In southern Italy, for example, ports were not only equipped with defensive structures, as befitted their role as military outposts against the Turks, but also with a new infrastructure (piers,

---

[9]Antonio Di Vittorio (ed.), *Tendenze e orientamenti della storiografia marittima contemporanea: gli Stati Italiani e la Repubblica di Ragusa secoli XIV-XIX* (Napoli, 1986).

[10]Di Vittorio and Barciela Lopez (eds.), *La storiografia marittima*.

[11]Fanfani, "Lo scenario generale," in Fanfani (ed.), *La penisola italiana*, 3.

dockyards, etc.) to fit the requirements of modern sail navigation.[12] Moreover, the arrival of ships from northern Europe in the Mediterranean marked a "revolution in trade." Until then trade with northern countries had been the preserve of Mediterranean ships and merchants, but from the late sixteenth century northern merchant ships first competed with and then replaced local vessels in the commerce between northern and southern Europe.[13]

In the more widespread crisis of the seventeenth century, Italian ports were affected by the difficult situation of the Mediterranean economy and the consolidation of the Dutch and English presence in the Mediterranean. In the eighteenth century, Italian ports and shipping experienced a recovery. This was due in part to the economic reforms launched in different Italian states, as well as the establishment or re-establishment of free ports in Genoa, Leghorn, Messina, Ancona and Trieste.[14] During the Revolutionary and Napoleonic periods, routes and trade were dislocated, especially because of the Continental Blockade. In the nineteenth century Italian ports went through a new phase of recovery, which consolidated not only the predominance of free ports (abolished in 1865) but also the stronger role of smaller ports.

In this brief sketch, mention should also be made of the numerous studies on individual ports. In this contribution I will only set out some of the more recent research on Italian states before Unification, specifically on the Republic of Genoa (in 1815 annexed by the Kingdom of Sardinia), the Grand-

---

[12]Simoncini, "L'architettura dei porti," in Simoncini (ed.), *Sopra i porti*, I, 37-125; Rita Binaghi, "Le macchine del porto," in *ibid.*, 127-173; and Giovanni Rebora, "Lavoro e tecnica nel porto di Genova: la manutenzione dei moli e dei fondali fra il XVI e il XVIII secolo," in Cavaciocchi (ed.), *I porti come impresa*, 59-63.

[13]Carmelo Trasselli, "Sul naviglio nordico in Sicilia nel sec. XVII," in *Homenaje a J. Vicens Vives* (Barcelona, 1967), 689-702; Edoardo Grendi, "I nordici e il traffico del porto di Genova 1590-1666," *Rivista storica italiana*, LXXXIII (1971), 23-72; and Gigliola Pagano de Divitiis, "L'arrivo dei nordici nel Mediterraneo," in *Storia d'Italia* (Milano, 1989), V, 49-72.

[14]Alberto Caracciolo, "Il dibattito sui porti franchi nel Settecento: genesi delle franchigie di Ancona," *Rivista storica italiana*, LXXV (1963), 538-558; Liana De Antonellis Martini, *Portofranco e comunità etnico-religiose nella Trieste settecentesca* (Milano, 1968); Giulio Giacchero, *Origini e sviluppo del Portofranco genovese 1590-1778* (Genova, 1972); Antonio Di Vittorio, "Porti e porto franco," *Mittailungen des Oesterreichischen Staatsarchiv Wien*, XXV (1972), 257-269; Lucia Frattarelli Fischer, "Livorno 1676: la città e il porto franco," in Franco Angiolini, Vieri Becagli and Marcello Verga (eds.), *La Toscana nell'età di Cosimo III* (Firenze, 1993), 45-66; Samuel Fettah, "Temps et espaces des trafics portuaires en Méditerranée: le cas du port franc de Livourne (XVII-XIX siècles)," *Ricerche storiche* (1998), 243-273; and Liliana Iaria, "La Fata Morgana: politica asburgica e portofranco a Messina," in *Scritti in ricordo di Gaetano Cingari* (Milano, 2001), 351-379.

Duchy of Tuscany, the Papal States, the Kingdoms of Naples and Sicily (from 1815 the Kingdom of the Two Sicilies), the Republic of Venice (in 1797 annexed by Austria) and the port of Trieste (Italian only since 1918, but in the past an important market for Italian trade).[15]

Research on Venice, Trieste, Genoa and Leghorn, ports which have always enjoyed privileged positions in maritime historiography, tends to widen the perspective towards more distant horizons.[16] This was certainly the case for Venice, according to Ugo Tucci, who argued that the twentieth century was a happy time for its historiography because of numerous publications. The sixteenth century remains the most studied period, but there have also been some publications which focus on the reasons for its rise beginning in the Middle Ages and for its decline in the eighteenth and the nineteenth centuries.[17] The studies on this area have also looked at Trieste. A free port since 1719, the

---

[15]For a review up to the 1980s see the following essays in Di Vittorio (ed.), *Tendenze e orientamenti*: Giorgio Felloni, "La storiografia marittima su Genova in età moderna," 29-46; Ugo Marchese, "Qualche spunto sulla storiografia marittima genovese relativa all'800," 47-52; Marcello Berti, "La storiografia marittima sulla Toscana (1950-1984)," 53-72; Ciro Manca, "La storiografia marittima sullo Stato della Chiesa," 73-94; Giovanna Motta, "La storiografia marittima siciliana," 95-122; Sergio Anselmi, "Il piccolo cabotaggio nell'Adriatico centrale: bilancio di studi, problemi, metodi, programmi," 125-150; Ugo Tucci, "La storiografia marittima sulla Repubblica di Venezia," 151-173; Giovanni Panjek, "La storiografia marittima su Trieste negli ultimi 40 anni (secoli XVI-XIX)," 175-234; and Tommaso Fanfani, "Riflessioni sulla storiografia marittima triestina," 235-239. For the period since the 1980s, see the following essays in Di Vittorio and Barciela Lopez (eds.), *La storiografia marittima*: Paola Massa Piergiovanni, "La Repubblica di Genova," 11-20; Giuseppe Bracco, "Il litorale sabaudo," 41-44; Giovanni Panjek, "Trieste e il litorale," 75-101; Giovanni Zalin, "Considerazioni sulla storiografia marittima veneziana tra Basso Medioevo e Settecento," 121-154; Marcello Berti, "La storiografia marittima sulla Toscana (1984-1999)," 179-235; Luciano Palermo, "La storiografia marittima sullo Stato della Chiesa (1980-2000)," 253-268; Frascani, "La storia marittima del Mezzogiorno," 297-314; Giuseppe Barbera Cardillo, "Il Regno di Sicilia," 337-350; and Giuseppe Doneddu, "La storiografia marittima sul Regno di Sardegna," 351-366.

[16]See, for example, Raffaele Belvederi (ed.), *Genova-Mediterraneo-Atlantico nell'età moderna* (Genova, 1983); and "Rapporti del porto di Livorno con Ragusa e le città dell'Adriatico Orientale (secoli XVI-XVIII)," *Studi Livornesi* (1988).

[17]Ugo Tucci, "La storiografia marittima sulla Repubblica di Venezia," 151. Among the endless references see, at least, Frederic C. Lane, *Venice and History* (Baltimore, 1966); Tucci, *Mercanti, navi, monete nel Cinquecento veneziano* (Bologna, 1981); Alberto Tenenti and Ugo Tucci, *Il mare*, in *Storia di Venezia* (12 vols., Roma, 1991); Tenenti, *Venezia e il mare* (Milano, 1999); and Elisabeth Crouzet-Pavan, *Venise triumphante. Les horizons d'un mythe* (Paris, 1999).

Habsburg port was an emerging centre in a sea which was witnessing the relentless decline of Venice.[18]

Over the last hundred years, the quantity and quality of maritime publications on Genoa – in 1861 the most important port in Italy in terms of both passengers and merchandise – has increased considerably. In an excellent bibliographical review covering the period up to the 1980s, Giorgio Felloni traced the development of trade in Genoa during the period of the Republic, while Paola Massa has analysed the more recent studies.[19]

Since the research by Braudel and Ruggiero Romano, the maritime historiography on Leghorn has included a series of long-term studies, above all on international trade. Established by the Medici family in the mid-sixteenth century, Leghorn was typical of those free ports in which trade thrived throughout the entire modern age because of the policies (neutrality, religious tolerance etc.) of the Grand-Duchy of Tuscany which attracted foreign ships and merchants. Research has hinged in particular on the activities of the Jews, who contributed to the development of trade with other Mediterranean ports, and the English, who made Leghorn the most important centre of their trade in the western Mediterranean.[20]

---

[18]Fulvio Babudieri, *Industria commercio e navigazione a Trieste e nella Regione Giulia. Dall'inizio del Settecento ai primi anni del Novecento* (Milano, 1982); and Ugo Cova, *Commercio e navigazione a Trieste da Maria Teresa al 1915* (Udine, 1992).

[19]Felloni, "La storiografia marittima su Genova," 29-46 (with bibliography); and Massa Piergiovanni, "La Repubblica di Genova," 11-20. See also Ugo Marchese, *Il porto di Genova dal 1815 al 1891* (Roma, 1959); Domenico Gioffrè, "Il commercio d'importazione genovese alla luce dei registri del dazio 1495-1537," in *Studi in onore di A. Fanfani* (6 vols., Milano, 1962), V, 113-241; Luigi Bulferetti and Claudio Costantini (eds.), *Industria e commercio in Liguria nell'età del Risorgimento (1700-1861)* (Milano, 1966); Edoardo Grendi, "Traffico portuale, naviglio mercantile e consolati genovesi nel Cinquecento," *Rivista storica italiana*, LXXX (1968); Ennio Poleggi, *1128-2000. Il porto di Genova* (Genova, 1971); and Giovanni Assereto, "Porti e scali minori della Repubblica di Genova in età moderna," in Cavaciocchi (ed.), *I porti come impresa*, 271-306.

[20]Besides Fernand Braudel and Ruggiero Romano, *Navires et Marchandises à l'entrée du Port de Livourne (1547-1611)* (Paris, 1951), see *Livorno e il Mediterraneo in età medicea* (Livorno, 1978); Carlo Mangio, "Commercio marittimo e reggenza lorenese. Provvedimenti legislativi e dibattito," *Rivista storica italiana*, XC (1978), 898-938; Jean Pierre Filippini, *Il porto di Livorno e la Toscana (1674-1815)* (Napoli, 1998); Silvana Balbi de Caro (ed.), *Merci e monete a Livorno in età granducale* (Firenze, 1998); and Marcello Berti, *Nel Mediterraneo e oltre. Temi di storia e storiografia marittima toscana (secoli XIII-XVIII)* (Pisa, 2000). On English trade, see *Gli inglesi a Livorno e all'isola d'Elba* (Livorno, 1980); Pagano De Divitiis, "Il porto di Livorno nelle carte della Levant Company," in *Economia e storia* (1984), 397-415; De

Maritime trade involving the Adriatic shores in general, and the Papal ports in particular, was the subject of research by Sergio Anselmi.[21] Studies on the maritime history of the Papal States, which had anchorages in the Tyrrhenian and Adriatic seas but had no naval or merchant fleets, have given prominence to the port of Ancona. But other, smaller ports have also received attention recently.[22]

As for Sardinia – an island which has always had a closer relationship with the land than with the sea – the role played by the maritime sector has been much less important. Still, some recent studies have looked at the decline of maritime activities during the Spanish period and its difficult modernization process under Savoy rule.[23]

In the Kingdom of Naples, the historiography relating to maritime matters reflects the clash between a favourable geographic condition and the

---

Divitiis, "Il porto di Livorno fra Inghilterra e Oriente," *Nuovi studi livornesi*, I (1993), 43-87; Carlo M. Cipolla, *Il burocrate e il marinaio. La "Sanità" toscana e le tribolazioni degli inglesi a Livorno nel XVII secolo* (Bologna, 1992); Michela D'Angelo, "La British Factory di Livorno tra la Corsica e l'Elba nel 1796," *Rivista di studi napoleonici*, XXXII (1999), 161-188; and D'Angelo, "The British Factory at Leghorn: A Kind of Chamber of Commerce *cum* Consulate," in Carmel Vassallo (ed.), *Consolati di Mare and Chambers of Commerce* (Malta, 2000), 113-125.

[21]Sergio Anselmi, *Venezia, Ragusa, Ancona tra '500 e '600* (Ancona, 1969); and Anselmi, *Adriatico. Studi di storia, secoli XIV-XIX* (Ancona, 1991).

[22]On Ancona, see Alberto Caracciolo, *Le port franc d'Ancone. Croissance et impasse d'un milieu marchand au XVIII siècle* (Paris, 1965); Jean Delumeau, *Ancone trait d'union entre l'Occident et l'Orient à l'epoque de la Reinassance* (Beirouth, 1966); P. Earle, "The Commercial Development of Ancona 1497-1551," *Economic History Review*, 2nd series, XXII (1969); and Michele Polverari (ed.), *Ancona tra Oriente e Occidente. Il Cinquecento* (Ancona, 1982). In addition to Mariano Gabriele, *I porti dello Stato Pontificio dal 1815 al 1880* (Roma, 1963), see also Giorgio Simoncini, "Porti e politica portuale dello Stato Pontificio dal XV al XIX secolo," in Simoncini (ed.), *Sopra i porti*, IV, 8-79; Luciano Palermo, "I porti dello Stato della Chiesa in età moderna: infrastrutture e politica degli investimenti," *ibid.*, 81-150; Giovanna Curcio and Paola Zampa, "Il porto di Civitavecchia dal XV al XVIII secolo," *ibid.*, 159-232; Claudio Varagnoli, "Corneto. Il porto clementino," *ibid.*, 233-249; Adriano Ghisetti Giavarina, "Da Porto Recanati a Porto d'Ascoli," *ibid.*, 251-262; Aloisio Antinori, "Il porto di Fano dal Rinascimento al periodo napoleonico," *ibid.*, 263-279; and Marinella Pigozzi, "Legazioni di Ferrara e di Romagna. Scali portuali e sbocchi a mare in età moderna," *ibid.*, 281-317.

[23]Giuseppe Doneddu, "Economia di scambio o movimento commerciale? I porti sardi del Settecento tra economia naturale ed economia monetaria," in Fanfani (ed.), *La penisola italiana*, 161-174; and Giuseppe Cavallo, *Il porto di Cagliari dal Medioevo alla fine del Settecento* (Cagliari, 1997).

perceived inability of the peoples of the south of Italy to enter the "virtuous circle" of a concrete development process from the late Middle Ages onwards.[24] In particular, research on ports and maritime trade in southern Italy in the modern age has emphasized the internal structural barriers to development and their economic dependence on foreign countries. Studies on Naples, Salerno and the smaller ports highlight the peculiar nature of a wide commercial area which played a dual role as both a distribution center and a market for consumption (in 1861, Naples was the most important Italian port in terms of the movements of ships).[25] Archival research has also been undertaken on anchorages and maritime trade in the other regions of the Kingdom – Abruzzi-Molise, Apulia, Calabria and the shores of the Messina Straits – in the eighteenth century.[26]

Sicily – an island which played an important part both in Spanish expansionism and Mediterranean trade – has not had an abundant maritime historiography. Nevertheless, there have been some positive developments in recent

---

[24]Frascani, "La storia marittima del Mezzogiorno," 297.

[25]Luigi De Rosa, "Navi, merci, nazionalità, itinerari in un porto dell'età preindustriale. Il porto di Napoli nel 1760," in *Studi sul Settecento Italiano* (Napoli, 1968), 332-417; De Rosa, "Napoli porto marittimo," *Nuova rivista storica*, LXXXVI (2002), 545-560; Maria Sirago, "Il porto di Salerno nel 'sistema' portuale del Regno meridionale in età moderna (1503-1806)," *Rassegna storica salernitana*, XXI (1994), 103-151; Sirago, "Attività economiche e diritti feudali nei porti, caricatoi ed approdi meridionali tra XVI e XVIII secolo," in Simoncini (ed.), *Sopra i porti*, II, 329-433; Giorgio Simoncini, "I porti del Regno di Napoli dal XV al XIX secolo," *ibid.*, II, 1-37; Maria Pessolano, "Il porto di Napoli nei secoli XVI-XVIII," *ibid.*, 67-123; and Alfredo Buccaro, "I porti flegrei e l'alternativa allo scalo napoletano dal XVI al XVIII secolo," *ibid.*, 125-154.

[26]On southern Italy, see Maria Sirago, *Le città e il mare. Economia, politica portuale, identità culturale dei centri costieri del Mezzogiorno moderno* (Napoli, 2004); Costantino Felice, *Porti e scafi. Politica ed economia sul litorale abruzzese molisano 1000-1980* (Vasto, 1983); Maria Pessolano, "Il sistema portuale abruzzese-molisano dal viceregno all'Unità," in Simoncini (ed.), *Sopra i porti*, II, 155-194; Maria Antonietta Visceglia, "Il commercio dei porti pugliesi nel Settecento. Ipotesi di ricerca," in Aldo Cormio (ed.), *Economia e classi sociali nella Puglia moderna* (Napoli, 1976); Filomena Fiadino, "I porti delle province pugliesi fra Settecento e Ottocento," in Simoncini (ed.), *Sopra i porti*, II, 195-259; Gaetano Cingari, *Scilla nel Settecento. "Feluche" e "venturieri" nel Mediterraneo* (Reggio Calabria, 1979); Cingari, "I traffici tra l'area calabro-sicula e la costa orientale adriatica nel '700," *Archivio Storico Sicilia Orientale*, LXXV (1979), 277-296; Cingari, "Uomini e navi nell'area dello Stretto di Messina nel '700," in Rogosta (ed.), *Le genti*, 1003-1029; and Clementina Barucci, "I porti delle Calabrie in periodo borbonico" in Simoncini (ed.), *Sopra i porti*, II, 261-318.

years.[27] The latest research, following in the footsteps of the pioneering work by Carmelo Trasselli in the 1950s, paints a picture of a well-structured maritime economy on the island and highlights the conditions and contradictions of Sicilian trade in the modern age.[28] The port of Messina, in particular, was well qualified to act as an emporium between East and West owing to its geographic position and its free-port status.[29] Despite this, it is also true that case studies, like those on Palermo and Trapani,[30] reveal Sicily's progressively subordinate role: it exported raw materials, such as silk and salt, which were subsequently transformed and re-exported to the island for consumption by northern Europeans as silk cloth, salted fish and so on.

---

[27]Motta, "La storiografia marittima siciliana," in Di Vittorio (ed.), *Tendenze e orientamenti*, 95; and Barbera Cardillo, "Il Regno di Sicilia," in Di Vittorio and Barciela Lopez (eds.), *La storiografia marittima*, 337.

[28]Carmelo Trasselli, "Les sources d'archives pour l'histoire du trafique maritime en Sicile," in Michel Mollat (ed.), *Les sources de l'histoire maritime en Europe du Moyen-Age au XVIII siècle* (Paris, 1962), 105-119; Trasselli, "Porti e scali in Sicilia dal XV al XVII secolo," in *Les grandes escales* (Bruxelles, 1972), 257-278; Trasselli, "Le routes siciliennes du Moyen-age au XIX siècle," *Revue historique*, XCVIII (1974), 27-44; Franco Benigno, "Le 'Risposte ai quesiti del console Balbiani' di Carlantonio Broggia: spunti per un'analisi del commercio marittimo siciliano," *Archivio Storico Sicilia Orientale* (1981), 447-462; Giorgio Simoncini, "La Sicilia marittima tra XV e XIX secolo," in Simoncini (ed.), *Sopra i porti*, III, 9-69; D'Angelo, "Porti e traffici marittimi in Sicilia fra Cinquecento e Seicento," *ibid.*, 71-110; and Rosario Battaglia, "Attività commerciali nei porti della Sicilia fra Settecento e Ottocento," *ibid.*, 111-157.

[29]Carmelo Trasselli, "Il traffico del porto di Messina nel 1587," *Economia e storia* (1955), 453-461; Rosario Battaglia, *Porto e commercio a Messina 1840-1880* (Reggio, 1977); Michela D'Angelo, "Aspetti commerciali e finanziari in un porto mediterraneo: Messina (1795-1805)," *Atti Accademia Peloritana*, LV (1979), 201-247; Liliana Iaria, "Il porto di Messina tra Austriaci e Borboni," *Atti Accademia Zelantea*, III (1983), 157-210; and Maria Giuffrè, "L'isola e il mare: il porto di Messina e altri porti," in Simoncini (ed.), *Sopra i porti*, III, 193-238.

[30]On Palermo, see Arianna Delle Vedove, "Il traffico del porto di Palermo dal 1790 al 1815," *Quaderni di geografia umana per la Sicilia e la Calabria*, I (1956), 51-81; Nicole Gotteri, "Gens, navires et marchandises à la Douane de Palerme (1600-1605)," *Mèlanges d'archeologie et d'histoire*, LXXXI (1969), 783-860; and Giovanni Cardamone and Maria Giuffrè, "La città e il mare: il sistema portuale di Palermo," in Simoncini (ed.), *Sopra i porti*, III, 159-192. On Trapani, see Carmelo Trasselli, "Il traffico del porto di Trapani nel 1598-99," *Annuario Facoltà Economia Commercio Palermo* (1947), 3-16; Orazio Cancila, *Aspetti di un mercato siciliano: Trapani nei secoli XVIII-XIX* (Caltanissetta, 1972); and Franco Benigno, *Il porto di Trapani nel Settecento. Rotte, traffici, esportazioni (1674-1800)* (Trapani, 1982).

Ships, Shipbuilding and Transport

In the modern age, ships and navigation underwent considerable changes as the mode of propulsion of the former shifted from oars to sails and then to steam. But studies on naval and merchant shipping of the different Italian states have centred much more on the military and nautical aspects and much less on economic and political considerations, although this is changing. Concurrently, there has been an increasing use of archives.[31] Indeed, the considerable bibliography on the merchant shipping of the pre-Unification Italian states now includes a number of studies dealing primarily with economic and social aspects rather than with the nautical.[32] In addition, studies at the local level have been decidedly more economic and social and less preoccupied with traditional concerns such as ship typologies, tonnage and numbers.[33]

Gaetano Cingari, for example, has highlighted the participation of an entire village in Calabria in the financing of the voyages undertaken by local *feluccas* in the eighteenth century, while Luciana Gatti and Antonio Di Vittorio have considered the market for ships (ownership, freights, etc.) in Genoa and

---

[31]Besides the somewhat dated publication by S. Romiti, *Le marine militari italiane nel Risorgimento 1748-1861* (Roma, 1961), see Lamberto Radogna, *Storia della marina militare delle Due Sicilie 1734-1860* (Milano, 1978); Fausto Piola Caselli, "La flotta pontificia tra il XIV ed il XVI secolo. Costo e finanziamento," in Fanfani (ed.), *La penisola italiana,* 89-106; Daniela Manetti, "Marina militare e costruzioni navali nel Granducato di Toscana (1815-1859)," *ibid.,* 391-410; and Pierangelo Manuele, *Il Piemonte sul mare. La marina sabauda dal Medioevo all'Unità d'Italia* (Cuneo, 1997).

[32]Giuseppe Di Taranto, "La marina mercantile del Mezzogiorno. Un bilancio storiografico (1950-1980)," in Di Vittorio and Barciela Lopez (eds.), *La storiografia marittima,* 285-295; Di Taranto, "La marina del Mezzogiorno nel Mediterraneo (secoli XVIII-XIX)," in Fanfani (ed.), *La penisola italiana,* 301-315; Ugo Tucci, "La marina mercantile veneziana del '700," *Bollettino dell'Istituto di storia della società e dello Stato,* II (1960), 155-200; Ruggiero Romano, "Per una valutazione della flotta mercantile europea alla fine del XVIII secolo," in *Studi in onore di A. Fanfani,* V, 573-591; Lamberto Radogna, *Storia della marina mercantile delle Due Sicilie 1734-1860* (Milano, 1982); Pierangelo Campodonico, *La marineria genovese dal Medioevo all'Unità* (Milano, 1989); Campodonico (ed.), *Dal Mediterraneo all'Atlantico. La marineria ligure nei mari del mondo* (Genova, 1996); and Cesare Ciano, *Navi, mercanti e marinai nel Mediterraneo* (Livorno, 1991).

[33]Paola Massa Piergiovanni, "Aspetti finanziari e funzioni economiche della gestione di una nave alla metà del '500," in Fanfani (ed.), *La penisola italiana,* 107-126; Ugo Tucci, "Traffici e navi nel Mediterraneo in età moderna," *ibid.,* 57-70; and Sergio Anselmi, "Tipologia navale italiana in età moderna (secoli XVIII-XIX)," *ibid.,* 219-232.

Apulia, respectively.[34] The role of small boats in the marketing of Sicilian wines, particularly the sweet malmsey of the island of Salina (Aeolian Islands), has also been examined.[35]

Merchant ships and shipbuilding have been the object of some specific research commissioned to coincide with the 100th anniversary of Unification and have outlined the condition of that sector of the industry in the Italian states in the first half of the nineteenth century.[36] More recent research on shipyards and shipbuilding has shifted the attention to economic and social aspects. In particular, participants in the above-mentioned 1991 conference on "Italy and the Sea" stressed the interaction between shipbuilding, transport systems and maritime trade between the fifteenth and the twentieth century.[37]

---

[34]Cingari, *Scilla nel Settecento*; Luciana Gatti, "Compravendita di imbarcazioni mercantili a Genova (1503-1645)," *Miscellanea storica ligure*, III (1973), 149-186; and Antonio Di Vittorio, "Il mercato delle imbarcazioni in Puglia 1801-1815," *Rivista italiana studi napoleonici*, XXXII (1999), 105-127.

[35]Marcello Saija and Alberto Cervellera, *Mercanti di mare. Salina 1800-1953* (Messina, 1997); and Enrico Iachello, *Il vino e il mare. Trafficanti siciliani tra '700 e '800 nella Contea di Mascali* (Catania, 1991).

[36]See, for example, Ugo Marchese, *L'industria armatoriale ligure dal 1816 al 1859* (Roma, 1957); Mariano Gabriele, *L'industria armatoriale nei territori dello Stato Pontificio dal 1816 al 1880* (Roma, 1961); Luigi Antonio Pagano, *L'industria armatoriale siciliana dal 1816 al 1880* (Roma, 1964); and Fulvio Babudieri, *Squeri e cantieri a Trieste e nella Regione Giulia dal '700 agli inizi del '900* (Trieste, 1986).

[37]Besides Fanfani (ed.), *La penisola italiana,* and Fratta (ed.), *La fabbrica delle navi*, see Mario Marzari (ed.), *Navi di legno. Evoluzione tecnica e sviluppo della cantieristica nel Mediterraneo dal XVI secolo ad oggi* (Trieste, 1998); Frederic C. Lane, *Le navi di Venezia fra i secoli XIII e XVI* (Torino, 1983); Ennio Concina, *L'Arsenale della Repubblica di Venezia* (Milano, 1984); Robert C. Davis, *Costruttori di navi a Venezia. Vita e lavoro nell'Arsenale di Venezia* (Vicenza 1997); Giorgio Bellavitis, *L'Arsenale di Venezia* (Venezia, 1983); Luciana Gatti, *Navi e cantieri della Repubblica di Genova, secoli XVI-XVIII* (Genova, 1999); Ennio Poleggi, "L'arsenale della Repubblica di Genova (1594-1597)," in Ennio Concina (ed.), *Arsenali e città nell'Occidente europeo* (Roma, 1987), 83-84; Catello Vanacore, *Il cantiere navale di Castellammare di Stabia 1780-1983* (Napoli, 1987); Marcello Berti, "Gli Arsenali toscani in età moderna," in *L'Arsenale militare marittimo di Taranto, tra politica, strategia di difesa e sviluppo industriale* (Taranto, 1991), 49-57; Romualdo Giuffrida, "L'arsenale militare di Palermo nell'ambito strategico mediterraneo dagli Asburgo ai Borboni," *ibid.*, 63-66; Nicola Aricò, Federico Martino and Giovanna Motta, "L'arsenale di Messina in età moderna," *ibid.*, 67-72; Ostuni, "L'Arsenale della Marina e l'economia del Regno di Napoli (secc. XV-XIX)," *ibid.*, 73-86; and Maria Sirago, "Attrezzature e costruzioni navali a Napoli e nelle antiche province di terra di Lavoro e di Principato Citra durante il Viceregno spagnolo," in Fanfani (ed.), *La penisola italiana*, 175-218.

The historiography of transportation is presently undergoing a shift from studies based on routes, tonnage and duration of voyage to an analysis of the maritime and the even-less-developed terrestrial transport systems: above all in southern Italy, where the sea provided the means to market the agricultural produce of the interior where the road network was deficient or even non-existent.[38]

Presence and Absence

In recent maritime historiography, the port has become the pivotal point in the analysis of various maritime activities (trade and economic enterprise, as well as financial, institutional and administrative management, etc.).[39] From a broader perspective, "port systems" have also been studied in various regions.[40] In the analysis of ports and commercial routes, particular attention has been devoted to foreign trade and, more generally, to the trade policies of the pre-Unification states.[41] In this context, trade relations with Great Britain have

---

[38]Giuseppe Mira, "Contributo alla storia dei trasporti marittimi nel '700," *Annali Facoltà Economia Commercio Bari*, XI (1951), 11-49; and Vito Dante Flore, *L'industria dei trasporti marittimi in Italia (sec. XVI-1860)* (3 vols., Roma, 1966-1973). See also Luigi De Rosa, "Trasporti terrestri e marittimi nella storia dell'arretratezza meridionale," *Rassegna economica* (1982), 689-721; Ostuni, "Strade liquide e terrestri nel Mezzogiorno in età moderna e contemporanea," in Simoncini (ed.), *Sopra i porti*, IV, 39-65; Giuseppe Cirillo, "I traffici del Regno. Strade e porti nel Mezzogiorno moderno," in *Le vie del Mezzogiorno* (Roma, 2002), 75-114; and Giuseppe De Gennaro, *Economia della terra, economia del mare* (Torino, 2001).

[39]Giorgio Doria, "La gestione del porto di Genova dal 1550 al 1797," in Cavaciocchi (ed.), *I porti come impresa*, 215-270; and Massa Piergiovanni, "Fattori tecnici ed economici dello sviluppo del porto di Genova tra Medioevo ed età moderna," *ibid.*, 169-214.

[40]For example, see Giorgio Doria and Paola Massa Piergiovanni (eds.), *Il sistema portuale della Repubblica di Genova (secc. XIII-XVIII)* (Genova, 1988).

[41]See Ruggiero Romano, *Le commerce du Royaume de Naples avec la France et les pays de l'Adriatique au XVIII siècle* (Paris, 1951); Augusto Graziani, *Il commercio estero del Regno delle Due Sicilie dal 1832 al 1858* (Roma, 1960); Vincenzo Giura, *Russia, Stati Uniti d'America e Regno di Napoli nell'età del Risorgimento* (Napoli, 1967); Antonio Di Vittorio, *Gli Austriaci e il Regno di Napoli 1707-1734* (Napoli, 1969-1973); Di Vittorio, *Il commercio tra Levante ottomano e Napoli nel secolo XVIII* (Napoli, 1979); Orazio Cancila, "Commercio estero (secoli XVI-XVIII)," in Rosario Romeo (coord.), *Storia della Sicilia* (10 vols., Napoli, 1978), VII, 150-161; Maria Luisa Cavalcanti, *Le relazioni commerciali tra il Regno di Napoli e la Russia 1767-1815* (Genève, 1979); and Rosario Battaglia, *Stelle e strisce sotto la Lanterna. Il commercio tra Stati Uniti e Genova 1813-1861* (Messina, 1999).

received more attention than intercourse with other countries.[42] A number of studies have also focussed on the activities of foreign merchants, in particular English merchants residing in Leghorn, Genoa, Naples and Sicily.[43]

The sea, the principal means of communication between the different Italian states, teemed with natural and man-made dangers. Ships, cargoes, crews and passengers were at the mercy of storms, shipwrecks, wars, piracy and other threats. But such threats also generated considerable economic opportunities. A considerable amount of work has been done on maritime insurance, but the financing of small-scale maritime enterprises has received less attention.[44] Piracy and privateering, on the other hand, have been the subjects of much valuable research covering the whole of Italy from Venice to the south.[45] There have also been several studies on the history of maritime law.[46]

---

[42]Pagano De Divitiis, "Il Mezzogiorno d'Italia e l'espansione commerciale inglese," *Archivio storico province napoletane*, XXI (1982), 125-151; De Divitiis, "Il Mediterraneo nel XVII secolo: l'espansione commerciale inglese e l'Italia," *Studi Storici* (1986), 109-148; Eugenio Lo Sardo, *Napoli e Londra nel XVIII secolo* (Napoli, 1991); Rosario Battaglia, *Sicilia e Gran Bretagna. Le relazioni commerciali dalla Restaurazione all'Unità* (Milano, 1983); Edoardo Grendi, "Sul commercio anglo-italiano del Settecento," *Quaderni storici* (1992), 263-275; De Divitiis and Vincenzo Giura (eds.), *L'Italia del secondo Settecento nelle relazioni segrete di William Hamilton, Horace Mann e John Murray* (Napoli, 1997); and Michela D'Angelo, "In the 'English' Mediterranean (1511-1815)," *Journal of Mediterranean Studies*, XII, No. 2 (2002), 271-285.

[43]Pagano De Divitiis, *Mercanti inglesi nell'Italia del '600. Navi, traffici, egemonie* (Venezia, 1990); Maria Christina Engels, *Merchants, Interlopers, Seamen and Corsairs: The Flemish Community in Livorno and Genoa 1615-1635* (Hilversum, 1997); Barbara Dawes, *British Merchants in Naples 1820-1860* (Napoli, 1991); and Michela D'Angelo, *Mercanti inglesi in Sicilia 1806-1815* (Milano, 1988).

[44]Alberto Tenenti, *Naufrages, corsaires et assurances maritimes à Venise 1592-1609* (Paris, 1959); Giorgio Coen, "Il contratto di cambio marittimo nella piazza di Ancona attraverso gli atti notarili," *Quaderni storici* (1967); *L'assicurazione in Italia fino all'Unità* (Milano, 1975); Franca Assante, *Il mercato delle assicurazioni marittime a Napoli nel Settecento* (Napoli, 1972); Carmelo Trasselli, "Banchieri, armatori, assicuratori," in Romeo (coord.), *Storia della Sicilia*, III, 485-500; Lucia Bonafede and Teresa Dispenza, "Note sull'assicurazione in Sicilia nella seconda metà del '500," *Atti Accademia Scienze Lettere Arti Palermo*, IV (1983-1984), 109-169; and Giulio Giacchero, *Storia delle assicurazioni marittime. L'esperienza genovese dal Medioevo all'età contemporanea* (Genova, 1984).

[45]Alberto Tenenti, *Venezia e i corsari* (Bari, 1961); Sergio Anselmi, *Pirati e corsari in Adriatico* (Pesaro, 1998); Salvatore Bono, *I corsari barbareschi* (Torino, 1964); Bono, *Corsari nel Mediterraneo* (Milano, 1993); Bono, *Il Mediterraneo. Da Lepanto a Barcellona* (Perugina, 2000); Mirella Mafrici, *Mezzogiorno e pirateria in età*

Today, the sea is also an object of study as an economic resource and a source of employment for fishermen and sailors. Yet few studies have focussed on the lives and working conditions of these men in areas such as recruitment, apprenticeship, wages and catering. Among the exceptions, besides *Peoples of the Mediterranean Sea*, it is worth mentioning the conference on "Life on Board Ships in the Mediterranean in the Sixteenth and Seventeenth Centuries" and some research on the fishermen of Apulia and on the porters of Genoa.[47]

In the last few decades, the maritime historiography of the different states prior to Unification has undergone a process of considerable renewal which has had a varying impact on the various areas of research. Fads in historiography and the many unexplored archival resources, as well as the political fragmentation, economic diversity and social complexity of the individual Italian states between the late fifteenth century and the mid-nineteenth century, can certainly explain the lack of long-term studies, on the one hand, and the research focussed on the individual realities, with sometimes too much detail and without a global vision.

Many of the recent studies carried out on ports and port infrastructures, on merchandise and merchants, on ships and seamen, on routes and navigation, and on resources and dangers at sea sketch a lively picture. Other

---

moderna (Napoli, 1995); Mafrici, "L'antica angoscia delle coste calabresi: la pirateria turca e barbaresca tra Cinquecento e Settecento," in Augusto Placanica (ed.), *Storia della Calabria* (12 vols., Roma, 1997), III, 313-347; Mafrici, "I mari del Mezzogiorno d'Italia tra cristiani e musulmani," in Walter Barberis (ed.), *Storia d'Italia. Annali 18. Guerra e pace* (Torino, 2002), 71-121; Daniele Tranchida, *Pirateria barbaresca e Regno di Napoli 1776-1799* (Messina, 1995); Antonello Savaglio (ed.), *Guerra di corsa e pirateria nel Mediterraneo* (Cosenza, 1999); and Luca Lo Basso, *In traccia de' legni nemici. Corsari europei nel Mediterraneo del '700* (Ventimiglia, 2002).

[46]Cesare M. Moschetti, "Gli studi di storia del diritto marittimo in Italia," in Di Vittorio (ed.), *Tendenze e orientamenti*, 289-344; and Vito Piergiovanni, "La storiografia del diritto marittimo," in Di Vittorio and Carlos Barciela Lopez (eds.), *La storiografia marittima*, 1-10.

[47]Tucci, "Marinai e galeotti nel Cinquecento veneziano," in Ragosta (ed.), *Le genti*, 677-692; Cesare M. Moschetti, "Aspetti organizzativi e sociali della gente di mare del golfo di Napoli nei secoli XVII e XVIII," *ibid.*, 937-973; Cingari, "Uomini e navi nell'area dello Stretto," *ibid.*, 1003-1029; Cingari, "La vita a bordo delle navi nel Mediterraneo nei secoli XVI-XVII," *Quaderni Stefaniani* (1987); Giuseppe Doneddu and Maurizio Gangemi (eds.), *La pesca nel Mediterraneo occidentale (sec. XVI-XVIII)* (Bari, 2000); Biagio Salvemini, "Comunità 'separate' e trasformazioni strutturali. I pescatori pugliesi fra metà '600 e gli anni Trenta del '900," in *Mèlanges Ecole Francaise de Rome*, XCVII (1985), 441-488; and Luisa Piccinno, *Economia marittima e operatività portuale. Genova secoli XVII-XIX* (Genova, 2000).

topics, such as coastal shipping, maritime companies and the like, remain to be explored. The state of maritime history is marked by what Giuseppe Galasso in his contribution on the history of shipbuilding in southern Italy has called *"più assenze che presenze."* In other words, maritime history is more notable for what it has yet to do than for what it has already done. Recent work, nevertheless, suggests that the gaps are slowly being filled in.[48]

Part II: Post-Unification Italy

At Unification, Italy was an economically-backward agricultural country that was poor in capital; possessed hardly any industrial raw materials or energy sources; and had a domestic communication system which was precarious and in parts non-existent.[49] During the years in which Italy was becoming unified, steam-powered shipping was gradually coming into its own, thus marking the most important revolution in world maritime history. As a consequence, the modernisation of both the merchant fleet and the navy emerged as crucial problems, as did many other compelling issues, such as the construction of an efficient land-based communications and transport network; the management of industrialisation; the fostering of an international trade network, closely linked to prospects of colonial expansion; and the management of emigration which became a mass phenomenon during the last quarter of the nineteenth century. All these problems had to be solved quickly in order to bridge the gap that separated Italy from the more advanced countries of Western Europe. The question of shipping thus became the centre of a debate around which raged furious controversies within the overall context of the country's industrialisation and the relationship between business and the state. Over the first fifty years of the history of a unified Italy, the debate over shipping involved economists, politicians and industrialists whose texts were published in trade journals such as *Rivista Marittima*, the official organ of the Navy General Staff published since 1868, *Rassegna nazionale*, *La Marina mercantile italiana* and various daily newspapers.

Ships, Shipping and Maritime Protectionism

The great importance that post-World War II historiography has given to the phenomenon of maritime protectionism – government intervention to support the maritime transport industry – that began in the 1880s within the context of

---

[48]Giuseppe Galasso, "Il Mezzogiorno e il mare," in Fratta (ed.), *La fabbrica delle navi*, 11.

[49]See, for example, Vera Zamagni, *Dalla periferia al centro. La seconda rinascita economica dell'Italia 1861-1981* (Bologna, 1990); and Zamagni, *The Economic History of Italy, 1860-1990* (Oxford, 1993).

the country's economic development can be traced to the compelling political debate about the issue at the time. In fact, a large number of contributions concentrated on the forms and methods of public intervention in the maritime sector.[50] Indeed, the same was true for extensive parts of works dealing with Italian economic and transport history and the state's economic policies in general.[51] State policy also affected shipbuilding, and the aforementioned studies

---

[50]Antonio Petino, "Il problema marittimo in Italia all'alba dell'unificazione," in Armando Sapori, *et. al.* (eds.), *L'economia italiana dal 1861 al 1961. Studi nel I centenario dell'Unità d'Italia* (Milano, 1961), 271-297; Cesare Ciano, "La marina mercantile nazionale dall'Unità ad oggi," in *ibid.*, 298-312; Ugo Spadoni, "Il canale di Suez e l'inizio della crisi della marina mercantile italiana," *Nuova Rivista Storica* (1970), 651-702; Spadoni, "Linee di navigazione e costruzioni navali alla vigilia dell'inchiesta parlamentare sulla marina mercantile italiana (1881-1882)," *Nuova Rivista Storica* (1973), 313-372; Spadoni, "L'Ansaldo e la politica navale italiana," in Giorgio Mori (ed.) *Storia dell'Ansaldo. 2. La costruzione di una grande impresa 1883-1902* (Roma, 1995), 67-88; Giuseppe Barone, "Lo Stato e la marina mercantile in Italia (1881-1894)," *Studi Storici*, No. 3 (1974), 624-659; Flore, *L'industria dei trasporti marittimi in Italia*; Ludovica de Courten, "Per una storia della marina mercantile italiana dall'Unità alla prima guerra mondiale," *Clio*, No. 4 (1981), 491-510; de Courten, "Marina mercantile e finanza. Il credito navale in Italia dall'Unità alla seconda guerra mondiale," *Clio*, No. 2 (1984), 233-260; de Courten, *La marina mercantile italiana nella politica di espansione (1860-1914); Industria, finanza e trasporti marittimi* (Roma, 1989); de Courten, "L'Ansaldo e la politica navale durante l'età giolittiana," in Peter Hertner (ed.), *Storia dell'Ansaldo. 3. Dai Bombrini ai Perrone 1903-1914* (Roma, 1996), 67-94; Daniel J. Grange, "Le convenzioni marittime in base alle Carte Stringher (1909)," *Storia Contemporanea*, No. 6 (1980), 905-932; Tommaso Fanfani, "Il difficile sviluppo di un settore protetto: la marina mercantile italiana dal 1861 al 1914," *Studi e Informazioni*, No. 2 (1990), 145-165; Fanfani, "Lo scenario generale," in Fanfani (ed.), *La penisola italiana e il mare*, 3-17; Fanfani, "Intervento pubblico e marina mercantile tra l'Unità e la fine dell'Ottocento: dalla 'tenda dell'arabo' alla ripresa produttiva," in Ilaria Zilli (ed.), *Fra Spazio e Tempo. Studi in onore di Luigi De Rosa* (Napoli, 1995), 383-418; Ezio Ferrante, "L'inchiesta parlamentare sulla marina mercantile italiana," *Guardia Costiera*, No. 1 (1992), 22-32; and L. Contini, "Pubblico e privato in età giolittiana: Luigi della Torre e le convenzioni marittime (1909-1910)," *Archivi e imprese*, Nos. 11-12 (1995), 193-232. On Genoa in particular, see Giorgio Doria, *Investimenti e sviluppo economico a Genova alla vigilia della prima guerra mondiale* (2 vols., Milano, 1969-1973).

[51]See, for example, Antonio Cardini, *Stato liberale e protezionismo* (Bologna, 1981); Vera Zamagni, *Lo Stato italiano e l'economia. Storia dell'intervento pubblico dall'unificazione ai nostri giorni* (Firenze, 1981); Istituto per lo Studio dell'Organizzazione Aziendale (IPSOA), *Annali dell'economia italiana* (14 vols., Mi-

must therefore be considered along with works on shipyards. Some examples that focus on shipyards that built iron and steel vessels for deep-sea shipping include the work by Tommaso Fanfani dedicated to the San Marco *squero* (a term that means shipyard in the Venetian dialect); the numerous essays contained in the nine-volume history of Ansaldo, the Genoese mechanical engineering company founded in 1853; the book by Paolo Fragiacomo on the Monfalcone shipyards founded in 1907 by the Cosulich family; and the chapters dedicated to the shipbuilding industry of Trieste and Venezia Giulia (which we include even though they were only annexed to Italy after World War I) in a very recent study by Giulio Mellinato.[52]

The studies on state policy to support shipping highlight the complex interaction between maritime transport companies, heavy industry, banking and political power; in the more dated works these problems are discussed with a polemical bitterness that recalls the heated debates of the past. In more recent contributions, which have been written in a more detached style, the close relationship between politics and business has been reasserted, but in overall terms public intervention has been judged as positive. Despite its limitations and inconsistencies, state policy did in fact lead to the modernisation and technological improvement of the Italian merchant fleet and the development of related shipbuilding, steel-making and mechanical industries. In Italy, however, unlike Britain, a solid and ongoing partnership between shipping companies and shipyards did not emerge. Indeed, this relationship developed only to a limited extent and not until the beginning of the twentieth century; most important, it came about on the basis of financial solutions "aimed at

---

lano, 1981-1985); Stefano Battilossi, *Storia economica d'Italia. 2. Annali* (Roma, 1999); and Stefano Maggi, *Politica ed economia dei trasporti (secoli XIX-XX)* (Bologna, 2001), 139-182. Aged but still valuable is the "classic" by Epicarmo Corbino, "Il protezionismo marittimo in Italia," *Giornale degli Economisti*, Nos. 11-12 (1921) and Nos. 2-4 (1922).

[52]Tommaso Fanfani, "Per una storia della cantieristica in Italia: dallo 'squero San Marco' all'Italcantieri," *L'Industria*, No. 2 (1988), 313-335; Paolo Fragiacomo, *La grande fabbrica, la piccola città. Monfalcone e il cantiere navale: la nascita di una company town (1860-1940)* (Milano, 1997); and Giulio Mellinato, *Crescita senza sviluppo. L'economia marittima della Venezia Giulia tra Impero asburgico e autarchia (1914-1936)* (Monfalcone, 2001). On Trieste's shipping, see also Fulvio Babudieri, *L'industria armatoriale di Trieste e della Regione Giulia dal 1815 al 1918* (Roma, 1964); and Babudieri, *Industria, commerci e navigazione a Trieste e nella Regione Giulia.*

creating pressure groups with regard to the State to obtain contributions and orders."[53]

Regarding the studies on maritime protectionism, the very evident preference for the first fifty years after Unification, with occasional incursions into the years of Fascism, should be noted.[54] In fact, the enormous importance of this issue during that phase of the country's history has led to an almost complete neglect of the latter half of the twentieth century, a period during which a new liberalisation emerged in maritime transport.[55]

It is well known that history is written by the victors, in this case steam shipping, and the vanquished are all but forgotten. This was the destiny of the sail-powered fleet whose technological eclipse, despite state protection, has been marked by a kind of historiographical amnesia at the national level which is difficult to justify in view of the fact that sail comprised most of the Italian merchant fleet up to 1907.[56] This deficiency was highlighted in, and to a great extent offset by, a recent essay by Marco Doria.[57] The author, with constant references to the national level, focussed on a Ligurian sailing fleet that reached the pinnacle of its success in the second half of the nineteenth century and that represented the most consistent element of the entire sailing fleet of post-Unification Italy.

Another maritime transport sector which has also been forgotten is short-haul shipping: regardless of its importance in quantitative terms, it is

---

[53]Fanfani, "Il difficile sviluppo," 163.

[54]Renato Giannetti, "I fattori del successo delle costruzioni navali mercantili nel periodo tra le due guerre mondiali: mercato, tecnologia, organizzazione," in Fanfani (ed.), *La penisola italiana*, 443-454; and Giuseppe Conti, "Finanza e industria nei cantieri navali dal primo dopoguerra agli anni '30," *ibid.*, 455-486.

[55]The only partial exception is Flore, *L'industria dei trasporti marittimi*, who deals with the period 1945-1970.

[56]Local historiography is instead extremely rich and therefore it is impossible to offer a complete set of references. As regards Ligurian sail-powered shipping see Gio Bono Ferrari, *Capitani di mare e bastimenti di Liguria del secolo XIX* (Rapallo, 1939); Campodonico, *La Marineria Genovese*; and Campodonico (ed.), *Dal Mediterraneo all'Atlantico*. A national perspective is adoped by Tommaso Gropallo, *Il romanzo della vela. Storia della marina mercantile a vela italiana nell'Ottocento* (Bogliasco, 1964), but this is a dated and anedoctical work.

[57]Doria, "La marina mercantile a vela in Liguria dalla metà dell'Ottocento alla prima guerra mondiale," in Paolo Frascani (ed.), *A vela e a vapore. Economie, culture e istituzioni del mare nell'Italia dell'Ottocento* (Roma, 2001), 83-107.

only fleetingly mentioned in studies about the maritime history of modern Italy. The issue was recently brought to the attention of historians in an essay by Giuseppe Moricola, who concentrated on short-haul shipping during the first post-Unification decades when, given the lack of an adequate road network, the sea was the main means of trade. In 1861, sixty percent of the traffic in Italian ports comprised short-haul shipping, and for an extended period of time it remained one of the principal factors in the emerging national market. The decline in the sector was due to the lack of modernisation that, according to Moricola, was the result of public policies that failed to support the construction of an integrated system of short-haul railways and maritime transport. Moricola's views on this subject are quite pertinent since land transportation has become unsustainable due to its negative impact on the environment, and there have been calls for a greater use of maritime "highways." A recent programme to bring this about has not progressed beyond the drawing board.[58]

The decisive role played by state intervention set the stage for the consideration of other issues, including publications devoted specifically to individual shipping companies and shipping families.[59] The merchant shipping sector has been dominated by the largest shipowners who, thanks to their influential political contacts, have been able to make greater use of public financing. But the historiography has also been characterized by some obvious deficiencies. For example, we lack a critical history of Navigazione Generale Italiana, founded in 1881 by a merger between Florio, a Sicilian company, and Rubattino, a Genoese firm. In 1931 it became Italia di Navigazione and in 1936 fell under the control of Finmare, a public holding company whose history also needs reassessment. Other companies and shipping dynasties that have played notable roles in the history of Italian transoceanic shipping in the nineteenth and twentieth centuries only receive brief mentions in general works that tackle Italian shipping during the contemporary period. These companies include La Veloce, belonging to the Genoese shipowners Lavarello; Lloyd Italiano, the property of Erasmo Piaggio; and Lloyd Sabaudo, founded in 1906 by the Genoese Alessandro Cerruti and Edoardo Canali.

---

[58]Giuseppe Moricola, "Il cabotaggio in età postunitaria," *ibid.*, 55-81.

[59]Maria Ottolino, *Commercio e navigazione marittima in Puglia. La Società di navigazione a vapore "Puglia"* (Napoli, 1981); Fulvio Babudieri, "I Cosulich, una stirpe di navigatori e imprenditori," *Archeografo triestino*, Nos. 43-44 (1983), 33-51; Simone Candela, *I Florio* (Palermo, 1986); Orazio Cancila, "La Società di Navigazione 'Tirrenia (Flotte riunite Florio-Citra)' 1932-1936," in Zilli (ed.), *Fra spazio e tempo*, 155-180; *Il Lloyd Triestino. Contributi alla storia di un cinquantennio 1936-1986* (Trieste, 1986); and Giorgio Doria, *Debiti e navi. La compagnia Rubattino 1839-1881* (Genova, 1990).

Again with regard to shipping, we do have general works about merchant and passenger maritime transport in Italy in the age of steam. Of particular importance are some studies that, at least in quantitatively terms, are quite extensive. These began with works by Giuseppe Annovazzi, Antonio Giordano and Ferdinando Tambroni, published in the mid-1950s, which focussed on the reconstruction of the national fleet after the Second World War.[60] Publications by Tommaso Gropallo, Francesco Ogliari and Lamberto Radogna followed in the 1970s and 1980s.[61] More recently, Maurizio Eliseo and Paolo Piccione have published on the topic.[62] These authors, who are often not scholars but professionals engaged in some capacity in the shipping sector, have focussed above all on the "Queens of the Seas," the huge transatlantic passenger liners (such as *Duilio, Giulio Cesare, Rex, Conte di Savoia, Raffaello* and *Michelangelo*) that were the antecedents of today's cruise ships. These studies provide construction and technical details, describe the routes, and through the use of extensive anecdotes chronicle the vicissitudes and salient facts of ships that, like beautiful and charming "ambassadors," effectively represented the values and skills of Italians abroad. The book by Eliseo and Piccione also contains an extensive analysis of the ships' interiors and a review of the innovative marketing strategies employed by the shipping companies.[63] Albeit repetitive, these works are nevertheless useful for reconstructing the overall evolution of the sector.

To obtain information about minor shipping firms and non-liner shipping we must refer to the numerous studies that focus on individual, local and regional maritime contexts. These case studies provide in-depth analyses of shipping-related manufacturing, the entrepreneurial and merchant environment and, in general, the economic strategies and professional behaviour of some

---

[60]Giuseppe Annovazzi (ed.), *La marina mercantile italiana. Nove secoli di storia cinque milioni Tsl* (Genova, 1958); Antonio Giordano, *La marina mercantile italiana dal 1900 al 1950* (Genova, 1951); and Ferdinando Tambroni, *La marina mercantile italiana* (Roma, 1953).

[61]Tommaso Gropallo, *Navi a vapore e armamenti italiani. Dal 1818 ai nostri giorni* (Milano, 1976); and Francesco Ogliari and Lamberto Radogna (eds.), *Trasporti marittimi di linea* (8 vols., Milano, 1977-1987).

[62]Maurizio Eliseo and Paolo Piccione *Transatlantici. Storia delle grandi navi passeggeri italiane* (Genova, 2001).

[63]Paolo Piccione had already dealt with this topic in *Costa crociere, cinquant'anni di stile* (Milano, 1998).

Italian maritime communities.[64] In this case as well, there are some very extensive gaps. A prime example is the case of Genoa, a city with merchant-marine
traditions so deep that it undoubtedly deserves to be called the "maritime capital" of post-Unification Italy. The major but somewhat dated work by Giorgio
Doria on the period between the Restoration and the eve of the First World
War should be reconsidered and extended.[65] This could be done through the
application of the same in-depth and lucid analysis to the recent years when
Genoa, after a very difficult period, once again became the leading Mediterranean maritime city.[66]

Returning to the subject of shipping companies, a well-known fact
that is reiterated persistently in publications about the Italian merchant navy
during the first decades after Unification is that the modernisation of the fleet
can be traced directly to the emigration "boom" of the late nineteenth and the
twentieth centuries.[67] In fact, emigration was such a profitable business that
Italian shipping companies benefited despite the technological backwardness of
their vessels. It should be emphasised, however, that Italian firms were heavily
affected by foreign competition: in the first decade of the twentieth century
only twenty to thirty percent of Italians who migrated to North America travelled on domestically-owned ships. The situation was somewhat better on Latin
American routes, where Italian ships transported about two-thirds of Italian
migrants during the same period.[68] While there is a considerable historiography on Italian emigration, we cannot say the same about the maritime transport

---

[64]Sergio Anselmi, *Da Goro a San Benedetto del Tronto: il commercio marittimo in Adriatico* (Ancona, 1991); Rosario Battaglia, *Mercanti e imprenditori in una
città marittima. Il caso di Messina (1850-1900)* (Milano, 1992); Saija and Cervellera,
Mercanti di mare; and Adriano Betti Carboncini, *Linee di navigazione marittima
dell'arcipelago toscano* (Cortona, 1999).

[65]Giorgio Doria, *Investimenti e sviluppo economico a Genova* (Milano 1969-
1973).

[66]See Federation of the Sea, Centre for Social Studies and Policies, *The Second Maritime Economy Report* (Milano, 2003).

[67]See Giovanni Roncagli, "L'industria dei trasporti marittimi," in *Cinquant'anni di storia italiana* (2 vols., Milano, 1911), I, 1-64. The topic was also taken
up, although only as a possible research field, by M. Elisabetta Tonizzi,
"L'emigrazione e lo sviluppo della marina mercantile: un'ipotesi di lavoro," in *I
fenomeni migratori dalla provincia di Genova nei secoli XIX e XX* (Genova, 1988), 50-
61.

[68]M. Elisabetta Tonizzi, *Le grandi correnti migratorie del '900* (Torino,
1999), 44.

involved in this phenomenon. If we exclude the book by Augusta Molinari on sanitary conditions on Italian vessels during the Atlantic crossing, the maritime aspects of migrant transport have been almost completely neglected.[69]

Ports and Port Policy

We will now focus briefly on the state of the literature on ports. There is a large corpus of publications on this subject, to be sure.[70] Most of it, however, is local or regional in scope.[71] To the best of our knowledge, the only comprehensive research carried out on Italian ports remains the work by Gino Bar-

---

[69]Augusta Molinari, *Le navi di Lazzaro. Aspetti sanitari dell'emigrazione transoceanica. Il viaggio per mare* (Milano, 1988). Up to the early 1900s Genoa was the country's leading migration port; see M. Elisabetta Tonizzi, *Merci, strutture e lavoro nel porto di Genova tra '800 e '900* (Milano, 2000), 39-58; and Andrea Carbone, "L'assistenza agli emigranti in partenza dal porto di Genova tra Otto e Novecento," in Adele Maiello (ed.), *L'emigrazione nelle Americhe dalla provincia di Genova. Questioni di storia sociale* (Bologna, 1992), 43-60. Some studies on the Genoese press focus on local shipping companies and their economic interests in migration transport, see Guido Ratti, *Il Corriere Mercantile di Genova dall'Unità al fascismo (1861-1925)* (Parma, 1973); Francesco Sudich, "Il problema dell'emigrazione in un giornale di armatori genovesi 'L'Italia all'estero' (1884)," *Porto e Aeroporto di Genova*, No. 8 (1980), 961-968; Mario Enrico Ferrari, *"L'Amazzonia." Una rivista per l'emigrazione nel Brasile settentrionale* (Genova 1983), 257-317; Ferrari, *Emigrazione e colonie: il giornale genovese 'La Borsa' (1865-1894)* (Genova, 1983); and Adele Maiello, "Stampa ed emigrazione a Genova: il caso del 'Cittadino,'" in Maiello (ed.), *L'emigrazione nelle Americhe*, 61-118.

[70]All Italian ports of any economic importance have been studied, and it is therefore impossible in this context to offer a complete set of references. With regard to Genoa, Naples, Barcelona, Marseilles and Piraeus in a comparative perspective, see M. Elisabetta Tonizzi (ed.), *Porti dell'Europa mediterranea (secoli XIX e XX)*, monographic issue of *Memoria e Ricerca*, XI (Milano, 2002).

[71]On Ligurian ports, see Giorgio Doria, "Il ruolo del sistema portuale ligure nell'industrializzazione dell'Italia nord-occidentale (1750-1918)," in Fanfani (ed.), *La penisola italiana*, 49-284; and Ugo Marchese, "Economia e sistema portuale," in Antonio Gibelli and Paride Rugafiori (eds.), *Storia d'Italia. Le regioni dall'Unità ad oggi. La Liguria* (Torino, 1994), 727-775. For Tuscany and Abruzzo, see Giuseppe Conti, "Livorno da centro mercantile a centro industriale e la 'diversità' con il resto della Toscana tra 800 e 900," in Zilli (ed.), *Fra Spazio e Tempo*, 167-186; and Ezio Ferrante, "Contributo allo studio della portualità abruzzese tra Ottocento e Novecento," *Proposte e Ricerche* (1996), 94-102.

bieri, but this dates back to the end of the 1950s.[72] Neither has there been much attention devoted to the history of a national port policy that, together with public action to support shipping and shipbuilding, has been a fundamental element of Italian "maritime policy." The chapters on this subject in the books published more than thirty years ago by Vito Dante Flore; an essay by Maria Ottolino that only covers the period between 1861 and 1880; and the concise and specific references to the phenomenon in an essay by Andrea Giuntini on the post-Unification development of the Italian infrastructure represent all that is available on this subject.[73]

Shipping-related Institutions

Among the many topics that maritime historians have hardly explored are the institutions created to manage maritime transport and the "bureaucracy of the sea," or administrative personnel who man them.[74] The only exceptions are the harbour masters, on whom there have been a couple of recent contributions,[75] and the "Registro Italiano Navale" (RINA), the shipping register founded in Genoa in 1860 that has played a fundamental role in modernising and upgrading the Italian merchant fleet. Giulio Giacchero chronicles RINA's history in a book that is now more than forty-years-old and which is somewhat flawed by the commemorative, if not hagiographic, aims which prompted its publication.[76] RINA is the fourth-oldest shipping register, after "Lloyd's Register" of

---

[72]Gino Barbieri, *I porti d'Italia* (Roma, 1959). With specific reference to the role played by the sea and ports within the framework of Italian industrialization, see Vera Zamagni, "Industrialization and the Sea," in Luciano Buzzetti, *et al.* (eds.), *Italy's Sea. Problems and Perspectives* (Roma, 1998), 111-117.

[73]Flore, *L'industria dei trasporti marittimi in Italia;* Maria Ottolino, "Navigazione commerciale e politica portuale in Italia (1861-1880)," in Istituto Formazione Operatori Aziendali (IFOA), *Mercati e consumi. Organizzazione e qualificazione del commercio in Italia dal XII al XX secolo* (Bologna, 1986), 407-417; Andrea Giuntini, "Nascita, sviluppo e tracollo della rete infrastrutturale," in Franco Amatori, *et al.* (eds.), *Storia d'Italia. Annali 15: L'industria* (Torino, 1999), 551-616.

[74]For this definition, see Frascani, "La storia marittima del Mezzogiorno," 313.

[75]Guglielmo Evangelista, "Il corpo delle Capitanerie di Porto. La storia dei primi decenni di vita," *Rivista Marittima*, No. 4 (1996); and Walter Gonzales, *Sentinelle in blu. Storia e vicende delle Capitanerie di porto e della Guardia Costiera* (Milano, 1997).

[76]Giulio Giacchero, *Il Registro Italiano Navale 1861-1961* (Genova, 1961).

London, "Bureau Veritas" of Antwerp and "Ufficio Veritas" of Trieste. The latter was founded in 1857 and recently has been studied by Sergio Maurel.[77]

The subject of shipping registers leads immediately to the field of maritime insurance. If we exclude works by Tommaso Fanfani and Giulio Sapelli for Trieste and the old, commemorative study by Giuseppe Annovazzi on Genoa, the subject has still to receive the attention of researchers.[78]

Much the same thing can be said about the historiography dedicated to the role of port authorities and the administrative and managerial personnel they employ. It is important to recall that this issue has been the subject of recent important legislative measures, such as Law 84/1994 that instituted Port Authorities. What we have instead are numerous publications about individual institutions, such as the Autonomous Port Trust of Genoa, the first Italian case of autonomous port management, which was founded in 1903.[79] In 1906, the Autonomous Port Trust of Genoa issued the first rules covering port labour, a subject that has been analysed in various recent studies.[80]

The periodical trade press devoted to shipping and maritime activities is another subject overlooked by historians. An exception is *Rivista Marittima*, the official organ of the Navy General Staff, which has been studied by Ezio Ferrante.[81] The publication in the 1980s and 1990s of extensive analytical catalogues of Genoa's periodical press provides a detailed and highly useful start-

---

[77]S. Maurel, "Un capitolo di storia dell'Ente Camerale triestino. L'istituzione dell'Ufficio Veritas austriaco," *Trieste economica*, No. 3 (1994), 57-65.

[78]Tommaso Fanfani, "Un modello di crescita economica. Trieste e le 'Assicurazioni Generali," in *Miscellanea di studi in onore di Mario Abrate* (2 vols., Torino, 1986), I, 411-425; Giulio Sapelli, "Uomini e capitali nella Trieste dell'Ottocento. La fondazione della Riunione Adriatica di Sicurtà," *Società e Storia*, no. 26 (1984), 821-874; and Giuseppe Annovazzi, *I cento anni del Comitato delle Compagnie di assicurazioni marittime di Genova 1860-1960* (Genova, 1961).

[79]Consorzio Autonomo del Porto di Genova (Cap), *Archivio Storico 1870-1945* (3 vols., Genova, 1988-1993).

[80]Aldo Giovanni Velardita (ed.), *Porto, lavoro portuale. Storia delle compagnie e dei gruppi portuali* (Genova, 1992); Tonizzi, *Merci, strutture e lavoro*, 143-160; and Marco Doria, "Les dockers de Gênes: le travail entre économie et politique de 1800 à la Seconde Guerre mondiale," in Jean Domenichino, Jean-Marie Guillon and Robert Mencherini (eds.), *Dockers de la Méditerranée à la Mer du nord* (Aix-en-Provence, 1999), 15-43.

[81]Ezio Ferrante, "La Rivista Marittima. La storia, le idee, gli autori," *Rivista Marittima*, No. 7 (1986).

ing point for those who would like to undertake a critical analysis of these numerous and often short-lived publications.[82]

On the other hand, attention has been paid to a phenomenon which was obviously crucial for the technological upgrading of Italian maritime transport: the technical education of seafarers. Indeed, Maria Stella Rollandi recently published an essay on Italian nautical schools in the period from 1859 to after the First World War.[83] The university education of marine engineers, professionals who furnished the technical and scientific expertise needed to design and build modern ships, has been the subject of a recent history of the Genoa Institute of Marine Engineering.[84] This institution, founded in 1870 to satisfy the need for new skills required by the advent of steam-powered navigation, was the only university-level educational centre specialising in this type of engineering up to the early twentieth century. The Genoa Institute was followed by the marine engineering institute of Naples and, after the First World War, by a similar institution in Trieste. The social profile and professional careers of Italian marine engineers are discussed in a 1999 study of graduates of the Genoa Institute which analyses their labour organisation in Italian shipyards in the period 1870-1914, with particular reference to how many were eventually employed in shipyards and the tasks they performed.[85] The essays by Alain Dewerpe and Giorgio Pedrocco on labour organisation and the manual trades in Italian shipyards are also of interest.[86]

---

[82]Marina Milan, *La stampa periodica a Genova dal 1871 al 1900* (Milano, 1989); and Roberto Beccaria, *I periodici genovesi dal 1473 al 1899* (Genova, 1994).

[83]Maria Stella Rollandi, "Imparare a navigare. Istruzione e marina mercantile dalla legge Casati al primo dopoguerra," in Frascani (ed.), *A vela e a vapore*, 139-176.

[84]Anselmo Marcenaro and M. Elisabetta Tonizzi (eds.), *Dalla Regia Scuola Superiore Navale alla Facoltà di Ingegneria* (Genova, 1997).

[85]M. Elisabetta Tonizzi, "Gli ingegneri della Scuola superiore navale di Genova (1870-1914)," in Andrea Giuntini and Michela Minesso (eds.), *Gli ingegneri in Italia tra '800 e '900* (Milano, 1999), 101-115. On marine engineers employed in Ansaldo's shipyards, see Anna Guagnini, "Gli ingegneri e la tecnologia dell'Ansaldo," in Valerio Castronovo (ed.), *Storia dell'Ansaldo. 4. L'Ansaldo e la Grande Guerra 1915-1918* (Roma, 1997), 165-189.

[86]Alain Dewerpe, "Construire des bateaux: Ansaldo 1900-1915," *Le Mouvement Social*, No. 156 (1991), 117-154; Dewerpe, "L'organizzazione del lavoro. Maestranze e dirigenti," in Mori (ed.), *Storia dell'Ansaldo. 2. La costruzione*, 111-138; Dewerpe, "Maestranze e quadri tecnici," in Hertner (ed.), *Storia dell'Ansaldo, 3. Dai Bombrini*, 201-224; and Giorgio Pedrocco, "Le origini della moderna

Sailors, Fishermen and Yachtsmen

Three essays have recently helped to shift the focus to the issue of maritime labour, another of the many "shadowy areas" in the maritime historiography on post-Unification Italy. Paolo Frascani, who uses the ship logs conserved at the State Archives of Naples as his main source of information, and M. Stella Rollandi have in fact studied the maritime labour market, recruitment, wages and living and working conditions of crews on merchant ships from 1861 to 1900.[87] A study by Annunziata Berrino analysed the maritime communities of the Sorrento peninsula whose economic vitality was closely connected to sea-related work in the second half of the nineteenth century.[88]

The extreme environmental and biological diversity of the many seas that surround Italy, and the inadequacy of statistical data, makes it particularly difficult, as Sergio Anselmi noted, to write a comprehensive history of Italian fishing and fishermen.[89] Nevertheless, the studies by Marco Armiero do shed some light on the subject.[90] With particular reference to the southern regions, but without neglecting the national scenario, he has undertaken a quantitative

navalmeccanica," in Fondazione Giangiacomo Feltrinelli (ed.), *La classe operaia durante il fascismo. Annali 1979-1980* (Milano, 1981), 951-972.

[87]Paolo Frascani, "Una comunità in viaggio: dal racconto dei giornali di bordo delle navi napoletane (1861-1900)," in Frascani (ed.), *A vela e a vapore*, 115-137; and Maria Stella Rollandi, "L'organizzazione a bordo delle navi mercantili fra Otto e Novecento," in Silvio Zaninelli and Mario Taccolini (eds.), *Il lavoro come fattore produttivo e come risorsa nella storia economica italiana* (Milano, 2002), 523-544. On maritime labour unions, see Guglielmo Salotti, *Capitan Giulietti. Il sindacalismo dei marittimi dal 1910 al 1953* (Roma, 1982). On the association of shipowners, see the somewhat dated and very hagiographical Giacchero Annovazzi, *Associazione Armatori Liberi. 60 anni al servizio dell'Armamento Libero Italiano 1901-1961* (Genova, 1961).

[88]Annunziata Berrino, "I sorrentini e il mare," in Frascani (ed.), *A vela e a vapore*, 29-53.

[89]Anselmi, *La pesca in Italia: note e indicazioni per un profilo storico* (Ancona, 1990).

[90]Marco Armiero, *L'Italia di Padron 'Ntoni. Pescatori, legislatori e burocrati tra XIX e XX secolo*, in Frascani (ed.), *A vela e a vapore*, 177- 213; Armiero, "La risorsa contesa: norme, conflitti e tecnologie tra i pescatori meridionali (XIX secolo)," *Meridiana*, No. 31 (1998), 179-206; and Armiero, "La risorsa invisibile: Stato, pescatori e comunità nell'Ottocento meridionale: il caso di Taranto," in Piero Bevilacqua and Gabriella Corona, *Ambiente e risorse nel Mezzogiorno contemporaneo. Appunti di ricerca* (Roma, 2000). On southern fishers, see also Salvemini, "Comunità 'separate' e trasformazioni strutturali," 441-488.

reconstruction of the size of the fishing fleet and the numbers of fishermen in the nineteenth and twentieth centuries. He also analysed the resource regulation policies in post-Unification Italy and concluded that the reactions of fishermen to government regulation are a fruitful area for future research.

The first yacht club in Italy, the Royal Italian Yacht Club in Genoa, was established in 1879, about a century after the first ones in Great Britain. The events involving the diffusion of boating and sailing as sports in Italy are the subject of a recent essay by Maria Malatesta.[91] The author constructs a collective social profile of Italian yachtsmen and emphasises the elitist and masculine nature of a sector whose "democratisation" only began in the 1930s.

Naval History

In the decades following the humiliating defeat at the battle of Lissa (1866), the Italian Navy entered an important period of growth, in line with the government's ever-increasing military expenditures.[92] During the years of Fascism, the Navy was the foremost supporter of the regime's imperialistic ambitions. Despite the Navy's increasing prominence, Italian naval historiography is relatively undeveloped compared to the renewal that has occurred in this field outside of Italy over the last twenty years. In addition, Italian naval historiography has nearly remained the exclusive preserve of scholars belonging to military circles; this has tended to exclude renewal in line with new research trends.

There are some general works of high quality on this topic.[93] But there are also many issues relating to both officers and other ranks which have received little attention, such as the social composition of crews; recruitment procedures; training systems; life on board; and the like.[94] Nicola Labanca, a "lay" scholar of military history, recently considered the problem of the recruitment of able seamen during the period between Unification and World

---

[91]Maria Malatesta, "Le élites e la vela," in Frascani (ed.), *A vela e a vapore*, 267-306.

[92]See Ezio Ferrante, "La politica delle costruzioni navali militari in Italia dall'Unità alla 'grande guerra,'" in Fanfani (ed.), *La penisola italiana*, 429-441.

[93]See, for example, Mariano Gabriele and Giuliano Fritz, *La flotta come strumento di politica nei primi decenni dello Stato unitario* (Roma, 1973); and Fritz, *La politica navale dal 1885 al 1915* (Roma, 1982). In English, see Brian R. Sullivan, "A Fleet in Being: the Rise and Fall of Italian Sea Power, 1861-1943," *International History Review*, X, No. 1 (1988), 106-124.

[94]See, as an exception Assunta Trova, "L'alimentazione della Marina militare italiana durante la seconda guerra mondiale," *Risorgimento*, No. 2 (1992), 423-435.

War I.[95] It is to be hoped that Labanca's research will stimulate other historians to produce similar contributions and to make a "new Italian naval history" a reality.

Conclusions

We can only put forward some brief closing remarks to try to make some very general observations. The historiographical "canvas" with regard to the issues at hand is very complex, although it is brightly coloured in some areas, such as the maritime protectionism, even though this is almost exclusively centred on the first fifty years following Unification. But in overall terms it is a decidedly frayed and faded picture. In other words, there are many more "gaps" than "filled-in" areas, and many more local studies than national and international perspectives. The recent emergence of some positive signs, supported by the recovery of neglected or forgotten sources, provides hope that the maritime historiography on post-Unification Italy has found a path that can lead towards substantial and significant progress.[96] Perhaps the best way to characterize the *status quaestionis* is to grade it as "unsatisfactory, but with strong signs of improvement."[97]

---

[95]Nicola Labanca, "Uniformi sul mare. Note sul reclutamento della Marina militare nell'Italia liberale," in Frascani (ed.), *A vela e a vapore*, 215-245.

[96]We make particular reference to the Fanfani (ed.), *La penisola italiana e il mare*; and Frascani (ed.), *A vela e a vapore*, published in 1993 and 2001, respectively.

[97]For a similar conclusion see, Ezio Ferrante, "La storiografia marittima dell'Italia contemporanea: bilancio e prospettive," in Di Vittorio and Barciela Lopez (eds.), *La storiografia marittima*, 417-425.

Maltese Maritime Historiography:
A Critical Assessment[1]

John Chircop

The most striking feature of the literature on Malta's maritime history is that it has been almost totally monopolized by naval and commercial themes to the exclusion of a wide range of other important matters about the relationship between people and the sea.[2] As a consequence, a substantial part of this essay will centre on publications in these two fields of inquiry, which have in common both similar perceptions of the sea's role in geopolitical events and a spatial focus on Valletta's Grand Harbour, the principal port of the small Maltese archipelago.

Equipped with a critical historical approach, and drawing on postcolonial and other theoretical perspectives, this paper will identify the key notions and methods that characterize the geo-strategic model adopted by traditional Maltese maritime historians. The works under review are marked by a "history from above," male-gendered approach that is largely Eurocentric. These preconceived notions pervade the bulk of the literature and exemplify Edward Said's claim that cultural practices, discourses and texts cannot be separated from the structures and relations of power.[3] The dominant power arrangements have decisively affected the selection of both the themes and the spatial focus to an astonishing degree, excluding groups such as fishers and those who live outside the Grand Harbour area. The spatial focus highlights privileged views of the past and excludes certain social groups, leading to a conventional history that is replete with "cultural prejudices," or what Pierre

---

[1]This essay is clearly not exhaustive and is limited to a review of a selection of the publications relating to the period from the sixteenth to the first half of the twentieth century.

[2]An analysis of *Melita Historica,* a history journal published by the Malta Historical Society, from its first issue in 1952 to the present demonstrates this uneven distribution in research. Over forty articles deal with naval or commercial matters or the Grand Harbour, while none centres on fishing or other coastal zone activities.

[3]E.W. Said, "Introduction," in Said, *Culture and Imperialism* (London, 1994).

Bourdieu has called "the cultural arbitrary."[4] This practice of selection nour-
ishes and reproduces the already entrenched geo-strategic model of history as
the sole "regime of truth" – the commonsense view of Maltese maritime history.[5] This totalising view of the past projects Malta's colonially-constructed,
maritime-frontier function in defence of Western European civilisation as a
"natural," all-determining law of history. More recently, the dominant post-
Cold War discourse has reaffirmed and validated the view of the island's history as a frontier within the Western European defence system.[6] In the fashionable discourse of Samuel P. Huntington, Malta therefore could be construed
as lying on one of the major "fault lines between Civilisations" which "will be
the battle lines of the future."[7]

Even a cursory review of the historiography of this model demonstrates the presence of the geopolitical perspectives of at least two rival European colonial powers with direct interests in the occupation of Malta in modern
times. Rival geopolitical approaches, each vying for hegemony, were articulated in two bodies of history texts marked by the overarching geo-strategic
perspectives of outsiders. On the one hand, the Anglophile and/or imperialist
view of the past, which portrayed the colonization of the islands as "progressive" and "civilizing," emphasized Malta's position as a key strategic naval-
military base of a "superior" Western European civilisation that legitimised
British colonial occupation.[8] The other historical perspective was articulated by
historians who favoured Italy's irredentist claims to Malta during the first four

---

[4]P. Bourdieu, *An Outline of the Theory of Practice* (Cambridge, 1972).

[5]M. Foucault, "Truth and Power," in C. Gordon (ed.), *Power/Knowledge:
Selected Interviews and Other Writings, 1972-1977* (New York, 1980), 130-131.

[6]Malta became politically independent from Britain in 1964. In 1979 the
NATO naval base was closed and the islands became neutral and non-aligned. Yet during these last two decades, NATO warships have called at Malta and used its ship-
repair facilities in full breach of the country's constitution. Malta became a full member
of the European Union in May 2004.

[7]S.P. Huntington, *The Clash of Civilizations and the Remaking of the World
Order* (New York, 1996). According to Huntington, "the survival of the West" depended on Westerners "uniting to renew and preserve it [their civilization] against challenges from non-western societies."

[8]See, for instance, A.V. Laferla, *British Malta* (2 vols., Malta, 1947); T.
Zammit, *Malta. The Maltese Islands and Their History* (Malta, 1971); and H. Lee,
Malta, 1813-1914: A Study in Constitutional and Strategic Development (Malta, 1972).
See also the works by two American scholars: H. Smith, *Britain in Malta* (2 vols.,
Malta, 1953); and E. Dobie, *Malta's Road to Independence* (Norman, OK, 1967).

decades of the twentieth century; scholars in this group have produced an impressive number of works on the naval history of the Order of the Knights of St. John, whose stay on the island was treated as a sort of "golden age."[9] In both sets of texts, Malta is depicted as "the key maritime fortress of Christian Europe" against the incursions of Muslim "infidels" or other foes. Although they have contrasting geopolitical outlooks, both perspectives share a common definition of the adjacent sea as a border between civilisations, cultures and people. This perception was subsequently maintained and nurtured by mainstream post-independence historical narratives and school texts.[10]

The above does not mean, however, that Maltese maritime historiography has not enjoyed any renewal. In fact, by the 1980s the influence of the *Annales* school, represented by foreign, mainly French, historians and some Maltese academics, had generated a fresh reading of Malta's early modern history based on a wider geo-historical perspective. Characterized by a pronounced Braudelian slant, this group of scholars conducted valuable research on a number of topics related to Malta's maritime past, including the patterns of seaborne trade; shipping; consular networks; and, most significantly, Maltese corsairing. Victor Mallia-Milanes, a prominent representative of this school, has claimed that this group has sought to lodge the island's history in a wider regional dimension.[11] This long-term perspective, which is more inclusive and utilises a more analytical methodology, is certainly positive. Nevertheless, the geo-historical perspective propounded by such scholars, which was essential for the development of local maritime history, has not been further articulated in line with contemporary theoretical advances, including the World System approach, which have had such a profound influence on Mediterranean

---

[9]E. Rossi, "La Marina dell'Ordine di S. Giovanni di Gerusalemme, di Rodi e di Malta," *Rassegna Italiana del Mediterraneo* (August 1925); O.F. Tencajoli, "Gl'Italiani nella marina dell'Ordine di Malta," *Giornale Politico Letterario* (May-June 1927), 337-339; F. Barlando, "Corsari Maltesi in Ragusa nel 1400," *Archivio Storico di Malta* (January 1936), 243-245; S. Salomone-Marino, "La cattura del galeone 'Gran Sultana' (1644)," *Archivio Storico Siciliano*, XXII (1936), 1-2 and 238-247; A. Baldieri, "La marina dell'Ordine di Rodi e di Malta," *Forze Armate*, No. 23 (September 1936), 3-5; R. Zeno, *Il Consolato del Mare di Malta* (Naples, 1936); and A. Aurigemma, *I Cavalieri gerosolimitani a Tripoli negli anni 1530-1550* (Roma, 1937).

[10]*Grajjet Malta* (3 vols. Malta, 1980-1993), I, vi-vii.

[11]See V. Mallia-Milanes (ed.), "Introduction," in Mallia-Milanes (ed.), *Hospitaller Malta 1530-1798. Studies on Early Modern Malta and the Order of St. John of Jerusalem* (Malta, 1993), viii-ix; on the influence of the *Annales* School on Mediterranean history, see M. Aymard, "The Impact of the *Annales* School in Mediterranean Countries," *Review*, No. 1 (Winter-Spring 1978), 53-64.

maritime history.[12] Consequently, the bulk of Malta's maritime history, covering the period from the sixteenth to the twentieth century, has revolved around the notion of Malta as a strategic point protecting Western Europe's southern flank, either during the early modern age on the *Frontiera Barbarorum* in defence of Christian Europe against the Muslims or as a strategic base to safeguard the expansion of Western European civilisation during British rule. This same historical tradition has made Valletta's Grand Harbour, which contains naval and commercial facilities of strategic importance, the sole maritime locus of Maltese history. Indeed, it has been the focus of considerable research and, perhaps more important, has been utilised as a "looking glass" through which Maltese maritime history has been reconstructed.[13]

Confronted with this "flat," unidimensional history, this critical review will endeavour to identify a suitable alternative research strategy and discuss ways of developing a comprehensive and multidimensional maritime history of the Maltese people. As I will make clear, it is imperative for this area of Maltese historiography to undergo what Peter Burke has called a "theoretical turn" to allow it to make an original contribution to the growth of a maritime history which must be comparative and international.[14] After all, as the late Frank Broeze put it, "satisfactory explanations and assessments can hardly be made without crossing borders and seas."[15]

Naval History Writ Large

Naval history has occupied such a central place in Maltese maritime history that the two terms have practically become synonymous. Indeed, mainstream historical narratives have tended to present the activities of the colonial naval fleets as the "most glorious," if not the only worthwhile, events in Malta's own history.[16] This misrepresentation has been nurtured by a shared nostalgic

---

[12]On the World System perspective on Mediterranean history, see the series of papers, including those by I. Wallerstein and R. Kasaba, in issues of *Review* published by the Fernand Braudel Center for the Study of Economies, Historical Systems and Civilisations.

[13]For a typical example of how the "Grand Harbour outlook" is used in the reconstruction of a nationalist type of history, see H. Frendo, "National Identity," in Frendo and O. Friggieri (eds.), *Malta. Culture and Identity* (Malta, 1994), 1.

[14]P. Burke, *History and Social Theory* (New York, 1992).

[15]F. Broeze, "Introduction," in Broeze (ed.), *Maritime History at the Crossroads: A Critical Review of Recent Historiography* (St. John's, 1995), x.

[16]P. Elliott, *The Cross and the Ensign. A Naval History of Malta, 1798-1979* (London, 1982); see also J. Bonnici and M. Cassar, *A Century of the Royal Navy at*

and celebrative discourse which highlights their role as the first line of defence of the islands' population against seaborne Muslim "predators" in the early modern period and the source of endless largesse and sustenance during the British era, particularly as a result of the lifeline maintained by the convoy system during the Second World War.[17] A more balanced naval history would need to take into account the wider role of the navies of both the Order of St. John and later of Britain, particularly their control of surrounding waters and naval operations in the wider Mediterranean. By making the imperial functions of these navies clear, and by coming to view them as instruments of overseas power projection, it is possible to make a more balanced assessment of the relationship between the fleets and the harbour area's inhabitants. The few scholarly economic histories of Malta demonstrate the direct connection between the level of employment in the naval establishments in Grand Harbour and the states of belligerency, or "armed peace," involving Mediterranean powers.[18] Research on either the long-term economic processes shaping the naval economy and its links with the commercial sector or on forms of social collaboration and conflict between the various social groups in the Harbour and the naval authorities, both as employers and colonial masters, has yet to be undertaken. The most positive developments in this line of inquiry are the historical-demographic studies, especially those which deal more specifically with

---

Malta (Malta, 1999), which is intended to provide a "celebration of the long association between Malta and the Royal Navy." The celebrative vein is even more evident in works on the encounters of the Order's navy with the "Turk." One of the most recent works which reflects this attitude is A. Cuschieri and J. Muscat, *The Naval Activities of the Order of St. John, 1530-1798* (Malta, 2002), especially the section entitled, "The Maltese Galley Always Victorious."

[17]Research on the strategic role of the island during the First and Second World Wars, but especially during the latter, has created a growing body of publications which would require a separate review. It will suffice here to mention just a few of the most important works which have dealt with naval and convoy operations during the Second World War: P. Shankland and A. Hunter, *Malta Convoy* (London, 1961); P. Smith, *Pedestal – The Malta Convoy of 1942* (London, 1970); P. Elliott, *The Cross and the Ensign*, especially chapters 8-11; and P. Woodman, *Malta Convoys, 1940-1943* (London, 2000).

[18]See C.A. Price, *Malta and the Maltese. A Study in Nineteenth Century Migration* (Melbourne, 1954); H. Bowen-Jones, J.C. Dewdney and W.B. Fisher, *Malta: Background for Development* (Durham, 1961); B. Blouet, *The Story of Malta* (London, 1972); S. Busuttil, *Malta's Economy in the Nineteenth Century* (Malta, 1973); and A.G. Clare, "Features of an Island Economy," in V. Mallia-Milanes (ed.), *The British Colonial Experience 1800-1964: The Impact on Maltese Society* (Malta, 1988), 127-154.

the effects of the Order of St. John and the British on population trends, in particular the patterns of marriage and births associated with the presence of the fleets.[19]

The bulk of research on Malta's naval history concentrates on the structure and evolution of the fleets stationed there, and even more specifically on their military operations in the Mediterranean. The fleet of the Order of St. John has been the focus of considerable research.[20] One sustained theme deals with construction techniques, classification, typology and nomenclature of the war vessels.[21] A small number of scholarly publications has followed in the footsteps of A. Cremona's seminal 1964 work on the maritime language used

---

[19]Studies on the demographic history of the harbour area are dealt with below in the discussion on the literature dealing with the Grand Harbour. But it is useful to mention here S. Bono, "Naval Exploits and Privateering," in Mallia-Milanes (ed.), *Hospitaller Malta*, 351-398, for his analytical remarks on the direct relationship between birth trends and the periodic entries of the Order's fleet.

[20]The chief studies shaping the historiographic tradition of the Order's naval history in Malta include Rossi, "La Marina dell'Ordine di S. Giovanni;" M.U. Ubaldini, *La Marina del Sovrano Militare Ordine di San Giovanni di Gerusalemme di Rodi e di Malta* (Roma, 1970); J.F. Grima, "Galley Replacements in the Order's Squadron (c. 1600-1650)," *Melita Historica*, VIII (1980), 46-80; R.L. Dauber, *Die Marine des Johanniter Malteser-Ritter Ordens* (Vienna, 1989); R. Launaguet, "Histoire des galères de Malte," *Quand voguaient les galères* (Paris, 1990), 254-264; M. Fontenay, "Les missions des galères de Malte, 1530-1798," in M. Verge-Franceschi (ed.), *Guerre et commerce en Méditerranée, IXe-XXe siècles* (Paris, 1991); A. Spada and R. von Dauber, *La Marina del Sovrano Militare Ordine di Malta* (Brescia, 1992); J. Muscat, "The Warships of the Order of St. John 1530-1798," in S. Fiorini (ed.), *Proceedings of History Week 1994* (Malta, 1996), 12-23; J.M. Wismayer, *The Fleet of the Order of St. John 1530-1798* (Malta, 1997); G. Scarabelli, *La squadra dei vascelli dell'Ordine di Malta agli inizi dell'settecento* (Taranto, 1997); J. Muscat, *The Maltese Galley* (Malta, 1998); and A. Quintano, *The Maltese Hospitaller Sailing Ship Squadron 1701-1798* (Malta, 2003), 48-60. The most recent contributors emphasizing the military operations of the galley squadron of the Order of St. John from Malta are Cuschieri and Muscat, *Naval Activities of the Order of St. John*; Wismayer, *The Fleet of the Order of St. John*; and Quintano, *The Maltese Hospitaller Sailing Ship Squadron.*

[21]For the technical details on the construction and the classification of different vessels in Hospitaller Malta, see J. Muscat's series of booklets published by Publikażżjonijiet Indipendenża, including *The Maltese Galley*; *The Xprunara* (Malta, 2000); and *The Lateen-Rigged Maltese Brigantine* (Malta, 2001). See also J. Abdilla and J. Muscat, "Ships of the Order of St. John – The *Caracca*," in *Heritage. An Encyclopedia of Maltese Culture and Civilization* (4 vols., Malta, 1977-1999), 191-195.

in the Order's fleet.[22] The overwhelming focus on naval exploits is accented by recent studies on other functions of the Order's navy, including the protection of merchant shipping; the policing of the sea; and the maintenance of political, diplomatic and other forms of communication with Southern Europe.[23] A small number of studies have examined the ceremonies and rituals on the Order's galleys, including the spectacles performed in Grand Harbour, but there has been no attempt at a theoretical analysis of their social significance.[24]

In contrast to the details of the construction, technical features and operations of the Order's fleet, which are the hallmark of this naval historiography, there has been scant attention to the workers required for these warships. Godfrey Wettinger's contributions, starting in 1956 and continuing to the present, are particularly worth mentioning. His most recent book, *Slavery in the Islands of Malta,* includes a section on slave oarsmen employed on the Order's galleys.[25] A number of other short contributions have looked at the various forms of labour utilized by the Order's galley squadron and the presence of Maltese sailors in foreign navies, but further research on these and other workers, as well as on work and living conditions on board, is required to create a more inclusive and balanced naval history which puts the typically

---

[22]A. Cremona, "La marina Maltese dal Medio Evo all'epoca moderna; storia e terminologia marittima," *Journal of Maltese Studies*, No. 2 (Malta, 1964), 177-197; J. Brincat, "Il Linguaggio marinaresco dei Cavalieri di Malta. Un dizionario della marina del Settecento inedito," *I dialetti e il mare. Atti del convegno Internazionale di Studi in onore di Manlio Cortelazzo, Chioggia, 1991* (Padova, 1997), 329-338.

[23]J. Debono, "The Protection of Maltese Shipping: A Late Eighteenth Century Report," *Melita Historica*, III, No. 3 (Malta, 1982), 204-212; Fontenay, "Les missions des galères de Malte;" Debono, "De Rhodes a' Malte: l'évolution de la flotte des hospitaliers au XVIe siècle," *Navi e navigazione nei secoli XV e XVI* (Genes, 1991), 109-133 ; Debono, "Des Galères. Pour quoi faire?" *Journal of Mediterranean Studies*, XII, No. 2 (2002), 287-306; and V. Mallia-Milanes, *Venice and Hospitaller Malta 1530-1798: Aspects of a Relationship* (Malta, 1992).

[24]G. Allen, "A Parish at Sea: Spiritual Concerns aboard the Order of St. John's Galleys in the Seventeenth and Eighteenth Century," in M. Barber (ed.), *The Military Orders, Fighting for the Faith and Caring for the Sick* (Aldershot, 1994); and J. Azzopardi, "Vestments and Furniture for Divine Service on the Galleys of the Order," in J. Azzopardi (ed.), *Portable Altars in Malta* (Malta, 2000), 76-81.

[25]G. Wettinger, *Slavery in the Islands of Malta and Gozo ca. 1000-1812* (Malta, 2002).

exploitative nature of the relationship between labouring people and the colonial power at the centre of the analysis.[26]

Surface Dealings: Shipping, Trade and the *Corso*

The history of Malta's maritime trade has for the past twenty years been characterised by substantial progress in the extent and depth of research and by a growing interest in the use of quantitative analysis. By making use of the archives of the Malta Chamber of Commerce and the shipping and quarantine registers at the National Archives, a number of studies have sought to quantify the volume of trade and shipping flowing through the Grand Harbour from the late eighteenth to the twentieth century. Researchers are currently branching out into related aspects, such as Maltese shipping, business firms, maritime insurance, banking and ancillary financial institutions, and so on, and these are providing us with a more comprehensive picture of the physical and institutional infrastructure.[27] Michela D'Angelo's pioneering work on British merchants in Malta during the first quarter of the nineteenth century has been a catalyst for further work in this field, especially regarding Maltese merchants, their corporate organisation and the development of their business networks, or

---

[26]G. Wettinger, "Coron Captives in Malta: An Episode in the History of Slave Dealing," *Melita Historica*, II, No. 4 (Malta,1956), 216-223; Wettinger, "The Galley-convicts and *Buonavoglia* in Malta during the Rule of the Order," *Journal of the Faculty of Arts (Malta)*, III, No. 2 (1965), 29-37; J.F. Grima, "The Rowers on the Order's Galley (1600-1650)," *Melita Historica*, XII (2001), 113-126; C. Vassallo, "El reclutamiento de marineros malteses en la armada española durante la segunda mitad del siglo XVIII," *Revista de Historia Naval*, VIII (1990), 21-30; S. Bono, "Schiavi musulmani a Malta nei secoli XVII-XVIII. Connessioni fra Maghreb e Italia," in P. Xuereb (ed.), *Karissime Gotifride. Historical Essays Presented to Godfrey Wettinger on His Seventieth Birthday* (Malta, 1999), 29-96.

[27]See J. Debono, "The Cotton Trade of Malta 1750-1800," *Archivum, Journal of Maltese Historical Research*, I, No. 1 (1981), 94-125; Debono, "The Wine Trade in the Eighteenth Century," *Melita Historica*, IX, No. 1 (1984), 74-92; and V. Wickman's series of articles on "Valletta Shipping," in *Civilization. An Encyclopaedia on Maltese Civilization, History and Contemporary Arts* (Malta, 1983-1985), 89-91, 141-144, 197-199, 271-275, 330-332 and 371-375. See also J.C. Sammut, *From Scudo to Sterling: Money in Malta, 1798-1887* (Malta, 1992), *passim*, which gives some attention to merchant banks and their role in shipping finance; H. Frendo, "Ports, Ships and Money: The Origins of Corporate Banking in Valletta," *Journal of Mediterranean Studies*, XII, No. 2 (2002), 327-350; and C. Vassallo, "The Maltese Merchant Fleet and the Black Sea Grain Trade in the Nineteenth Century," *International Journal of Maritime History*, XIII, No. 2 (December 2001), 19-36.

diasporas, in Southern European ports, particularly in Spain.[28] This pool of works has also included a series of papers on the consular networks of the Order of St. John and Malta in the early modern period, with particular reference to their commercial functions.[29]

The perception of Malta as a strategic entrepot has conditioned the island's maritime commercial history, and several studies have endeavoured to demonstrate that over and above its naval functions, the principal harbour was a transit port between Southern Europe and North Africa at least as early as the eighteenth century.[30] Michela D'Angelo and Desmond Gregory, for example, have studied Malta's role as a British trade centre during and after the

---

[28]M. D'Angelo, *Mercanti Inglesi a Malta, 1800-1825* (Milano, 1990); C. Vassallo, *The Malta Chamber of Commerce 1848-1979. An Outline History of Maltese Trade* (Malta, 1998); Vassallo, "Los malteses en la Valencia del siglo XVIII," in C. Martínez Shaw (ed.), *Actas primer coloquio internacional hispano-maltés de historia* (Madrid, 1991), 65-79; Vassallo, "Los malteses en el Cádiz del siglo XVIII," *Gades. Homenaje a Don José Muñoz Perez*, No. 20 (Cádiz, 1992), 361-374; Vassallo, *Corsairing to Commerce. Maltese Merchants in XVIII Century Spain* (Malta, 1997); Vassallo, "La colonia mercantil maltesa en la Barcelona del siglo XVIII," in C. Martinez Shaw (ed.), *Historia moderna. Historia en construcción: Economía, mentalidades, cultura* (2 vols., Lleida, 1999), I, 221-236; and Vassallo, "Diaspora Entrepreneurial Networks: The Maltese in Eighteenth-Century Spain, a Comparative Perspective," in M.B. Villar García and P. Pezzi Cristóbal (eds.), *Los extranjeros en la España moderna* (2 vols., Malaga, 2003), II, 667-680. See also J.J. Iglesias Rodriguez, "Les mercaderes malteses de la Bahía de Cádiz en el siglo XVIII. La colonia de El Puerto de Santa María," in Martínez Shaw (ed.), *Actas primer coloquio*, 81-97; E. Martin-Corrales, "Comerciantes malteses e importaciones Catalanas de algodón," in *ibid.*, 119-161; and A.D. Brito González, "La colonia maltesa en Las Palmas en el Antiguo Régimen," in Cristóbal (ed.), *Los extranjeros,* 229-240.

[29]On consular networks in the early modern period, see A. Mifsud, "I nostri consoli e le arti ed i mestieri," *Archivum Melitense*, III, Nos. 2-3 (Malta, 1917-1919), 36-82; V. Mallia-Milanes, "The Maltese Consulate in Venice during the XVIII Century: A Study in the Manner of Appointment of Maltese Consuls Overseas," *Melita Historica*, V, No. 4 (1971), 321-43; Mallia-Milanes, "The Price of Hospitaller Crusading Warfare in the Eighteenth Century: The Maltese Consulate on Zante," in H. Nicholson (ed.), *The Military Orders. Welfare and Warfare* (2 vols., Aldershot, 1998), II, 173-182; C. Vassallo, "The Consular Network of XVIII Century Malta," in Fiorini (ed.), *Proceedings*, 51-62; and S. Bottari, "Geopolitical and Commercial Interests in the Mediterranean Sea. The Reports of Angelo Rutter, English Vice Consul in Malta (1769-1771)," *Journal of Mediterranean Studies*, XII, No. 2 (2002), 249-257.

[30]See, for instance, the works by V. Mallia Milanes mentioned in this section; and Blouet, *Story of Malta*, 122-140.

Continental Blockade in the early nineteenth century.[31] In his various publications, Carmel Vassallo has attributed the emergence of this entrepot role to, among other things, "the presence of benign foreign masters...[who] ensured an inflow of foreign resources."[32]

Studies on the "Maltese" *Corso* have proliferated due to a constant flow of contributions from domestic and foreign scholars. Taking a more analytical perspective and adopting a broad regional and long-term approach, historians of the early modern period have examined corsairing in the Mediterranean in general and the "Maltese" variant in particular. Scholars such as Michel Fontenay, David Panzac, Salvatore Bono, Gonçal Lopez Nadal and Alberto Tenenti have been particularly active, especially as a consequence of their redefinition of the concept of corsairing.[33] Fontenay, for example, has

---

[31]D'Angelo, *Mercanti Inglesi*; and D. Gregory, *Malta, Britain and the European Powers, 1793-1815* (London, 1996). See also Price, *Malta and the Maltese*; and Clare, "Features of an Island Economy."

[32]C. Vassallo, "Preface," in Vassallo (ed.), *Consolati di Mare and Chambers of Commerce. Proceedings of a Conference held at the Foundation for International Studies* (Malta, 2000).

[33]S. Bono, *I corsari barbareschi* (Turin, 1964); Bono, "Naval Exploits and Privateering," in Mallia-Milanes (ed.), *Hospitaller Malta*; Bono, *Corsari nel Mediterraneo. Cristiani e musulmani fra guerra, schiavitù e commercio* (Milan, 1993); M. Fontenay and A. Tenenti, "Course et piraterie méditerranéennes de la fin du Moyen Age au début du XIXe siècle," in P. Adam (ed.), *Actes du congrès de la commission international d'histoire maritime, 14th congrès international des sciences historiques, San Francisco* (Paris, 1975), 78-131; Fontenay, "Corsaires de la foi ou rentiers du sol? Les chevaliers de Malte dans le corso méditerranéen au XVIIIe siècle," *Revue d'Histoire Contemporaine*, XXXV (1988), 361-384; Fontenay, "La place de la course dans l'économie portuaire: l'exemple de Malte et des portes barbaresques," in S. Cavaciocchi (ed.), *I porti come impresa economica (sec.XII-XVIII)* (Firenze, 1988); A. Blondy, "The Barbary Regencies and Corsair Activity in the Mediterranean from the Sixteenth to the Nineteenth Century. From the Community of Origin to Evolutionary Divergence," *Journal of Mediterranean Studies*, XXII, No. 2 (2002), 241-248; G. Lopez Nadal, "Malta en la estrategia del corsarismo mallorquín en la segunda mitad del siglo XVII," in Martínez Shaw (ed.), *Actas primer coloquio*, 51-64; X. Labat Saint Vincent, "Course et commerce en Méditerranée au XVIIIe siècle: étude de la présence maritime française a Malte au cours de quatre conflits majeurs," in S. Requemora and S. Linon-Chipon (eds.), *Les tyrans de la mer. Pirates, corsaires et flibustiers* (Paris, 2002), 83-98; and Labat Saint Vincent, "La guerre de course et ses effets sur le commerce en Méditerranée des guerres Sept ans et d'Indépendance américaine: l'exemple de Malte," in M. Verge-Franceschi (ed.), *La guerre de course en Méditerranée (1515-1830)* (Paris, 2000). J. Godechot, "La course maltaise le long des côtes barbaresques à la fin du XVIIIe siècle," *Revue Africaine*, XCV (1952), 105-113, although dated, still remains significant.

made a clear distinction between "la guerre de *Corso*," which accompanied the war between the Christian and Muslim powers, and the habitual privateering practices of both sides which he termed "le *corso a danno d'infedeli.*"[34] This distinction has been taken up by other historians, including Bono in his *Corsari nel Mediterraneo*, as well as by Maltese historians studying the structure and organisation of the Maltese *Corso* in its multifarious economic, political and diplomatic aspects.[35]

A comparative methodological approach needs to be widely adopted and developed to permit more in-depth exploration of the wide spectrum of formal and informal commercial practices and exchanges practiced by the Maltese. Research on the commercial links between Malta and its trading partners is at present sparse, as is work on various "hidden" seaborne exchanges in the central Mediterranean.[36] An exception is the present author's own attempt at

---

[34]M. Fontenay, "Les missions des galères de Malte: 1530-1798," in M. Vergé-Franceschi (ed.), *Guerre et commerce en Méditerrané IX-XXe siècles* (Paris, 1991), 103-122.

[35]Bono, *Corsari nel Mediterraneo*; R.E. Cavaliero, "The Decline of the Maltese Corso in the XVIII Century. A Study in Maritime History," *Melita Historica*, II, No. 4 (1959), 224-238; P. Cassar, "The Maltese Corsairs and the Order of St. John of Jerusalem," *Catholic Historical Review*, XLI, No. 2 (1960), 137-156; J. Busuttil, "Pirates in Malta," *Melita Historica*, VI, No.4 (1971), 308-311; V. Mallia-Milanes, "Venice and Maltese Privateering in the Levant 1572-1589," *Bank of Valletta Annual Report and Financial Statement* (Malta, 1989); Mallia-Milanes, "Corsairs Parading Crosses: The Hospitallers and Venice, 1530-1798," in Barber (ed.), *Military Orders*, 103-112; C. Vassallo, "Maltese Corsairing or Christian Corsairing based in Malta," *L'Ordre de Malta, el regne de Mallorca i la Mediterrània. Actes congrés cientific internacional, Palma, 25-28 d'Octubre de 2000* (Palma, 2001), 285-290; Vassallo, "Corsairing and Piracy in Malta," in R. Gertwagen and A. Zemer (eds.), *Pirates. The Skull and Crossbones* (Haifa, 2002), 202-206; and J. Muscat, "Rules and Regulations for Maltese Corsairs," in T. Cortis, T. Freller and L. Bugeja (eds.), *Melitensium Amor: Festschrift in Honour of Dun Gwann Azzopardi* (Malta, 2002), 185-198.

[36]J. Pons and A. Bibiloni, "Las relaciones comerciales entre Malta y Mallorca durante la segunda mitad del siglo XVII," in Martínez Shaw (ed.), *Actas primer coloquio*, 29-49; L. Valensi, "Les relations commerciales entre la Régence de Tunis et Malte au XVIIIe siècle," *Cahiers de Tunisie*, No. 43 (1963), 70-83; J. Pignon, "Aperçu sur les relations entre Malte et la côte orientale de Tunisie au début du XVIIe siècle," *Cahiers de Tunisie*, Nos. 45/48 (1964), 58-87; C. Vassallo, "Trade between Malta and the Barbary Regencies in the Nineteenth Century with Special Reference to Tunisia," in A. Fehri (ed.), *L'Homme et la Mer. Actes du colloque des 7-8-9 mai 1999 a Kerkennah* (Sfax, 2001), 169-185; Vassallo, "Commercial Relations between Hospitaller Malta and Sicily and Southern Italy in the Mid-Eighteenth Century," *Atti del Convegno Internazionale 'Rapporti diplomatici e scambi commerciali nel Mediterraneo moderno', Salerno 22-23 ottobre 2002* (in press). Work on the Middle

establishing a framework within which to lodge these "narrow sea" complexes.[37] Related investigations on maritime traffic between the smaller ports and anchorages within the Maltese islands are also meagre, with only a few short articles which nevertheless provide detailed descriptions of the evolution of transportation between Malta and its sister island, Gozo.[38] Studies on the different types of sailing vessels that carried commodities and people in Maltese and neighbouring waters, on the other hand, are abundant.[39] Unfortunately, though, the intricate web of exchanges practised in neighbouring waters by inhabitants of coastal villages, landing places and smaller ports remains unstudied.

The Grand Harbour: Infrastructure, Institutions and Policies

Technical studies on the port's spatial layout have been published by established specialist historians and others with a background in military history.[40]

Ages can also contribute to our understanding of this issue; see G. Wettinger's "Malta and Jerba, 1240-1798," in J. Schiro, *et al.* (eds.), *Liber Amicorum, Dr. Albert Ganado* (Malta, 1994), 33-44; C. Dalli, "Medieval Island Societies: Reassessing Insularity in a Central Mediterranean Context," *Al Masaq*, No. 10 (1998); and J. Jones, "Arabic Contracts of Sea-exchange from Norman Sicily," in Xuereb (ed.), *Karissime Gotifride*, 55-78.

[37]J. Chircop, "The Narrow Sea Complex: A Hidden Dimension in Mediterranean Maritime History," in G. Boyce and R. Gorski (eds.), *Resources and Infrastructure in the Maritime Economy, 1500-2000* (St. John's, 2002), 43-61.

[38]J. Attard, "Maritime History of Malta: Sea Transport between Malta and Gozo," *Heritage*, 1696-1700; G. Sommer, *Ferry Malta. Il Vapuri ta Ghawdex* (Kendal, 1982); and J. Bezzina, *The Gozo-Malta Ferry Service: Il Vapuri ta' Għawdex: From Prehistory to the Present Days* (Valletta, 1991).

[39]Many of these were written by a group of dedicated sailing ship modelling experts working at the National Maritime Museum in Vittoriosa, one of the towns on Malta's Grand Harbour, led by J. Muscat, who has published extensively on the subject. See J. Muscat, *The Gozo Boat* (Malta, 2001); his series of entries on the "Maritime History of Malta" in *Heritage*, 1736-1739, 1768-1773; and 1793-1796; Muscat, *The Dguajsa and Other Traditional Boats* (Malta, 1999); Muscat, "Maltese Eighteenth-Century Merchant Ships," in Fehri (ed.), *L'Homme et la Mer*, 105-130; C. Briffa, "Ancient Vessels: The Story of Sea-Crafts in Malta," *Civilisation* (Malta, 1989), 1065-1067; and C. Pule, *Qxur, Billiet u Opri tal-Ba'ar* (Malta, 2000).

[40]Q. Hughes, *Fortress: Architecture and Military History in Malta* (London, 1969); Hughes, *The Buildings of Malta during the Period of the Knights of St. John of Jerusalem 1530-1795* (London, 1967); and A. Hoppen, *The Fortification of Malta by the Order of St. John 1530-1798* (Edinburgh, 1979). Maltese historians who have fur-

The essay by Lorenzo Bartolini Salimbeni on the port's infrastructure is one of the most carefully researched and analytical of a number of studies which have investigated the infrastructure of both the mercantile and naval sectors of the port, as well as its organisation and management under the Order of St. John and the British.[41] The Order's arsenal, with its ship construction and repair facilities, has also received some attention, although it is still not possible to gauge this facility's importance in the overall economy during the early modern period.[42] John Debono's *Trade and Port Activity in Malta, 1750-1800*, gives a detailed picture of both the naval and mercantile port complexes and their supporting institutions during the period of transition from the Order to British colonial rule.[43] While no discussion on the infrastructure of the Grand Harbour can be complete without some knowledge of technology, only a small number of scholarly works have treated this subject, leaving a lacunae in our understanding of the functions of lighthouses, cable telegraphy, hydraulic docks, dredging equipment and the like, or of the Admiralty's experiments

---

ther extended this area of research include R. Degiorgio, *A City by an Order* (Malta, 1985); and D. De Lucca, *Giovanni Battista Vertova. Diplomacy, Warfare and Military Engineering Practice in Early Seventeenth Century Malta* (Malta, 2001). On the development of one specific fortress, see M. Ellul, *Fort St. Elmo - Malta* (Malta, 1988); more specifically on the British period, see A. Sammut Tagliaferro, *The Coastal Fortifications of Gozo and Comino* (Malta, 1993); Sammut Tagliaferro, "British Fortifications and the Defence of Malta, 1800-1860," *Archivum. Journal of Maltese Historical Research*, I, No. I (1981), 73-94; and S. Spiteri, *British Military Architecture in Malta* (Malta, 1996).

[41]L. Bartolini Salimbeni, "Il Porto di Malta," in G. Simoncini (ed.), *Sopra I Porti di Mare, Sicilia e Malta, III* (Firenze, 1997), 239-312.

[42]L. Zahra, "Maritime History in Malta. The Order's Arsenal," *Civilization* (Malta, 1989), 1425-1428; J. Muscat, "Maltese Shipping and Boatbuilding in the 18th and 19th Centuries," in K. Damianidis (ed.), *The Evolution of Wooden Shipbuilding in the Eastern Mediterranean during the 18th and 19th Centuries* (Athens, 1993), 70-78; J.F. Darmanin, "The Building of the Order at H.M.S. Victualling Yard," *Melita Historica*, II, No. 2 (1957), 66-72; J. Muscat, "The Arsenal 1530-1798," in L. Bugeja, M. Buhagiar and S. Fiorini (eds.), *Birgu: A Maltese Maritime City* (2 vols., Malta, 1991-1993), II, 25-29; J. Debono, *Port and Trade Activity in Malta, 1750-1800* (Malta, 2000); and J. Muscat, *The Birgu Galley Arsenal* (Malta, 2001). For the British period, see G. Ellul Galea, *L-Istorja tat-Tarzna* (Malta, 1973); A. Zammit Gabarretta, "The Royal Navy and Vittoriosa - Old and New Documents," *Melita Historica*, VIII (1980), 34-38; P. MacDougall, "The Formative Years, Malta Dockyard 1800-1812," *Mariner's Mirror*, LXXVI (August 1990), 205-213; and J. Bonnici and M. Cassar, *The Malta Grand Harbour and the Dockyard* (Malta, 1994), 66-72.

[43]Debono, *Port and Trade Activity*.

with new equipment and armaments.[44] In addition, there is no discussion of the colonial function of the port's infrastructure, especially in relation to the expansion of British imperialism in the region between 1815 and the 1930s.

The role of institutions in the maritime sector has lately received a considerable amount of attention. The *Consolato di Mare* (Consulate of the Sea), which was established in 1697 in response to an increasing Maltese presence in international trade, played an important role in the promotion and regulation of the island's maritime economic sector during the Order's administration. R. Zeno's 1936 publication, *Il Consolato del Mare di Malta*, was considered the main reference on this institution until the publication in 2000 of a selection of papers drawn from a 1998 conference that also examined another institution, the Chamber of Commerce, which inherited some of the functions of the *Consolato*.[45] Other institutions, such as the Malta-based Admiralty Court, have not attracted scholars. Yet during the nineteenth century this institution played a key role in exercising Royal Navy control over Mediterranean waters.

Tariff and other policies at the port have received some mention in general histories. They evolved from mercantilist and protectionist ideas under the Order to the more generally *laissez-faire* characteristics of the British period, but no specific work has been devoted to them.[46] By way of contrast, the history of health and quarantine measures in Valletta has been one of the most extensively researched topics in Maltese maritime historiography. Historians of medicine have studied the organisation of state sanitary institutions in some depth, with particular emphasis on the quarantine system from the sixteenth to the twentieth century. The facilities and operations of the *Lazzaretto*, and especially the methods of disinfection employed, including the fumigation of letters, have also received some attention.[47] Paul Cassar's work is still unrivalled

---

[44]R. Ghirlando, "Birgu – Birthplace of Malta's Technological Society," in Bugeja, Buhagiar and Fiorini (eds.), *Birgu*, II, 537-550; and G. Bonello, "The Telegraph in Malta during the Victorian Era," *PSM Magazine*, XX, Nos. 2/3 (August 1991), 30-58.

[45]Zeno, *Il Consolato del Mare*; and Vassallo (ed.), *Consolati di Mare*.

[46]Excluding the paper by J. Mea, "Custom Tariffs in Malta since 1530," *Melita Historica*, II, No. 2 (1956), 88-94.

[47]M. Carnevale-Mauzan, *La purification des lettres en France et a Malte* (Gap, 1960); N.A. Cutajar, "The History of the Maltese Postal Service," *Heritage*, 2271-2274; P. Cassar, "Slitting of Letters for Disinfection in the 18th Century, in Malta," *British Medical Journal*, I (January 1967), 105-106; and G. Bonello, "Malta and the French Naval Postal Services," *PSM Magazine*, XX, Nos. 2/3 (1996). 40-48.

and has prompted a series of fine studies based upon hitherto unused sources.[48] But again, very little is available when it comes to the study of the long-term health issues or the quality of life of the people living in this densely-populated harbour area, although the prospects are good due to a number of demographic studies currently under way.[49] One focus has been the flow of immigrants into the Valletta Harbour area during selected periods from the sixteenth to the eighteenth century.[50] The few published works on the demographic history of Malta in general have already set out the main outlines of population movements to the Grand Harbour's fortified enclosures and have established that the main pull factor in this process was the growing demand for labour from the naval and commercial establishments.[51] Focusing on the inner-harbour settlement of Cottonera, Dominic Fenech's excellent paper on "Birgu during the

---

[48]P. Cassar, *Medical History of Malta* (London, 1965) dedicates sections (especially 298-307) to the maritime *Lazzaretto*. See also Cassar, "A Tour of the *Lazzaretto* Buildings," *Melita Historica*, IX, No. 4 (1987), 369-380; and J. Galea, "The Quarantine Service and the *Lazzaretto* of Malta," *Melita Historica*, IV, No. 3 (1966), 184-209. V. Mallia-Milanes, "La Buona Unione: An Episode in Veneto-Maltese Relations in the Late XVIII Century," *Journal of the Faculty of Arts (Malta)*, IV, No. 4 (1971), 309-326, discusses the regulations and sanitary quarantine system adopted by the Order of St. John. See also D. Cutajar, "The Malta Quarantine, Shipping and Trade 1654-1694," *Mid-Med Bank Limited, Report and Accounts* (Malta, 1987), 19-66; and Gregory, *Malta, Britain*, chapter sixteen.

[49]Apart from Cassar's work on the medical history of Malta, which refers to the sanitary system in the Harbour area, see the more specific works on maritime health and sanitary institutions, which include Cassar, "Malta's Role in Maritime Health under the Auspices of the Order of St. John in the 18th Century," *Lombard Bank (Malta) Limited. Report 1989* (Malta, 1989); J.F. Darmanin, "The British Naval Hospitals in Malta with Particular Reference to Bighi," *Archivum Melitense*, X (1939), 160-166; S. Savona-Ventura, "Malta and the British Navy: The Medical Connection during the Nineteenth Century," *Journal of the Royal Naval Medical Service*, No. 78 (1991), 171-176; No. 79 (1992), 33-36; and No. 80 (1993), 100-105; and C. Savona Ventura, "An Outbreak of Cerebrospinal Fever in the 19th Century British Mediterranean Naval Base," *Journal of the Royal Army Medical Corps*, No. 140 (1994), 155-158.

[50]See, for instance, S. Fiorini, "The Rhodiot Community of Birgu: A Maltese City 1530-c.1550," *Library of Mediterranean History*, I (1994), 172-175; M. Fontenay, "Le development urbain du port de Malte du XVIe au XVIIIe siècle," *Revue du monde musulman et de la Méditerranée*, No. 71 (1994), 259-271; and S. Mercieca, "The Spatial Mobility of Seafarers in the Mediterranean : A Case Study Based on the *Status Liberi* Documentation (1581-1640)," *Journal of Mediterranean Studies*, XXII, No. 2 (2002), 385-410.

[51]Blouet, *The Story of Malta*; and Bowen-Jones, Dewdney and Fisher, *Malta*.

British Period" has analysed the social structure and political-cultural dimensions of this highly urbanised industrial landscape during the British period.[52]

The current paucity of research on the origins and expansion of the working population in the Grand Harbour area is remarkable. Apart from the few works on the men employed on the Order's galleys, there are few other studies on the various forms of forced and "free" labour employed afloat or in the naval and mercantile port establishments ashore. As a result, we know little about their work culture, standard of living or quality of life. Significantly, the unionisation of the naval workforce and the mercantile port workers from the late nineteenth century has been examined by a small number of non-academic historians, most of whom are ex-dockyard employees with trade-union backgrounds.[53] Written without any scholarly pretensions, often in the Maltese language and based mostly on original archival documentation, it is a genre deserving of a separate analysis, since it represents another form of historical discourse. Setting aside the latter exception, it is probably safe to say that the bulk of scholarly research on the history of the Grand Harbour is characterised by a lack of concern for the welfare of working people, the poor and women. In sharp contrast, the colonial authorities and the native elites, specifically the leading native merchants, have been highlighted as the principal protagonists in the Harbour's history, and their views of the past, their system of values, and their meanings and perceptions dominate the literature.

Reclaiming the Hidden Dimensions of the Sea: Absent People, Silent Voices

Grand Harbour, the location of the colony's strategic naval and commercial facilities, has similarly dominated the attention of maritime historians to the exclusion of the rest of the littoral. The extent of the exclusion of other coastal dwellers, especially those dependent on fishing, from mainstream history, is remarkable.[54] Aside from some short, albeit informative, works, no significant

---

[52]D. Fenech, "Birgu during the British Period," in Bugeja, Buhagiar and Fiorini (eds.), *Birgu*, 125-188.

[53]See, for instance, Galea, *L'Istorja tat-Tarzna*; Galea, *L'Istorja tat-Trejdunionizmu f'Malta* (3 vols., Malta, 1998); and J. Fino, *B'Rilet l-Guaqda* (Malta, 1983). The historiography of the naval dockyard, for instance, has a tradition of research contributions made by trade union activists but still needs to be seriously analyzed.

[54]Fishing is referred to only once in each of the general works on Maltese history: Bowen-Jones, Dewdney and Fisher, *Malta*, 117; and C. Cassar, *A Concise History of Malta* (Malta, 2000), 18. See also footnote 2.

scholarly research has been published on other coastal locations, small ports, anchorages, enclaves and creeks which were utilised for shelter, provisioning and the exploitation of shore and sea resources.[55] Indeed, the only available information is in a handful of non-academic publications which deal with seasonal fishing habits, methods and the construction of fishing boats.[56] This gap is usually justified by the "commonsense" argument that the fishing population has never been significant in Malta and that it dwindled rapidly during the last century. This hypothesis is founded, however, on a perfunctory reading of the official statistics available after the 1840s, and the supposition that these people and their sea-related activities were insignificant during the early modern age. The scarcity of official documentation contrasts sharply with the relatively abundant data available on the Grand Harbour and clearly poses a problem. One way around this lack of archival sources is to use a more inclusive method of research which integrates a combination of materials, some of which have traditionally been used by folklorists who have maintained an on-going interest in the maritime lore of the coastal inhabitants without excluding the common people of the Grand Harbour area.[57] These scholars have focused mainly on community structure, traditional work and leisure practices, ancient sea cultures and rites of maritime communities.[58] It is partly due to their pioneering

---

[55]See the short pamphlet by J. Muscat, *Maltese Ports (1400-1800)* (Malta, 2002); and the more dated A. Zeri, "I porti dell'isole del gruppo di Malta," *Monografia storica dei porti dell'antichita' nell'Italia insulare* (Roma, 1906), 361-382.

[56]F. Evans and M. Micallef, *The Marine Fauna of Malta* (Malta, 1968); G. Lanfranco, *The Fish around Malta* (Malta, 1993); S. Farrugia Randon, *The Fishing Industry in Malta* (Malta, 1995); and R. Sammut and S. Farrugia Randon, *Fishes of Maltese Waters* (Malta, 1995).

[57]On the use of the sea by the common people inside and outside the Grand Harbour area for leisure, see J. Serracino, *L-Istorja tat-Tigrija tal-Vitorja* (2 vols., Malta, 1983), which deals with the traditional regatta races held in the Grand Harbour on 8 September to commemorate the Victory of the Order of St. John over the Turks during the Siege of 1565. On the origins and development of the sport of water polo on the island, see A.J. Leaver, "History of Water Polo," *Civilization* (Malta, 1983-1984), 266-267, 289-290, 313-316, 345-349 and 382-387. On traditional forms of leisure near the seaside. see "Il-Banjijiet ta' L-Guawm," *L-Imnara*, IV, No. 3 (1992); A. Dougal, "Seashells in Folk Art," *L-Imnara* , IV, No. 3 (1992); and R. Attard, "Il-Barklori," *L-Imnara*, VI, No. 3 (2000).

[58]There are some exceptions, such as M.O. Henriet, "L'organisation sociale villageoise a Gozo," *Journal of Maltese Studies*, No. 9 (1973), 72-95, which includes a section on Gozitan fishing communities. On the smaller islands, some historical information can be found in C. Boffa, *The Islets of Comino and Filfla* (Malta, 1966). The fishing villages of Marsaxlokk and Zejtun have been treated with some insight in the now-dated E.B. Vella, *Storja tas-Zejtun u Marsaxlokk* (Malta, 1927). See also P.P.

field work that authentic representations of fisherfolk and others associated with the sea have been recorded and can be utilised by a younger generation of maritime historians. For instance, there is a considerable potential for the use of maritime art, specifically votive paintings, as original sources for the reconstruction of a people's own perception of the sea. These paintings have attracted the attention of A.H.J. Prins, a modern cultural anthropologist, whose book *In Peril on the Sea* is unsurpassed.[59] Still, the historically-oriented research on these visual maritime representations has so far been characterised by an antiquarian mentality and has been used largely to reconstruct in detail the vessels which plied the central Mediterranean.[60] Yet this art form constitutes an authentic source from which maritime historians can draw not only detailed information but also a more comprehensive understanding of the people's lifestyles, perceptions of the sea and views of the past. To some extent, it compensates for the absence of archival documentation and enables us to put these maritime communities at the centre of an historical analysis. At the same time, it is also imperative to integrate oral history as part of this new methodology. The oral testimonies of the inhabitants of these coastal areas provide us with information on their fishing practices and customs as well as the survival strategies of their families who relied on seasonal fishing for their subsistence but who frequently failed to appear in official statistics. Practical knowledge of the various "patches of water" and "resource locations," as well as weather forecasting and other necessary skills, has been embedded in the collective memory and transmitted orally from generation to generation. For this purpose, the Oral History Centre at the University of Malta has launched a project to trace and record the vast indigenous knowledge of these coastal/fishing people as expressed in their own voices.[61] The recorded oral testimonies already

---

Borg, *Selmun u l-Inhawi* (Malta, 1989). There are in addition a series of folklorist studies mainly found in the journal of the Malta Folklore Society *L-Imnara*; see, for instance, S. Borg, "Kif jghamlu x-xkal f'Wied il-Ghajn," *L-Imnara*, VII, No. 2 (2003).

[59]A.H.J. Prins, *In Peril on the Sea. Marine Votive Paintings in the Maltese Islands* (Valletta, 1989).

[60]For the use of votive paintings as sources to reconstruct different sea crafts, see Muscat, *Xprunara*, 13 and 24-25; and Muscat, *The Lateen-Rigged Maltese Brigantine*, 12. See also A. Cuschieri and J. Muscat, "Maritime Votive Paintings in Maltese Churches," *Melita Historica*, IX, No. 2 (1989). For an attempt at a broader use of these paintings, see P. Cassar "The Nautical Ex-votos of the Maltese Islands," *Maltese Folklore Review*, I (1966), 226-231; and A. Kisic, "Maritime Relations between the Republic of Dubrovnic and Malta: Votive Paintings of Ragusan Seamen in Malta," *Journal of Mediterranean Studies*, IX, No. 1 (1999).

[61]The recording of oral recollections of members of fishing communities in Gozo and Malta forms part of the "Maltese Voices of the Twentieth Century" project

available provide us with unique perceptions and an alternative historical discourse in which the sea and shore are omnipresent.

The essentially geo-ecological awareness inherent in these maritime people's perceptions of the sea and their collective view of the past, and made available through such alternative sources, needs to be incorporated as a fundamental part of any analysis in local maritime history. This can be done through a multidisciplinary approach, or in other words, by an interface of the relevant social and physical sciences with history. Excellent scientific studies on physical environmental issues, topography and coastal/marine ecology, in addition to recent work on the toponomy of the Maltese coastline, are indispensable for the inclusion of an eco-geological dimension into the maritime history of the Maltese archipelago.[62] The widening of the spatial and social area of research to include the coastal locations at a distance from the Grand Harbour, with particular reference to fishing communities and working people both within and without the capital district, with their alternative perceptions and discourse of the sea, is indispensable for the emergence of maritime history as a proper sub-discipline which challenges the currently dominant Grand Harbour-centred, geo-strategic model with its unidimensional definition of the sea as a frontier or border which divides neighbouring civilizations, cultures and peoples.

---

launched three years ago by the Oral History Centre of the Department of History at the University of Malta: see http://home.um.edu.mt/history/oralhistorycentre.pdf.

[62]S.M. Haslam and J. Borg, *The River Valleys of the Maltese Islands. Environment and Human Impact* (Bari, 1998); L.F. Cassar and D.T. Stevens, *Coastal Sand Dunes under Siege: A Guide to Conservation for Environmental Managers* (Malta, 2002); and M. Pedley, M. Hughes Clarke and P. Galea, *Limestone Isles in a Crystal Sea: The Geology of the Maltese Islands* (Malta, 2002). On Maltese toponomy, the best work so far is G. Wettinger's *Place-names of the Maltese Islands* (Malta, 2000); J. Zammit Ciantar, *The Placenames of the Coast of Gozo* (Malta, 2000); and the dated, yet still useful, J.S. Rouff, "Some Features of the Coastal Topography of Malta," *Malta Yearbook 1955* (Malta, 1955).

Slovenia

Flavio Bonin

The Slovenian littoral, which is forty-six kilometres long and is comprised of three councils – Koper, Izola and Piran – has a very turbulent history. It is an integral part of the Istrian Peninsula, which is distinctly transitional in character and has been directly affected by political and economic changes in the neighbouring countries. Following centuries of economic and political control by the Venetian Republic, the Istrian Peninsula came to be ruled by Austria, and so it remained until the end of the First World War. Between the two Great Wars, the area formed part of the Kingdom of Italy. After the Second World War, the territory became part of the Republic of Slovenia within the framework of Yugoslavia and remained in this position until 1991 – although there was a transitional period during the so-called Free Territory of Trieste, which existed until 1954. Since 1991, the Republic of Slovenia has been an independent state.

Until the end of the Second World War, the historiography of the Slovenian coastal region was mainly a product of Italian historians, who wrote predominantly political rather than economic history. As a consequence, there are no significant works on seamanship or maritime activities. Indeed, it was not until the second half of the twentieth century that Slovenian historians began to write about their own maritime history. As a consequence of their research in the archives of Piran, Koper, Ljubljana, Trieste, Venice, Graz and Vienna, these historians have concluded that maritime activities have had a great historical impact on the economy of Slovenia. The most prolific writers, as we shall see, have been Ferdo Gestrin and Miroslav Pahor, but they have subsequently been joined by a younger generation of scholars.[1]

In 1967, on the tenth anniversary of the Port of Koper, the main public library prepared an exhibition and the first catalogue of maritime literature entitled *About the Sea and Seamanship*, covering the library holdings on this subject produced by local and foreign authors. The main objective was to assist researchers working in the fields of maritime history, the problems of the sea

---

[1]Slovenian maritime historiography after 1991 was also the focus of Giovanni Panjek, "Trieste e il litorale," in Antonio di Vittorio and Carlos Barciela López (eds.), *La storiografia marittima in Italia e in Spagna in età moderna e contemporanea* (Bari, 2001).

and the maritime economy. An attempt was also made to secure the collaboration of the Croatian Library Service, but this was not forthcoming. The material covered by the catalogue is divided into vocational bibliographies, encyclopaedias, vocabularies and dictionaries, periodicals, chronicles, almanacs, calendars, museums, collections of scientific papers, international and national maritime law, maritime administration, naval warfare, navies, marine insurance, navigation, merchant navy schools, nautical astronomy and navigation, oceanography, naval hydrography and meteorology, flora and fauna, marine medicine, ship engines, salt-pans, maritime constructions, naval signals and rescues at sea, ships and shipbuilding, fishing, fish canning, sport fishing, anthologies, geography and great sea voyages. The book contains details of 1087 texts, of which twenty-eight were written by Slovenian authors, including six dealing with maritime history or the maritime economy.[2] All other contributions related to marine zoology or fauna.

One of the most important works was the first Slovenian monograph dealing with the "Slovene Sea" and the role of the people in maritime affairs. The 1933 book, entitled *Our Sea,* was written by Valter Bohinec, Silvo Kranjec and Karel Dobida. The term "Slovene Sea" is enclosed in quotation marks because between 1918 and 1943 the coast of Slovenia was an integral part of the Kingdom of Italy.

After 1954, when the Free Territory of Trieste was abolished and the Slovenian coastal area was annexed by the Slovene Federal Republic of Yugoslavia, it enjoyed rapid economic development. Some large companies were established, such as Piran General Shipping (subsequently Portorož General Shipping) and the Port Authority of Koper, while the Portorož Shipbuilding Yard was greatly enlarged. At the same time, some educational and cultural institutions were established, such as the Portorož Merchant Navy Secondary School and the Piran Municipal Museum (subsequently renamed the Sergej Mašera Maritime Museum of Piran). As the maritime economy expanded, so did interest in maritime history and other related disciplines. Ferdo Gestrin played an important role in the development of the maritime historiography of

---

[2]Valter Bohinec, Silvo Kranjec and Karel Dobida, *Naše morje* (*Our Sea*) (Celje, 1933); Miroslav Pahor, "Solan pogodba med Piranom in Benetkami iz leta 1616" ("A Salt Agreement between Piran and Venice from the Year 1616"), *Kronika,* V (1957); Pikril Boris, *Borba za Sredozemlje* (*War for the Mediterranean*) (Ljubljana, 1959); Gradišnik Janez, Ernest Kopriva and Vladimir Naglič, *Pomorska slovenščina* (*Slovenian Coastal Language*) (Ljubljana, 1961); Miroslav Pahor and Tatjana Poberaj, *Stare piranske soline* (*Piran's Old Salt Pans*) (Ljubljana, 1963); and Ferdo Gestrin, "Piranska komenda v 14. stoletju" ("Piran Council Buildings from the Fourteenth Century"), *Razprave,* V (1966).

the area.[3] The first Slovene historian to conduct research in various Italian archives from Trieste and Venice to Fano and Sinigalia, Gestrin contributed a number of fundamental works on the history of the maritime economy of Slovenian ethnic territory from the fourteenth century onwards. In his publications he dealt with most branches of the maritime economy, from shipbuilding in the coastal region to iron foundries in Carniola and Styria, as well as the transit trade of the coastal towns with the towns in the Apennine Peninsula and its hinterland, and the various types of businesses that were formed. Together with Miroslav Pahor, he also laid the foundations for the establishment of the Maritime Museum of Piran. Gestrin's research has been an important source of encouragement for Pahor and a number of other scholars.

Miroslav Pahor, the Head of the Maritime Museum from 1954 until his death in 1981, was very much influenced by Gestrin, although his research focused more on the role of Slovenian seamen and sailors. He was also very interested in Slovenia's recent history, including the National War of Liberation, and art, especially marine paintings.[4] One of his initiatives was the publi-

---

[3]Ferdo Gestrin, "Pregled pomorstva v Slovenskem primorju" ("Summary of the Maritime Business of the Slovene Coast"), *Pomorski zbornik*, II (1962); Gestrin, "Oris razvoja pomorstva v Slovenskem primorju" ("The Chronology of Maritime Affairs in the Slovene Sea"), *Kronika*, X, No. 2 (1962); Gestrin, "Trgovina slovenskega zaledja s primorskimi mesti od XIII. Stoletja do konca XVI. Stoletja" ("Trade between the Islands and Slovene Coastal Cities from the Thirteenth Century to the End of the Sixteenth Century"), *Kronika*, XI, No. 1 (1963); Gestrin, "Piranska komenda v 14. stoletju prispevek k problemu tehnike trgovine v srednjem veku" ("Piran's Council in the Fourteenth Century and Its Contribution to the Logistics of Trade"), *Razprave SAZU*, V (1966); Gestrin, "Gospodarske povezave jugoslovanskih dežel in Italije v. 15. in 16. stoletju" ("Trade Corridors between the Yugoslav Nations and Italy in the Fifteenth and Sixteenth Centuries"), *Istorijski časopis*, XIII (1971); Gestrin, "Mitninske knjige 16. in 17. stoletja na Slovenskem" ("Toll Books as a Source for the History of Slovenia"), *Viri za zgodovino Slovencev*, V (1972); Gestrin, "Gospodarstvo in družbe zahodno jugoslovanskih dežel od 15. do srrede 17. stoletja" ("Trade and Social Issues of the Western Yugoslav Regions from the Fifteenth to the Middle of the Seventeenth Centuries"), *Zgodovinski časopis*, XXIX (1975); Gestrin, "Pomorstvo Pirana v poznem srednjem veku" ("Maritime Pirana in the Late Middle Ages"), *Kronika*, III (1977); Gestrin, *Pomorstvo srednjeveškega Pirana* (*Maritime Pirana in the Middle Ages*) (Ljubljana, 1978); Gestrin, "Ljubljanski Lanthieriji in trgovina v Fanu" ("Ljubljanski Lanthieriji and Trade in Fanu"), *Zgodovinski časopis*, No. 3 (1985); Gestrin, "Karta obsoške poti iz 17. stoletja" ("Maps of Seventeenth-century River Paths"), *Zgodovinski časopis*, No. 1 (1987); Gestrin, *Darja Mihelič, Tržaški pomorski promet 1759/1760* (*Maritime Traffic of Trieste in 1759-1760*) (Ljubljana, 1990); and Gestrin, *Slovenske dežele in zgodnji kapitalizem* (*The Slovenian Regions in the Early Years of Capitalism*) (Ljubljana, 1991).

[4]Miroslav Pahor, "Statuti Izole, Kopra, in Pirana ter istrski zakoni o solarjih, solarnah in tihotapcih" ("Legal Statutes of Izole, Kopra and Pirana on Salt Workers,

cation of an historical journal entitled *The Slovene Sea and Its Hinterland*, but this regrettably ceased publication after only a couple of issues following Pahor's premature death.

With the arrival of a new generation of historians in the late 1980s and early 1990s, maritime historiography was given a new impetus. The Primorska Historical Society was founded in 1991 and began publishing a journal entitled *Annales*, which eventually also included contributions on the social and natural sciences. Young historians with new ideas joined a number of cultural and research institutions in Slovenia in a period coinciding with the country's independence and the founding in 1994 of the Koper Science and Research Centre of the Republic of Slovenia, which in 2002 become the University of Primorska.

The 1990s were marked by a proliferation of articles by up-and-coming historians in journals such as *Chronicle, History Journal* and *Annales*. Two collections of scientific papers were also published by the University of Ljubljana in 1993 and 2002, respectively.[5] The first collection included a couple of articles of interest to maritime historians. Leo Čeh and Flavio Bonin contributed a paper entitled "The Slovenes and Seamanship from Ancient Times to the Twentieth Century," in which they sought to delineate the role of the Slovenians in maritime affairs, from trade to shipbuilding and the typology of ships. Zora Žagar's contribution, entitled "Salt-making on the Northwestern Coast of the Adriatic Sea," analysed the development of the area's salt-pans,

---

Salts Plants and Smugglers"), *Kronika*, V, No. 3 (1957); Pahor, "Oblastni in upravni organi Pirana v dobi Beneške republike" ("Laws and Law Enforcement Bodies in Piran during the Time of the Venetian Republic"), *Kronika*, VI, No. 3 (1958); Pahor, "Nastanek apelacijskega sodišča v Kopru" ("The Organization of the Kopru Appeal Court"), *Kronika*, VI (1958); Pahor and Tatjana Poberaj, *Stare piranske soline (The Salt Pans of Old Piran)* (Ljubljana, 1963); Pahor, "Pomen piranskega patricjata v mestni upravi od XVI. do XVIII. Stoletja" ("The Influence of the Patriarch of Piran in the Council from the Fourteenth to the Eighteenth Centuries"), *Kronika*, XVI, No. 2 (1968); Pahor, "Sto let slovenskega ladharstva" ("A Hundred Years of Slovenian Shipbuilding"), *Priloga Informatorja* (1969); Pahor, *Socialni boji v Občini Piran od XV. do XVII. Stoletja (Social Unrest in the Region of Piran from the Fifteenth to the Seventeenth Centuries)* (Ljubljana, 1972); Pahor, "Ladjedelništvo v preteklosti Pirana" ("Shipbuilding in the History of Piran"), *Informator*, II/III, No. 4 (1975); and Pahor and Janez Šumrada, *Statut piranskega komuna od 13. do 17. stoletja (Statutes of Piran's Council from the Thirteenth to the Seventeenth Centuries)* (Ljubljana, 1987).

[5] *Kultura narodnostino mešanega ozenlja slovenske Istre (Culture of the Multi-national Slovenian Istrian Territory)* (Ljubljana, 1993); and *Kultura narodnostno mešanega ozemlja slovenske Istre – Varovanje naravne in kulturne dediščine na področje konservatorstva in muzeologije (Culture of the Nationalities of the Mixed Slovenian-Istrian Territory. Natural and Cultural Heritage in the Protected Area)* (Ljubljana, 2002).

with a special emphasis on those in Piran; it underlined the strategic importance of salt in the past and delineated the economic advantages accruing to the communities that produced the commodity.

Six researchers on the staff of the Piran Maritime Museum contributed to the second collection published by the University of Ljubljana in 2002. Peter Čerče, the librarian, gave details of the Museum's library holdings, with a particular emphasis on the *Biblioteche civiche – Istrico*. This refers to a collection of books belonging to the town's old library, some of which date from the sixteenth century; among the most important is a volume by the cartographer Pietro Coppo. Historian Nadja Terčon's, "The Fish Processing Industry in Slovene Istria (1867-1918)," describes the establishment of fish factories in the town of Izola and their impact on the immediate hinterland. Ethnologist Bogdana Marinac's, "The Ship is My Home: Residential Places in Merchant Ships," describes living conditions on ships during the two World Wars of the twentieth century. Another ethnologist, Zora Žagar, looks at the development of private fishing and its complexity in view of new economic trends in her work entitled "Private Sea-fishing on the Slovene Coast with Particular Reference to Anchovy Fishing." In her contribution entitled "Late Roman Ports on the Coast of Slovenia," Snježana Karinja, the Museum's archaeologist, describes the development of Roman ports in the area and their current state. Finally, historian Flavio Bonin's "The Role of Venetian Naval Shipping in the Area of Slovene Istria," describes the role, maintenance and manning of Venetian ships stationed off the Slovenian coast.[6] Other contributions by Bonin have included a study of Venetian naval operations against Tunisian pirates in the latter half of the eighteenth century based on the logbook of the Venetian frigate *Siren* which is held at the Koper Regional Museum;[7] a paper on the development of wooden vessels in Slovenian Istria given at the Congress of Wooden Ships held in Grado;[8] and a 2001 contribution on the production of

---

[6]See also Flavio Bonin, "Vloga vojaških ladij v primorskih mestih v 16. in 17. stoletju" ("The Role of the Navy in the Coastal Cities in the Sixteenth and Seventeenth Centuries"), *Annales*, I (1991).

[7]Flavio Bonin, "Beneška vojna proti tuniškim gusarjem" ("The Venetian War against Turkish Pirates"), *Annales*, III (1993).

[8]Flavio Bonin, *Un breve cenno sulla marineria e sui tipi di imbarcazioni in uso nel litorale sloveno, Navi di legno. Evoluzione tecnica e sviluppo della cantieristica nel Mediterreneo dal XVI secolo ad oggi* (Trieste, 1998).

salt in the Piran salt-pans with a special emphasis on experiments to produce "thick salt" in the 1720s.[9]

Other publications on maritime history have been contributed by Nadja Terčon, Bogdana Marinac and Darko Darovec. In an article entitled "Organisation of the Port and Naval Medical Service in the Austrian Armed Forces," the first author described the factors affecting sailors' health during their time at sea.[10] In the same issue of *Annales*, the second author recounted the history of the so-called "sea baptism" and its past significance compared with the present.[11] Marinac has also written on victualling the ships of the merchant navy in the Kingdom of Yugoslavia, while Darovec has carried out research into the development of marine insurance in the area of northern Istria during the Venetian Republic.[12]

The Sergej Mašera Maritime Museum in Piran has published a number of catalogues to accompany its major exhibitions, as well as monographs containing the research carried out by its experts. The latter include works by Miroslav Pahor, as well as ethnologist Igor Presl's article marking the 160th anniversary of the testing by Josef Rissel of a screw propeller he had invented during a trial voyage by the steamer *Civette*.[13] In 1992 a number of experts participated in the preparation of an extensive catalogue for the Museum of Salt-making, setting out the history of salt-making in the area, salt-making technology and associated folk traditions. The catalogue was published in Slovenian, Italian, English and German and was reprinted just two years later.[14] In 1994 the Museum organised an exhibition on the development of the

---

[9]Flavio Bonin, "Proizvodnja soli v piranskih solinah od 16. do druge polovice 18. stoletja" ("Salt Production in Piran's Salt Plants from the Sixteenth Century to the Second Half of the Eighteenth Century"), *Annales*, XI (2001).

[10]Nadja Terčon, "Organizacija pristaniške in pomorsko-sanitetne službe v avstrijski vojski" ("Organisation of the Port and Naval Medical Service in the Austrian Armed Forces"), *Annales*, III (1993).

[11]Bogdana Marinac, "Pomorski krst kot inicijacijski obred" ("The Cross of the Sea as a National Emblem"), *Annales*, III (1993).

[12]Bogdana Marinac, "Brez jela di dela. Prehrana pomorščakov na trgovskih ladjah Kraljevine Jugoslavje" ("'No Food – No Work.' The Nutriton of Seamen in the Merchant Navy of the Kingdom of Yugoslavia"), *Annales*, X (2000); and Darko Darovec, "Oblike zavarovalstva v severni Istri v obdobju Beneške republike" ("Types of Insurance in Northern Istria in the Time of the Venetian Republic"), *Annales*, I (1991).

[13]Igor Presl, *Ressel in pomorstvo – Ressel e la marineria* (Piran, 1991).

[14]AA.VV, *Muzej solinarstva – Museo delle saline* (Piran, 1992).

harbour of Piran. In a catalogue accompanying the exhibition, a number of authors described the historical development and growth of the harbour and its architectural heritage.[15]

Over the past dozen years or so, a generation of young experts has been maturing and broadening its experience and knowledge, at the same time building on the firm foundations laid by Ferdo Gestrin and Miroslav Pahor. A number of monographs and catalogues are currently being prepared for publication in the near future which should constitute a substantial contribution to Slovenia's growing maritime historiography.

---

[15]AA.VV, *Piranski pristanišče od starega mandrača do današnje podobe - Il porto di Pirano dall'antico mandracchio all'aspetto odierno* (Piran, 1993).

Greek Maritime History Steaming Ahead[1]

Gelina Harlaftis

Maritime history opens the way to comparative history and communication beyond national boundaries. One major weakness of Greek historiography is linguistic isolation, which to a large extent prevents Greeks from participating to international dialogues. Shipping is an international sector *par excellence* in any coastal economy, and the activities of Greeks during the last three centuries have taken place primarily beyond domestic waters. The small communities of seamen onboard vessels are traditionally international, and the space of a ship is the most globalised and homogeneous workplace in the world. The wind, sea, sails and masts engender a common language whether in the China Seas, the Gulf of Mexico or the Aegean Sea.

An important branch of the so-called "new" Hellenic historiography began in the early 1970s "onboard ships."[2] The first studies of Greek shipping within the framework of the modernization of the economy and society of the Greek state by Vassilis Kremmydas and Constantinos Papathanassopoulos reflected the scholarship of that period.[3] The beginning of Greek maritime history was marked by a volume on Greek merchant shipping published by the National Bank of Greece and edited by Stelios Papadopoulos in 1972. It not only contained a unique and comprehensive overview of Greek merchant shipping under Ottoman rule by George Leontaritis but also used an integrated approach to study Greek ships and seamen up to the mid-nineteenth century.[4]

---

[1]Part of this paper was originally presented as "Historiography of Modern and Contemporary Greece, 1833-2002" at the Fourth International Congress of History, Centre of Neo-Hellenic Research/Institute of National Research, November 2002.

[2]See the introduction by Harlaftis and Vassalo in this volume.

[3]Constantinos Papathanasopoulos, *Elliniki Emporiki Naftilia (1833-1856). Ekseliksi kai prosarmogi* [*Greek Merchant Shipping (1833-1856). Development and Readjustment*] (Athens, 1983); and Vassilis Kremmydas, *Elliniki Naftilia, 1776-1835. Opseis Mesogeiakis Nafsiploias* [*Greek Merchant Shipping, 1776-1835. Facets of Mediterranean Navigation*] (2 vols., Athens, 1985-1986).

[4]Stelios Papadopoulos (ed.), *Elliniki Emporiki Naftilia (1453-1850)* [*Greek Merchant Shipping (1453-1850)*] (Athens, 1972).

It is no coincidence that most of the authors who wrote about trade also wrote about shipping. The latter is the thread that links the history of diaspora communities with Greece and is closely bound with the development of Greek commerce with the West during the eighteenth and nineteenth centuries. Indeed, Kremmydas wrote about the commerce of the Peloponnese before he wrote about Greek shipping.[5] Christos Hadziiossif, who has written about the Greek commercial community in Alexandria, has also produced a series of important studies on various issues of Greek shipping.[6] Olga Katsiardi-Hering has published not only about the Greek community of Trieste and Sennigalia but also about eighteenth-century Adriatic shipping.[7] Vassilis Kardasis wrote about the first Greek shipping centre, Syros, and Greek merchant shipping during the transition from sail to steam, in addition to works about Greek merchants in Russia.[8] Research on Greek shipping activities on the Danube and

---

[5]Vassilis Kremmydas, *To emporion tis Peloponnisou sto 18o aiona, 1715-1792* [*The Trade of the Peloponnese in the Eighteenth Century, 1715-1792*] (Athens, 1972); and Kremmydas, *Sigiria kai emporio stin pro-epanastatiki Peloponisso, 1793-1821* [*Conjucture and Commerce in the Pre-revolutionary Peloponnese*] (Athens, 1980).

[6]Christos Hadziiossif, "La colonie grecque en Egypte (1833-1856)" (Unpublished Doctorat de troisième cycle, Université de Paris-Sorbonne, 1980); Hadziiossif, "Constructions navales et constructeurs de navires en Grèce. De l'indépendance à l'introduction de la navigation à vapeur (1833-1856)," in *Navigations et Gens de Mer en Méditerranée* (Paris, 1980); Hadziiossif, "Conjunctural Crisis and Structural Problems in the Greek Merchant Marine in the Nineteenth Century: Reaction of the State and Private Interests," *Journal of Hellenic Diaspora*, XII, No. 4 (Winter 1985); and Hadziiossif, "Social Values and Business Strategies in the Naming of Ships in Greece, 18th-Twentieth Centuries," in Spyros Vryonis, Jr. (ed.), *The Greeks and the Sea* (New York, 1992).

[7]Olga Katsiardi-Hering, *I elliniki koinotita tis Tergestis, 1751-1830* [*The Greek Community, 1751-1830*] (2 vols., Athens, 1986); Katsiardi-Hering, *Lismonimenoi Orizontes Ellinon Emporon: To panigyri tis Sennigalia* [*Forgotten Horizons of Greek Merchants: The Senigallia Fair*] (Athens, 1989); and Katsiardi-Hering, "I Afstriaki Politiki kai I elliniki nafsiploia, 1750-1800" ["The Austrian Policy and Greek Shipping, 1750-1800"], *Parousia*, É (1987), 445-537.

[8]Vassilis Kardasis, *Syros, to Stavrodromi tis Anatolikis Mesogeiou (1832-1857)* [*Syros: Crossroads of the Eastern Mediterranean (1832-1857)*] (Athens, 1987); Kardasis, *Apo tou Istiou eis ton Atmon. Elliniki Emporiki Naftilia, 1858-1914* [*From Sail to Steam. Greek Merchant Shipping, 1858-1914*] (Athens, 1993); Kardasis, *O Ellinismos tou Euxeinou Pontou* [*The Greeks of the Euxene Pontos*] (Athens, 1997); and Kardasis, *Diaspora Merchants in the Black Sea. The Greeks in Southern Russia, 1775-1861* (Lanham, MD, 2001).

their commercial activities in Smyrna, Marseilles and Livorno has been conducted.[9] So have studies of the Mediterranean, Black Sea and northern European commercial communities which have proven indispensable for understanding the networks of sea trade (not to mention the existence of an important number of Greek commercial communities beyond Europe and the Mediterranean, as in the Indian Ocean).[10] The entrepreneurial organizations and business practices of Greek diaspora merchants and shipowners of the eighteenth and nineteenth centuries laid the foundations for the development of the large shipowning groups of the twentieth.

The use of "networks" (by which we mean entrepreneurial networks of people with common interests) as analytical tools has aided tremendously in the understanding and interpretation of trade and shipping. The most integrated theoretical analysis of the networks of the Greek diaspora commercial communities is by Christos Hadziiossif in his still unpublished study of the Greek commercial community in Alexandria. Central to his approach is the notion that "Greek history cannot be understood as the history of the Greek state but as the history of Greek people," as the prominent historian Nikos Svoronos has noted.[11] Greek maritime history can only be understood as the story of Greeks dispersed in various port cities, nodal points of international trade. Greek merchant shipping has built upon the commercial and maritime networks that were created in the Mediterranean and northern Europe after 1830. It became an international tramp shipping fleet, trading between third countries, carrying cheap bulk cargoes and responding to the demand for sea transport in an increasingly integrated international economy during the nineteenth and twentieth centuries. The apogee of Greek shipping in the international arena in the sec-

---

[9]Spyridon Fokas, *Oi Ellines eis tin Potamoploian tou Dounaveos* [*The Greeks in the River Traffic of the Lower Danube*] (Thessaloniki, 1975); Elena Frangakis-Syrett, *The Commerce of Smyrna in the Eighteenth Century (1700-1820)* (Athens, 1988); Anna Mandylara, "The Greeks in Marseille, 1816–1900: Resources and Strategies of a Business Community" (unpublished PhD thesis, European University Institute, 1999); and Despina Vlami, *To fiorini, to sitari kai I odos Kipou. Ellines emporoi sto Livorno, 1750-1768* [*The "Fiorini," Grain and Garden Street. Greek Merchants in Livorno, 1750-1768*] (Athens, 2000).

[10]There is valuable information in Dioni Markou-Donde, *The Chronicle of the Greeks in India, 1750-1950* (Athens, 2002). See also Richard Clogg (ed.), *The Greek Diaspora in the Twentieth Century* (Oxford, 1999).

[11]N. Svoronos, *The Unsaid in Modern Greek History and Historiography* (Athens, 1987), 36.

ond half of the twentieth century can only be analysed through the notion of the "network," a tight web based on common language, religion and culture.[12]

Maritime trade of the nineteenth and the twentieth centuries and the diaspora merchant communities, along with the studies on the Greek shipping fleet and its effects on economic and social modernization, have absorbed the larger part of the new historiography: navigation, ships and their technology, along with the maritime infrastructure, have been the central focus of the studies published by the Cultural Foundation of the Hellenic Bank of Industrial Research (ETBA).[13] The rich contributions of Captain A.I. Tzamtzis stand out among the works produced by ex-officers of the merchant marine for their quality and consistency.[14] John S. Vlassopulos, a member of the shipowning circle, has done a superb job publishing and annotating logbooks of cargo sailing ships in the first half of the nineteenth century.[15]

The bulk of Greek naval history is concerned with the War of Greek Independence of 1821, although a few studies on the Greek Navy during the two World Wars have also been produced. Publications of log books of warships are both rare and valuable.[16] The history of the Greek Navy has been

---

[12]For a general view of Greek-owned shipping and the formation of international entrepreneurial networks in the nineteenth and twentiethcenturies, see Gelina Harlaftis, *A History of Greek-Owned Shipping. The Making of an International Tramp Fleet, 1830 to the Present Day* (London, 1996). For the development of postwar Greek-owned shipping and its effects on the development of the Greek economy, see Harlaftis, *Greek Shipowners and Greece, 1945-1975. From Separate Development to Mutual Interdependence* (London, 1993).

[13]Along the lines of the two big commercial banks, the state-owned Hellenic Bank of Industrial Development (HBID) created the Cultural and Technological Foundation in the 1980s. This Foundation, which has now been privatized and is part of the Bank of Piraeus, promotes research and publications on the history of technology and has published in a short period an impressive number of books relating to maritime history: six of the seven monographs published since 1989 fall within the area.

[14]See A.I. Tzamtzis, *Ta Liberty kai oi Ellines* [*The Liberties and the Greeks*] (Athens, 1984; 2nd ed., Athens, 2001); Tzamtzis, *Ta Ellinika Yperwkeaneia, 1907-1977* [*The Greek Transatlantics, 1907-1977*] (Athens, 1996); and Tzamtzis, *Elliniki Epivatiki Aktoploia. I proti periodos, 1830-1840* [*Greek Passenger Shipping. The First Period, 1830-1840*] (Athens, 1999).

[15]John S. Vlassopulos, *Odysseas: Ena Karavi tis Ithakis* [*Odysseas: A Ship from Ithaca, 1837-1841*]; and Vlassopulos, *Fourtounes kai bounatses. Ta karavia mas sti Mesogeio to 19o aiwna. Anekdota imerologia triwn emporikwn karaviwn* [*Tempest and Calm. Our Ships in the Mediterranean in the Nineteenth Century*] (Athens, 2003).

[16]Georgia Koulikourdi, *O "Alexandros" tou Hadzi Alexandri.Ena polemiko karavi ton Psaron. Imerologio kai drasi (1821-1838)* [*The Alexander of Hadzi Alexan-*

written almost exclusively in the last thirty years by rear admirals of the Greek Navy, and has been published either through the War Museum and the Hellenic Maritime Museum, both of which are partially financed by the Ministry of Defence, or by the Historical Department of the Navy.[17] But it is only since the time of Admiral Dimitrios Fokas in the 1950s that an overview of the operations of the Greek Navy based on archival material has been written.[18]

Corsairing and piracy in the eastern Mediterranean, despite their appeal to the popular imagination and tradition through the romantic poetry of Lord Byron, the books of Robert Louis Stevenson and Jules Verne in the nineteenth century, and Hollywood cinematic productions of the twentieth century, have not triggered a wider historical interest in Greece. This is probably because a lack of sources has hindered the synthesis of information in the various Mediterranean nations. The study by Despoina Katifori on the first Greek prize courts, which were formed to punish piratical actions in the Capodistrian period, remains unique.[19] Indeed, few historians have conducted comparative

---

dris. A War Ship of Psara. Logbook and Action (1821-1838)] (Athens, 1972); and Dimitri Saprandis (ed.), *Georgiou Sachtouri, Imerologio tou polemikou istioforou Athina, 1823-1824 [George Sachtouri, Logbook of the War Sailing-Ship Athina, 1823-1824]* (Athens, 1997).

[17]These Departments publish the journals *Periplous* and *Naftiki Epitheorisi*, which contain articles on Greek naval history of the nineteenth and twentieth centuries. The main historical studies by naval officers are Kostis Varfis, *Poros 1831. To Kinima-oi Protagonistes [Poros 1831. The Movement and the Protagonists]* (Athens, 1986); Varfis, *To Elliniko Naftiko kata tin Kapodistriaki periodo. Ta Hronia tis Prosarmogis [The Greek Navy during the Capodistrian Period. The Years of Adjustment]* (Athens, 1994); Varfis, *I Kypros kai ta nisia tou Aigaiou. O stohos tis Leopoldianis Apoikiakis Politikis [Cyprus and the Aegean Islands. The Aim of the Leopoldian Colonial Policy]* (Athens, 1985); and Varfis, *Venetotourkikoi kai rossotourkikoi polemoi stis ellinikes thalasses, 1453-1821 [Veneto-Greek and Russo-Turkish Wars in the Greek Seas, 1453-1821]* (Athens, 1995). See also P.E. Konstas, *Naftiki Epopoiia tou 1821 [The Naval Epos of 1821]* (Athens, 1971); and Const. Metallinos, *Vassilissa Olga. Ena antitorpilliko sth dini tou polemou [Vassilissa Olga. A Destroyer in the Vortex of War]* (Piraeus, 1996).

[18]See Zisis Fotakis, "Greece, Its Navy and the Foreign Factor, November 1910-March 1919" (Unpublished DPhil thesis, Oxford University, 2003).

[19]Despina Themeli-Katefori, *I dioksis tis peirateias kai to Thalassion Dikastirion kata tin protin kapodistriakin periodon, 1828-29 [The Prosecution of Piracy and the Marine Court during the First Capodistrian Period, 1828-29]* (Athens, 1973); and Themeli-Katefori, "Ai apofaseis tou Thalassiou Dikastiriou, 1828-1829" ["The Decisions of the Sea Law"], *Epetiris tou Kentrou Erevnis tou Ellinikou Dikaiou tis Akadimias Athinon [Journal of the the Research Centre for Greek Law of the Academy of Athens]*, XX-XXI (1973-1974).

research on Greek corsairing and piracy.[20] An extensive investigation, presented chronologically, of corsairing and pirate attacks in the eastern Mediterranean from French and Greek sources, however, has been carried out.[21]

Despite the work that has already been done, particularly in the Venetian-conquered regions, the activities of the Greeks in the seas of the Levant during the Ottoman period remain blurry.[22] Sea trade, shipping, the slave trade, island communities and inter-island communication and the economic

---

[20]See Olga Katsiardi-Hering, "Mythos kai Istoria. O Lambros Katsonis, oi hrimatodotes tou kai h politiki taktiki" ["Mythos and History. Lambros Katsonis, His Sponsors and Political Tactics"], in *Rodonia. In Honour of N. Manousakas*, A' (1994), 195-214. See also Apostolos Vakalopoulos, *I Peirateia sta paralia tis Halkidikis gyrw sta 1830* [*Piracy on the Coast of Halkidiki around 1830*] (Thessaloniki, 1987); Vakalopoulos, *I peirateia kata ta teleftaia hronia tou polemou tis ellinikis aneksartisias* [*Piracy in the Last Years of the War of Greek Independence*] (Thessaloniki, 1988); and Nikos Belavilas, *Limania kai oikismoi sto Archipelagos tis Peirateias, Fifteenth-Nineteenth ai.* [*Ports and Settlements in the Archipelago of Piracy, Fifteenth-Nineteenth Centuries*] (Athens, 1997).

[21]See Alexandra Krandonelli, *I Istoria tis peirateias stous protous hronous tis Othomanikis Aftokratorias (1390-1538)* [*The History of Piracy during the first Years of the Ottoman Empire (1390-1538)*] (3 vols., Athens, 1985); Krandonelli, *I Istoria tis Peirateias stous mesous xronous tis Tourkokratias (1538-1699)* [*The History of Piracy during the Middle Years of the Ottoman Empire (1538-1699)*] (Athens, 1991); and Krandonelli, *Elliniki Peirateia kai Koursos ton IH' aiona kai mehri tin elliniki epanastasi* [*Greek Piracy and Corsairing in the Eighteenth Century until the Greek Revolution*] (Athens, 1998).

[22]See, for example, Krista Panayotopoulou, "Ellines ploioktites kai naftikoi apo ta palaiotera oikonomika vivlia tis Elliniki Adelfotitas tis Venetias" ["Greek Shipowners and Seamen from the old Economic Books of the Greek Fraternity of Venice"], *Thesaurismata*, XI (1974), 308-328; George S. Ploumidis, *Oi Venetokratoumenes Ellinikes hores metaksy tou defterou kai tritou tourkovenetikou polemou (1503-1537)* [*The Venetian-conquered Greek Lands between the Second and Tthird Turkish-Venetian Wars*] (Ioannina, 1974); Chryssa Maltezou, "Ta ploia tis Monis tis Patmou, 16os-17os ai." ["The Ships of the Monastery of Patmos, Sixteenth-Seventeenth Centuries"], *Praktika I. Monis Agiou Ioannou Theologou. Enniakosia hronia istorikis martirias, [Proceedings of the Holy Monastery of Agios Ioannis Theologos. Nine Hundred Years of Historical Evidence]* (Athens, 1989); and Aliki Nikiforou, "I diakinisi tou emporiou sto limani tis Kerkyras kata to 17o ai." ["Trading Goods at the Port of Corfu in the Seventeenth Century"], in Nikiforou (ed.), *Kerkyra, mia mesogeiaki synthesi: nisiotismos, diasyndeseis, anthropina perivallonta, 16os-19os ai. [Corfu, A Medieterranean Synthesis: "Insularité," Interlinkages and Human Environments]* (Corfu, 1998). For an overview of the bibliography of that period, see Gerassimos D. Pagratis, "Greek Commercial Shipping (Fifteenth to Seventeenth Centuries). Literature Review and Research Perspectives," *Journal of Mediterranean History*, II, No. 2 (2002).

relation to the sea (not only that of the Greeks) are issues that still wait to be investigated in the archives of the western Mediterranean and in local island communities. It is encouraging to see younger scholars turning to older and under-researched periods.[23]

Another important theme concerns the historiography of the port cities of continental Greece and the Ionian and Aegean islands. Spyros Asdrachas has approached this issue in his own particular way since the 1970s and has brought to the fore the concept of "insularity," the perception of the sea by agricultural societies that has paved the way for research on the societies of the Greek isles.[24] Studies on Syros and Piraeus are perhaps the most thorough in emphasizing the relation between commercial activities in the ports and shipping and the development of local industry.[25] There is a large gap, however, in research on local maritime societies. *The Sailing Ships of Andros* by Dimitrios Polemis is worth mentioning as an example of a solid study of local shipping based on archival material.[26] Multi-volume studies of the shipping activities of Galaxidi and the Ionian islands have also been compiled.[27]

---

[23]Gerassimos Pagratis has given a new dimension to the continuity of Greek trading and maritime practices in his study on partnerships, co-ownerships and the general shipping activities of merchants and shipowners on Venetian-conquered Corfu at the end of the fifteenth and beginning of the sixteenth century. See Gerassimos D. Pagratis, "Thalassio Emporio sti Venetokratoumeni Kerkyra, (1496-1538)," ["Sea Trade in Venetian-conquered Corfu"] (Unpublished PhD thesis, Ionian University, 2001).

[24]Spyros Asdrachas (ed.), *I Oikonomiki domi ton Valkanikon horon, 15th-19th ai.* [*The Economic Structure of the Balkan Countries, 15th-19th Centuries*] (Athens, 1979); and Asdrachas, *Oikonomia kai Nootropies* [*Economy and Mentalities*] (Athens, 1988). For studies of the Greek islands see, for example, Eleftheria Zei, *Paros dans l' Archipel grec, 17e-18e siècles: les multiples visages de l'insularité* (Paris, 2001).

[25]Vassilis Kardassis, *Syros. Stavrodromi tis anatolikis Mesogeiou (1832-1857)*, [*Syros. Crossroads of Eastern Mediterranean*] (Athens, 1987). See also Vasias Tsokopoulos, *Pireas (1835-1875). Eisagogi stin istoria tou ellinikou Manchester* [*Piraeus (1835-1875). Introduction to the History of the Greek Manchester*] (Athens, 1984); and V. Tsokopoulos, "Piraeus in the 20th Century," in George Steinhauer, Matina G. Malikouti and Vasias Tsokopoulos (eds.), *Piraeus. City of Shipping and Culture* (Piraeus, 2000).

[26]Dimitrios Polemis, *Ta istiofora tis Androu* [*The Sailing Ships of Andros*] (Andros, 1992).

[27]Nikos Vlassopulos, *I Naftilia ton Ionion Nison* [*Shipping in the Ionian Islands*] (Athens, 1996). Efthymios Gourgouris, *To Galaxidi ston kairo ton karavion* [*Galaxidi in the Time of Sailing Ships*] (3 vols., Athens, 1983) is also of great interest.

There is still, of course, a wide range of subjects that await study. A subject among Greek historians that is still unclear is the issue of flag. In the twentieth century, a distinction can be made between the nationality of owner-ship of a vessel and the nationality of its flag with the adoption of the so-called "flags of convenience."[28] When we want to study "Greek" merchant shipping in the eighteenth and nineteenth centuries, which ships should be included? The islanders learned to work in an open, free sea that had no boundaries. The Chiot captain registered his ship in Zante in 1850 if he wanted to sail under the Ionian flag, in Santorini if he wanted to adopt the Greek flag, or on his home island if he wanted to sail under Ottoman colours. The Ithacan captain built his ship in Samos, Castellorizo or Kasos and adopted either the Ionian or the Brit-ish flag, or he registered his ship in Syros and adopted the Greek flag. And when steam came puffing, the Kassiot captain or shipowner did not sail his steamers under the Italian flag even though his island was under Italian occu-pation from the Balkan Wars to the Second World War but established himself instead in Piraeus. Thus, we regard as "Greek" and "Greek-owned" all ships and shipping-related operations owned by Greeks of the islands and ports of the Ionian and the Aegean seas.

Considering the importance of shipping in Greece, minimal research has taken place on Greek seamen. There are rich and completely unused ar-chives with full details regarding Greek seamen from the late nineteenth cen-tury to the present day kept by the Seamen's Pension Fund and the Ministry of Merchant Shipping. Few academic studies of Greek seamen have been under-taken, but it is rather encouraging to find that the "silence has been broken" by an increasing number of seamen who are writing their memoirs.[29]

I have saved for last a discussion of the business history of shipping. Vassilis Kremmydas can be regarded as a pioneer in this facet of scholarship, having studied and published on the organization and function of Greek com-

---

[28]Gelina Harlaftis, "Greek Shipowners and State Intervention in the 1940s: A Formal Justification for the Resort to Flags-of-Convenience?" *International Journal of Maritime History*, I, No. 2 (December 1989), 37-63.

[29]Alexander Kitroeff, "The Greek Seamen's Movement, 1940-1944," *Journal of Hellenic Diaspora*, VII (Fall/Winter 1980). See also the recent study of Constantinos Tsousmanis, *I elliniki emporiki naftilia kai to naftergatiko kinima (1939-1945)* [*Greek Merchant Shipping and the Seamen's Labour Movement (1939-1945)*] (Athens, 2001). Seamen's memoirs are extremely valuable; examples include Yannis Paizis, *Thalassines Anamniseis, 1939-1956* [*Memoirs of the Sea, 1939-1956*] (Athens, 1996); Manolis Ro-donakis, *Yper pleontwn* [*For the Ones that Sail*] (Piraeus, 1996); Andrea Tsesmeli, *To Odoiporiko enos paliou naftikou, tou capetan Andrea Tsesmeli* [*The Travelogue of an Old Seaman, Captain Andreas Tsesmelis*] (Athens, 1994); and Nicholaos I. Fykaris, *To Naftiko ton Kardamylon ston B Pagosmio Polemo* [*Shipping in Kardamyla during the Second World War, 1939-1945*] (Chios, 2002).

mercial and shipping houses during the pre-revolutionary period. Also ground-breaking is his book on Hadzipanayotis Politis, published in 1973. Written during a period in which he had no comparable studies to guide him, it re-mains unique because it reveals the structure, organization and administration of a typical Greek family business with an international orientation functioning within a triad of trade, shipping and finance. Based on the coast of the south-eastern Peloponnese, Hadzipanaytis Politis operated as an investor-merchant and shipowner and acted in direct co-operation with shipowners from the nearby island of Spetses. Because of his activities he became a leading figure in the "Peloponesian-Spetsiot" commercial and maritime network that thrived during the Napoleonic wars and the continental embargo.[30]

Thirty years after this book appeared we are still seeking to under-stand the nucleus of maritime activity, the business. This is probably because business history was never in the mainstream of the new Greek historiogra-phy.[31] Or it is equally possible that because shipping is a service industry it was never considered by Marxist-oriented theoretical analysts of the develop-ment of capitalism to be the "right" leading sector. In a country where the third-sector traditionally has held a leading position (and since the last third of the twentieth century has been driven largely by tourism) and has enjoyed the highest rates of growth, it is time to reconsider this approach. It might also be the case that the discussion of capitalist development in this part of the world should not be guided by preconceptions of what should or should not have been important according to other models of development. In his excellent article "The Belle Epoque of the Capital," which discusses twentieth-century Greek history, Christos Hadziiossif wrote that:

The study of the third sector of the economy is extremely important for the understanding of the Greek economy and its position in the international division of labour at the be-ginning of the century. It concerns facts and situations that, with the exception of shipping, did not have any continuity, after the changes brought to the international environment by the First World War.

---

[30]Vassilis Kremmydas, *Archeio Hadjipanagioti* [*Hadjipanayoti Archive*] (Ath-ens, 1972).

[31]Margarita Dritsas was the first to enter the international circle of business historians; in the 1980s she organized in Greece some important international confer-ences. See Alice Teichova, Hakan Lingren and Margarita Dritsas (eds.), *L'Enterprise en Grèce et en Europe, XIXe-Xxe siècles* (Athens, 1991); and Margarita Dritsas and Terry Gourvish (eds.), *European Enterprise. Strategies of Adaptation and Renewal in the Twentieth Century* (Athens, 1997).

An adherence to the model of industrial development prevails. The identification of modernization in the secondary sector with that of the tertiary can lead to erroneous interpretations, as Hadziiossif observed:

> During the largest period of the history of Greek shipping, the survival and success of Greek shipowners was based on archaic models..The famous networks and the high productivity of the Greek seaman, who for many historians form the basis of the impressive success of Greek shipping can be interpreted as the consequence of the weak technological and capitalist basis and the difficulty they encountered in implementing modern forms of organization.[32]

According to the above, the adherence of Greek shipowners to the family form of business is a sign of their inability to adjust to modern types of organizations – in other words, of backwardness and failure – and they are referred to as "archaic elements of organization" based on a "weak technological basis." There must be a mistake somewhere, since the most prominent Greek shipowning groups of the second half of the twentieth century owed their expansion not to a "weak technological basis" but to their timely adoption of technological innovations, which they sometimes introduced through orders for new ships in the yards of Germany, the United States and Japan, not only for tankers but also for dry-bulk cargo ships.[33] The family shipping companies of the Ionian and Aegean islands and their "archaic models of organization" were archetypes of entrepreneurial success.[34]

The study of the firm, which thirty years ago was regarded as not sufficiently scholarly, has proved to be a lively field internationally. Making the firm the centre of modern economic development has triggered a debate on

---

[32]Christos Hadziiossif, "I bel epok tou kefalaiou," in Hadziiossif (ed.), *Istoria tis Elladas tou 20ou ai., 1900-1922. Oi aparhes* ["The Belle Époque of Capital," in Hadziiossif [ed.], *A History of Greece in the Twentieth Century, 1900-1922. The Beginnings]* (Athens, 1999), 335.

[33]In the field of tankers, for example, the Greeks were pioneers in technological innovation and in placing orders for new vessels. See John Theotokas and Gelina Harlaftis, *Eupompe. Ellinikes Naftiliakes epiheiriseis 1945-2000. Organosi kai stratigiki* [*Eupompe. Greek Shipping Firms, 1945-2000, Organisation and Strategy]* (Athens, 2004).

[34]Gelina Harlaftis and John Theotokas, "European Family Firms in International Business: British and Greek Tramp Shipping Firms," *Business History*, XXXVI (April 1994).

family capitalism in a large number of twentieth-century firms in a period when the trend was towards managerial capitalism.[35] The family firm has survived the first and second phases of the industrial revolution. Family firms today form more than seventy-five percent of all companies in the European Union; even in the United States one-third of the Fortune 500 are family firms. And in the non-western world, with the exception of Japan, the family firm is the rule and not the exception.[36] It has been demonstrated on an international level that the family-type organization in the western world is a distinct and strong category in the service sector, particularly in trade and shipping.[37]

A large part of the archival material that would enlighten us about the success of Greek shipping during the last two centuries forms part of the individual histories of the families involved in shipping and are thus basically private family archives. Because there is a suspicion of researchers and a tradition of secrecy among shipowning circles in Greece and abroad, the history of Greek shipping companies has remained until recently a *terra incognita*. It has been only during the last few years that researchers have been able to gain access to private archives. The company that first attracted the interest of historians, because of the existence of a large volume of archival material and because of the financial resources the Historical Archive of the National Bank has provided through research projects, is the Greek Steamship Company, which was established in 1856 and functioned until the end of the nineteenth century. But research into a single company, which was also involved in coastal and passenger shipping, has not been enough to uncover the entrepreneurial strategies, organizations, investments and, more generally, the diverse activities of the hundreds of Greek shipping companies of the nineteenth and twentieth centuries.[38]

---

[35]Alfred D. Chandler, Jr., *The Visible Hand: The Managerial Revolution in American Business* (15th ed., Cambridge, MA, 1999); and William Lazonick, *Business Organisation and the Myth of the Market Economy* (Cambridge, 1991).

[36]Geoffrey Jones and Mary Rose, "Family Capitalism," in Jones and Rose (eds.), *Family Capitalism* (London, 1993).

[37]Geoffrey Jones, *Merchants to Multinationals. British Trading Companies in the Nineteenth and Twentieth Centuries* (Oxford, 2000).

[38]For the business history of shipping, see Constantinos Papathanassopoulos, *Etaireia Ellinikis Atmoploias (1855-1872). Ta adiexoda tou prostateftismou [Greek Shipping Companies (1855-1872). The Impasses of Protectionism]* (Athens, 1988); Vassilis Kremmydas, *Emporikes praktikes sto telos tis Tourkokratias. Mykoniates Emporoi kai ploioktites [Commercial Practices at the End of Turkish Rule. Merchants and Shipowners from Mykonos]* (Athens, 1993); Kremmydas, *Emporoi kai emporika diktya sta hronia tou Eikosiena (1820-1835) [Merchants and Shipowners from the Cyclades (1820-1835)]* (Athens, 1996); Vassilis Kardasis, "Greek Steam Liner Companies, 1858-

As I indicated years ago, the greatest hurdles that most historians faced in analysing Greek-owned shipping of the nineteenth and twentieth century arose from the lack of a systematic series of shipping statistics, along with the resulting dangers inherent in interpretations made without such archival resources.[39] This gap has recently been filled by the historical register *Pontoporeia*.[40] The name is taken from a Nereid who was believed to be a protector of deep-sea seamen in Ancient Greece and is a data bank of 20,000 Greek-owned vessels from 1830 to the Second World War. The data were drawn from twelve sources in Greece and abroad – ship registers, customs archives, commercial and shipping journals and the like – and represents the fruits of many years of research and information collection. These data provided more information on who and how many were involved in shipping, where they were located, what sorts and how many ships they used, and where these ves-

---

1914," *International Journal of Maritime History*, IX, No. 2 (December 1997), 107-127; Kardasis, "International Trends and Greek Shipping: The Business Strategy of Demetrios Moraitis, 1893-1908," in David J. Starkey and Gelina Harlaftis (eds.), *Global Markets: The Internationalization of Sea Transport Industries since the 1850s* (St. John's, 1998); and John Theotokas, "Organizational and Managerial Patterns of Greek-owned Shipping Enterprises and the Internationalization Process from the Inter-war Period to 1990," in Starkey and Harlaftis (eds.), *Global Markets*. Biographies, memoirs and local histories of members of shipowning families are of particular interest. Andreas Lemos has been a prolific writer, as has Manuel (Manolis) Kulukundis, a leading figure in twentieth-century Greek shipownering. See Andreas Lemos, *To naftiko tou genous ton Ellinon* [*The Greek Shipping Gender*] (Athens, 1968); Lemos, *Neoellines aeinaftai* [*Greek Seamen*] (Athens, 1976); Lemos, *The Greeks and the Sea. A People's Seafaring Achievements from Ancient Times to the Present Day* (London, 1976); Manuel Kulukundis, *Ships Loved and Painted* (London, 1978); Kulukundis, *Voyages on My Father's Ships and Others* (Piraeus, 1986); and Kulukundis, *Eis tin ypiresian tis naftilias. 1960-1984* [*To the Service of Shipping, 1960-1984*] (Piraeus, 1984). See also John K. Hadjipateras (ed.), *Aftobiografia Konstantinou Ioannou Hadjipatera* [*Autobiography of Konstantinos I. Hadjipateras*] (London, 1963); and Hadjipateras (ed.), *Grammata sta paidia tou* [*Letters to His Children*] (Athens, 1994). Eustathios Batis, one of the most important shipping journalists of the second half of the twentieth century, has also written a number of books; see Eustathios Batis, *Portraita se ble fondo. Prosopa pou egrapsan istoria sti naftilia tou 20ou aiona* [*Portraits in Blue Fond. Persons who Wrote the History of Twentieth-Century Shipping*] (Athens, 1999); and Batis, *Ek tis thalasis ta kreito* [*From the Sea the Best*] (Athens, 2001). This last book is on the charities established by Greek shipowners during the twentieth century.

[39]Harlaftis, *History of Greek-owned Shipping*, 106-112.

[40]Gelina Harlaftis and Nikos Vlassopulos, *Pontoporeia. Pontopora Istiofora kai Atmoploia, 1830-1939* [*Pontoporeia. Deep-sea Sailing Ships and Steamships, 1830-1939*] (Athens, 2002).

sels were built and registered.[41] The continuation of shipping activities to the present day, and the involvement of many generations of a single family in the business, provides an incredible wealth of material, not only for business history but also for the history of the islands from which these families came.[42]

Furthermore, the history of the sea has not yet included the "invisible" women who dealt with the family and agricultural responsibilities back on the island. Greek shipping has the scent of the Aegean and the Ionian seas and its soul is of a female gender. This may be why it has reproduced and expanded so abundantly over the years, transferring the expertise of work at sea from one generation to the next.

---

[41]We draw valuable information from the second, and still unfinished, volume of *Pontoporeia*, which will cover an unknown period in Greek-owned shipping, 1700-1829. Research thus far completed has "discovered" 3500 sailing ships from local Greek historical archives, particularly those on the Ionian Islands, as well as from the archives of Venice, Malta, Florence and Marseilles.

[42]*Pontoporeia 1830-1939* "gave birth" to the second volume on the history of Greek shipping businesses, *Ploto:* see Gelina Harlaftis, Manos Haritatos and Eleni Beneki, *Ploto. Greek Shipowners from the End of the Eighteenth Century to the Second World War* (Athens, 2002) (in Greek and English). Based on the information provided in *Pontoporeia, Ploto* was written to present the largest shipping families of the main maritime areas of Greece. The trilogy on the history of Greek shipping companies has been completed with the recent publication of *Eupompe,* a study that contains an overview of the organization and strategy of Greek shipping in combination with 150 histories of companies that functioned for at least thirty years between 1945 and 2000; see Theotokas and Harlaftis, *Eupompe.* The names of the volumes in the trilogy, *Pontoporeia, Ploto* and *Eupompe,* are taken from the names of three Nereids, the daughters of the ancient god Poseidon, who protected Greek seamen on long-haul voyages. *Eupompe* is based on a third data bank of 25,000 Greek-owned ships, a statistical series every five years from 1945 to 2000 from an unpublished data bank (ELIA, 2003). The entire research and publication project, which lasted for six years (1998-2004), was sponsored by the Stavros S. Niarchos Foundation and was led by Gelina Harlaftis.

Sources for the Maritime History of Greece (Fifteenth to Seventeenth Century)

Gerassimos D. Pagratis

The historiography on Greek commercial shipping for the period prior to the mid-eighteenth century is quite limited.[1] In general terms, the commercial and maritime activities of Greeks from the fall of Constantinople (1453) to the early eighteenth century are perceived as being of relatively minor importance and limited mostly to playing a subservient role to the trade networks of Western European countries struggling for supremacy in the Levant. Yet there are plenty of indications that Greeks were actually very active seamen at that time. This evidence is heterogeneous and by and large remains unexplored; as a consequence, we are not in a position to reach solid conclusions. In order to reach such general conclusions on Greek commercial shipping we require extensive research based on a substantial corpus of data. The aim of this paper is to systematise and assess sources that might be useful to this end.

The publication of selected archival records is a necessary precondition for the widening of the scope of Greek maritime history. Modern Greek historiography is marred by a lack of published sources. Although a great number of records have been published by Sathas and other such "generous" scholars, the existing collections of Greek primary sources are small compared to known unpublished material. Moreover, they are not part of a series but constitute individual and fragmentary publications. Their shortcomings become even more conspicuous when compared to collections such as *Monumenta Germaniae Historica, Calendar of State Papers, Colección de documentos para la historia de España* and *Collection des documents inédits relatifs à l'histoire de France*.[2] The absence of special publications of sources pertaining to economic history should also be stressed.

---

[1]Gerassimos D. Pagratis, "Greek Commercial Shipping (Fifteenth to Seventeenth Centuries). Literature Review and Research Perspectives," *Journal of Mediterranean Studies*, XII, No. 2 (2002), 411-433.

[2]For Greek and non-Greek collections of primary sources, see Ioannis D. Psaras, *Theoria ke Methodoloyia tis Istorias* (*Theory and Methodology of History*) (Thessaloniki, 2001), 40-42; Georgios Ploumidis, "Ta Chania sta teli tou 16ou aiona. I ekthessi tou Provlepti B. Dolfin" ("Chania in the Late Sixteenth Century. The Report of *Provveditore* B. Dolfin"), *Dodoni*, II (1973), 79.

The quest for archival and bibliographical sources from which quantitative data on Greek maritime history can be obtained should be concerned with considerations of space and category. In the case of the former, we have to identify the vast geographic area, extending well beyond the boundaries of the modern Greek state, within which Greek seamen transported goods to and from the Levant. The seaports and cities of nations which enjoyed "Capitulations" and had strong interests and widespread diplomatic networks in the Near East have to be studied as foci of Greek maritime activity: first, ports in Italy (Venice, Ancona, Bari, Messina, Leghorn, Genoa, etc.) but also the south of France (Marseilles, Toulon), Malta, Spain, Portugal, Britain (Southampton, London) and the Netherlands (Amsterdam, The Hague).

The different categories of sources that could provide important information on maritime history have by and large been identified by Frederic C. Lane and other historians who participated in the *Colloques d'Histoire maritime* during the 1950s and 1960s.[3] Nine main categories apply to the Greek case: records of administrative authorities of foreign suzerains and great powers trading in the Levant; diplomatic reports; records of port and customs offices; judicial records; records of provisioning authorities; personal records (notarial deeds, commercial correspondence, etc.); travel literature; diaries and chronicles; and commercial manuals. Each of these categories is discussed in detail below.

The so-called "official sources" consist of the records of state institutions that formulated commercial and shipping policies. Their main concerns were to regulate economic life to ensure the regular flow of taxes on maritime trade to the state treasury and to ensure the readiness of the navy for war. In implementing state policies, public officials supervised shipyards and regulated the technicalities of shipbuilding, determined the composition and size of crews and drew up policies regarding their own commercial vessels and those of foreign citizens.[4]

---

[3]See Michel Mollat (ed.), *Les sources de l'histoire maritime en Europe du Moyen âge au XVIIIe siècle. 4e Colloque d' Histoire maritime* (Paris, 1962). For Venice in particular, see Frederic C. Lane, "La marine marchande et le trafic maritime de Venise a travers les siècles," *ibid.*, 7-32; and Ruggiero Romano, "La marine marchande vénitienne au XVIe siècle," *ibid.*, 33-68.

[4]In the State Archives of Venice there are records of the three main legislative bodies: the Senate (*Senato*), Council of Ten (*Consiglio di Dieci*) and College (*Collegio*). There was also a special service that dealt with the shipyards, the so-called *provveditori e patroni all'Arsenal*. See Maria Francesca Tiepolo, *et al.*, "Archivio di Stato di Venezia," in *Guida Generale degli Archivi di Stato Italiani* (4 vols., Rome, 1981-1994), IV, 889-891, 894-902 and 955-956.

The "official sources" also include reports written by state officials, especially Venetian ones (*baili, provveditori* and *capitani*).[5] Most often these were produced when their term of office ended or during a scheduled or random mission overseas to inspect local administrations (*sindici inquisitori*).[6] A voluminous correspondence between these officials and the central administration (*Senato Mar, registri e filze, Provveditori da Terra e da Mar*) is attached to their reports.[7] Of particular historical importance are the surviving records of the local administrations (*reggimenti*), which contain plentiful information on the events that took place in the eastern Mediterranean at the time.[8]

---

[5]The reports of the *provveditori* and *baili* are included in the College series of the State Archives of Venice [Collegio (Secreta), Relazioni di Ambasciatori, Rettori e altre cariche]. Copies of certain reports are preserved in the Museo Correr at Venice as well as in the National Library in Paris. Frederic C. Lane, *Storia di Venezia* (Turin, 1983), 548.

[6]In Venice, they were called "Inspectors of the Levant" or "Inquisitors of the Levant" (*Sindici Orientis, Sindici et Inquisitori in Levante*). See Ermannos Luntzis, *Peri tis politikis katastaseos tis Eptanisou epi Veneton* (*About the Political Situation in the Seven Islands during Venetian Rule*) (Athens, 1856), 106-108; Bruno Dudan, *Sindacato d'Oltremare e di Terraferma. Contributo alla storia di una magistratura e del processo sindacale nella Repubblica veneta* (Rome, 1935); and Georgios Ploumidis, *I venetokratoumenes Ellinikes chores metaxi tou defterou ke tou tritou tourcovenetikou polemou, 1503-1537* (*The Venetian-ruled Lands between the Second and the Third Turco-Venetian Wars*) (Ioannina, 1974), 26-27.

[7]On archival sources and libraries in Venice that are of interest to Greek researchers, see Spyridon Theotokis, *Eisayoyi eis tin erevnan ton mnimeion tis istorias tou Ellinismou ke idia tis Kritis en to Kratiko Archeio tou Venetikou Kratous* (*Introduction to the Research of Records Pertaining to Greek and Especially Cretan History in the State Archives of Venice*) (Corfu, 1926); Georgios Ploumidis, *Diagramma ton archeiakon pigon tis Neoellinikis Istorias* (*Outline of Archival Sources Pertaining to Modern Greek History*) (Athens, 1983), 26-34; and Michela Dal Borgo, "Archivio di Stato di Venezia. Fonti per la storia delle Isole Ionie: Corfù, Cefalonia, Zante e Santa Maura," in Massimo Costantini and Aliki Nikiforou (eds.), *Levante Veneziano, Quaderni di Cheiron* (2 vols., Rome, 1996), II, 177-222. A detailed index of the State Archives of Venice is found in Tiepolo, "Archivio di Stato di Venezia."

[8]A considerable volume of Venetian records has survived in Crete. See E. Gerland, *Das Archiv des Herzogs von Kandia im Königl. Staatsarchiv zu Venedig* (Strasbourg, 1899); Maria Francesca Tiepolo, "Note sul riordino degli Archivi del Duca e dei Notai di Candia nell' Archivio di Stato di Venezia," *Thisavrismata*, X (1973), 88-100; and Tiepolo, "Archivio di Stato di Venezia," 1008-1010. For the records on Corfu, see Aliki Nikiforou, "L'Archivio di Stato di Corfù: da ieri ad oggi," in Costantini and Nikiforou (eds.), *Levante Veneziano*, II, 223-255. For sources in Cephalonia, see Nikos Moschonas, "Topikon Istorikon Archeion Kefallinias" ("The Local Historical Archive of Cephalonia"), *Symmeikta*, II (1970), 459-501. For records

In reports dispatched by Venetian officials in the Levant to the Senate and in their correspondence with other central authorities, statistics and other evidence relating to shipping and commerce in various areas were often included; these proved extremely important in case of war. These data refer to the number of merchant ships which, if suitably equipped, could become part of the navy; the names of their owners; the strength of their crews; and their tonnage. For instance, the retiring Venetian *Provveditore* of Zakynthos (Zante), Antonio Venier, reported that thirty frigates and numerous smaller ships, manned by skilled sailors experienced in managing galleys, were stationed at the island in 1584.[9]

Similar registers of the mercantile and naval fleets were compiled with regularity by the Venetian authorities. Two such lists of Venetian warships, compiled by Marino Sanudo in 1499, on the vigil of the Second Turco-Venetian War, have been published.[10] Another census of the Venetian mercantile fleet was carried out in 1558 under the auspices of the authorities and is preserved in the archive of the Museo Correr in Venice. It contains the names and ages of the captains in the Venetian merchant navy at the time (comprising ships of 300 to 720 tonnes, i.e., 500-1200 *botti*); sixteen of the fifty-nine ships, or twenty-seven percent, were Greek.[11]

The administrative correspondence sheds light on the relations between citizens and the central administration. Through petitions, the so-called "embassies" *(ambascerie)*, emissaries from Venetian dominions asked the metropolitan authorities to solve the various problems faced by their communities.

---

in Kithyra (Cerigo), see Chryssa Maltezou, "Les archives vénitiennes de Cythére. Un fonds historique négligé," *Byzantinische Forschungen*, V (1977), 249-252). There is also material pertaining to the second period of Venetian rule in the Peloponnese in Tiepolo, "Archivio di Stato di Venezia," 1120, *passim*; Andrea Nanetti, *Il fondo archivistico Nani nella Biblioteca Nazionale di Grecia ad Atene* (Venice, 1996); and Anastasia Stouraiti (ed.), *Memorie di un ritorno. La guerra di Morea (1684-1699) nei manoscritti della Querini Stampalia* (Venice, 2001).

[9]Museo Correr di Venezia (MCV), Donà dalle Rose (DDR), codice 21, "Dello Stato da Mar," primo libretto, f. 18r.

[10]Frederic C. Lane, *Navires et Constructeurs à Venise pendant la Renaissance* (Paris, 1965), 253-256.

[11]MCV, DDR, codice 217, ff. 36r and 39r. The register has been published by Stefanos Kaklamanis, "Markos Defaranas (1503-1575). Zakinthios stichourgos tou 16ou aiona" ("Markos Depharanas (1503-1574), Zakynthian Rhymester of the 16th Century"), *Thisavrismata*, XXI (1991), 302-305; and analysed by Jean Claude Hocquet, "La gente di mare," in Alberto Tenenti and Ugo Tucci (eds.), *Storia di Venezia. III: Il Mare* (Rome, 1991), 482-483.

These petitions and the official replies of the central authorities provide information on state policies and the political situation in the provinces.[12]

Records of public bodies entrusted with the regulation of seaborne trade constitute another important source. A characteristic example is the office of the *Cinque Savi alla Mercanzia* (Five Sages on Trade), which was established in 1517 to improve state commercial policies and to attract as much merchandise as possible to Venice using land and sea routes. It faced problems emanating from changes in international politics (and the marginalisation of Venice in the global market), as well as from the malfunctioning of the Venetian state apparatus. Within its jurisdiction was the regulation of maritime and terrestrial commerce; issues pertaining to the organisation of shipping and handicraft production; the levying of import-export and transit taxes; the provision of relief to victims of shipwrecks; the security of seafaring; problems with intermediaries; the interdiction of illicit traffic; the coordination of Venetian consuls; and the like. In its capacity as a counselling and executive body it co-operated with other authorities. Its records are preserved in an extensive archive of 1130 files in which, apart from decisions, there are also lists of Venetian ships calling at various ports abroad, declarations of cargo (*manifesti*) and copies of decrees issued by state authorities relating to shipping.[13]

It will by now have become clear that the archival material researched and/or published thus far is skewed in that it originates mostly in Western European, particularly Venetian, sources. We can in fact posit the existence of a "Venetian" and an "Ottoman" Greek historiography for this epoch.[14] That Greek economic historiography on the fifteenth to seventeenth centuries is based almost exclusively on Venetian sources can be partly explained by the importance of Venice for its Greek subjects as well as by the easy access to the material offered to the researcher by the Hellenic Institute for Byzantine and Post-Byzantine Studies in Venice. On the other hand, a major shortcoming of "Ottoman" historiography is that it is not derived from Ottoman sources and

---

[12]A large number of petitions from Cretan communities has already been published; see Georgios Ploumidis, *Presveies Criton pros ti Venetia, 1487-1558* (*Petitions from Cretans to Venice*) (Ioannina, 1986). The publication of those from Corfu is forthcoming by E. Yotopoulou-Sissilianou. For the institution of "embassies," see Freddy Thiriet, *La Romanie Vénitiénne au Moyen age* (Paris, 1975), 204-209.

[13]Maria Borgherini-Scarabellin, "Il Magistrato dei Cinque Savi alla Mercanzia dalla istituzione alla caduta della Repubblica," in *Miscellanea di Storia Veneto-Tridentina* (2 vols., Venice, 1925-1926), II.

[14]See the categorisation of the relevant literature in Nikos Svoronos, *Episkopissi tis Neoellinikis Istorias. Vivliografikos Odigos Spirou I. Asdracha* (*Survey of Modern Greek History. Bibliographical Guide by Spyros I. Asdrachas*) (Athens, 1994).

by and large ignores the historical framework of the Ottoman state.[15] The tension between Greece and Turkey, difficulties in reading Classical Turkish and problems emanating from the archival policies of the Turkish and Greek states explain these shortcomings. As a consequence, writing on the Ottoman period in Greek history has been based on non-Ottoman sources, written by states that traded with the Empire, and on European travel literature and the works of Turkish historians who have published studies in English on the economic and social aspects of the Empire for the period from the fifteenth to the seventeenth century, such as Ömer Lufti Barkan, Halil Inalcik, Lütfi Güçer and others.[16]

Information on the Ottoman merchant navy can also be found in various European repositories, such as the Venetian archives (especially in the reports of the Venetian *Bailo* in Constantinople), where information on Ottoman traders, shipowners and sailors, both Christian and Muslim, may be encountered;[17] the State Archives of Ancona, a town which from the late fifteenth century competed with Venice for Ottoman commerce; the State Archives of Florence, a town which lay behind the Papal city of Marche; the archives of Dubrovnik (Ragusa), a free city which enjoyed a special status under joint Venetian and Ottoman suzerainty;[18] the State Archives of Genoa (Genoese mer-

---

[15]For Ottoman primary sources held in Greece, see Evaghelia Balta, "Othomanika archeia stin Ellada. Prooptikes tis erevnas" ("Ottoman Archives in Greece. Research Prospects"), *Mnimon*, XII (1989), 241-252; and Balta, "Oi othomanikes spoudes stin Ellada" ("Ottoman Studies in Greece"), *Historica*, XVI (1999), 455-460. For sources of Greek historical interest in Turkish archives, see Ploumidis, *Diagramma ton archeiakon pigon*, 38-39. An annotated bibliography of published Ottoman sources and European archival material relating to the history of Greek lands under Ottoman rule is to be found in Svoronos, *Episkopissi tis Neoellinikis Istorias*, 163-169 and 219-259.

[16]For an economic history of the Ottoman Empire see, for example, Robert Mantran, *Istanbul dans la seconde moitié du XVII siècle. Essai d' Histoire institutionnelle, économique et sociale* (Paris, 1962); and H. Inalcik and D. Quataert (eds.), *An Economic and Social History of the Ottoman Empire, 1300-1914* (Cambridge, 1994), which includes an updated bibliography.

[17]Ploumidis, *Diagramma ton archeiakon pigon*, 27; Chrissa Maltezou, *O thesmos tou en Konstantinoupoli Venetou Vailou (The Office of the Venetian Bailo in Constantinople)* (Athens, 1970), 16-17 and 133-221; Fani Mavroidi, *O Ellinismos sto Galata (1453-1600). Kinonikes ke ikonomikes pragmatikotites (The Greek Population of Galata. Social and Economic Aspects)* (Iaonnina, 1992), 11-13; and Tiepolo, "Archivio di Stato di Venezia," 981 and 1011-1012, where a list of relevant titles is provided.

[18]Ekaterini Aristeidou has published material from the archives of Dubrovnik (Ragusa) on the maritime trade of Cyprus; see Aristeidou, "Oi emporikes etaireies sti Ragusa ke oi schesseis ton me tin Kypro apo to 14o os to 16o aiona" ("The Trading Companies of Ragusa and Their Relations with Cyprus from the Fourteenth to the Six-

chants traded with the Aegean islands throughout the sixteenth century);[19] and various archives in Spain, which in the fifteenth to seventeenth centuries tried to undermine the Ottomans in the Levant.[20]

Diplomatic reports constitute another category of "official sources." In general terms, they include reports and correspondence between the consuls, who usually also held the office of state commercial agent, and the ambassadors, on the one hand, and the state authorities on the other. These types of documents shed light on political as well as commercial issues, on the legal framework of trade and on the means of transport, but also contain quantitative data on mercantile transactions. Pointing to the work of Ruggiero Romano,[21] Lane has highlighted the value of diplomatic reports as a particularly rich source of quantitative data.[22] Especially informative are the diplomatic archives of nations which enjoyed "Capitulations" and had commercial contacts with the Ottoman Empire. Several excellent Greek studies on mercantile shipping in the eighteenth century are based on Marseilles Chamber of Commerce records and French diplomatic reports, which were more frequent from the seventeenth

---

teenth Century"), *Kypriakos Logos*, I (n.d.), 65-66; and Aristeidou, "I parayoyi ke to emporio tis Kyprou kata tous 18o-19o aiones" ("The Products and Trade of Cyprus in the Eighteenth and Nineteenth Century"), in *I zoi stin Kypro ton 18o ke 19o aiona* (Nicosia, 1984), 33-62.

[19]For Ancona's archives, see Lucio Lume, *et al.*, "Archivio di Stato di Ancona," in *Guida Generale degli Archivi di Stato Italiani*, I, 333-357; Alberto Caracciolo, "I fondi di interesse veneto nell' Archivio Comunale di Ancona," *Bollettino dell' Istituto di Storia della Società e dello Stato Veneziano*, IV (1962), 241-248; and Caracciolo, *Le port franc d' Ancone. Croissance et impasse d' un milieu marchand au XVIII siècle* (Paris, 1965). Information on records which are of Greek historical interest in the State Archives of Genoa is provided by Phillipe Argenti, "Chief Primary Sources for the Medieval and Modern History of Chios," in *Is mnimin K. Amantou 1874-1960* (Athens, 1960), 231-256; and Argenti, *Diplomatic Archive of Chios 1577-1841* (Cambridge, 1954).

[20]For sources of Greek historical interest preserved in Spain and in other non-Greek archives, as well as for the relevant literature, see J. Hassiotis, "Fuentes de la Historia Griega Moderna en Archivos y Bibliotecas Españoles," *Hispania*, XXIX (1969), 133-164; Ploumidis, *Diagramma ton archeiakon pigon*, 26-34; and Psaras, *Theoria ke methodologia tis Istorias*, 108-109.

[21]Ruggiero Romano, *Le Commerce du Royaume de Naples avec la France et les pays de l'Adriatique au XVIIIe siècle* (Paris, 1951).

[22]Lane, "La marine marchande," 11.

century onwards.[23] Research on the records of the Venetian *Bailo* in Constantinople has also produced much interesting information.[24] The shortcomings of Greek literature in this field become more evident when compared to the series of *Bailo* reports published in other countries.[25]

Within the institutional context of shipping and commerce one can also mention the Ottoman consulates in Venetian territories, and of Venetian or Greco-Ottoman ones at other ports. Archives relating to these consulates contain notarial deeds on the appointment of Ottoman diplomatic/mercantile agents at Venetian ports, as well as the *exequatur* or *placet* issued by the Venetian authorities confirming their appointment and delineating their jurisdiction. Consular archives shed light on the development of Greek Ottoman trade and shipping: on the quantitative and qualitative aspects of the transactions; on the types of ships used; and on the geographic and social origin of the merchants and seamen and their professional associations. These records also contain many indirect references and other "subsidiary" archival data that if properly analysed could shed light on various issues that have not yet been researched.[26]

---

[23]See, for example, Nicolas G. Svoronos, *Salonique et Cavalla (1686-1792). Inventaire des correspondances des consuls de France au Levant conservées aux Archives Nationales* (Paris, 1951); Svoronos, *Le commerce de Salonique au XVIII siècle* (Paris, 1956); Vassilis Kremmydas, *To emporio tis Peloponnissou sto 18o aiona, 1715-1792 (The Commerce of the Peloponnese in the Eighteenth Century)* (Athens, 1972); Kremmydas, *Sygkyria ke emporio stin proepanastatiki Peloponnisso 1793-1821 (Circumstances and Commerce in the Pre-Revolutionary Peloponnese)* (Athens, 1980); and Georgios Siorokas, *To galliko proxeneio tis Artas, 1702-1789 (The French Consulate at Arta)* (Ioannina, 1981). For the French archives, see Serafeim Voreios [Maximos], "Yia mia neoelliniki oikonomiki istoria" ("For a Modern Greek Economic History), *Nea Estia*, XXXII (1942), 1246-1251; Ploumidis, *Diagramma ton archeiakon pigon*, 35-36; and Psaras, *Theoria ke methodologia tis Istorias*, 109-111.

[24]See Mavroidi, *O Ellinismos sto Galata*.

[25]G. Berchet and N. Barozzi, *Relazioni degli stati europei lette al Senato dagli ambasciatori veneti nel sec. decimosettimo* (9 vols., Florence, 1856-1872); Berchet and Barozzi, *Relazioni degli ambasciatori e baili veneti a Costantinopoli* (2 vols., Venice, 1873); and Eugenio Alberi, *Le relazioni degli ambasciatori Veneti al Senato durante il secolo decimo sesto. Serie III. Relazioni dell' Impero Ottomano* (15 vols., Florence, 1839-1863).

[26]On the office of consul, see Mitsa Oikonomou, "O thesmos tou proxenou ton Ellinon emporon kata tin periodo tis Tourkokratis. To emporio tou Archipelagous ke to elliniko proxeneio tis Venetias" ("The Office of the Consul of Greek Merchants during Ottoman Rule. The Trade in the Aegean and the Greek Consulate in Venice") (Unpublished PhD thesis, University of Athens, 1990); Oikonomou, "O thesmos tou proxenou ton Ellinon emporon: To proxeneio tou Archipelagous sto venetokratoumeno Nafplio" ("The Office of the Consul of Greek Merchants: The Consulate of Archipel-

The rebuilding of Saint George's church in Venice obliged the Greek Confraternity to impose a special tax on Greek ships which sailed into the port. The names of more than 400 Greek seamen and of the owners of about thirty ships in the years 1536-1576 are recorded in these tax registers.[27] In the years 1588-1589, twenty-one captains sailed into Venice and paid anchorage tax (*anchoraggio*). They were in charge of low- to medium-tonnage vessels (*karamoussalia, skiratzia*) and originated from the Aegean islands (mainly from Patmos, Lesbos, Lindos in Rhodes and Skyros) and from Lefkas.[28] The aforementioned registers were compiled for the use of the Venetian coast guard offices that were authorised to levy taxes on mercantile transactions.

In addition to keeping tax registers, the port authorities also recorded the inspections carried out on incoming and outgoing ships to check for smuggling and to prevent the spread of epidemics. This category of primary sources includes the sworn declarations made to the coast guard authorities of Irakleion (Candia) to permit clearance of the cargo in departing vessels. The captains had to declare that they were not transporting male or female slaves and that the amount of olive oil on board did not exceed the established limits. The name and type of ship, the name of the captain and owner, and the ports it had come from and was sailing to were recorded. The individuals making the declarations were usually merchants, shipowners or owners of the ship's cargo. Cretan notarial records give further information on their socio-economic activities, especially in the town of Irakleion.[29]

---

ago in Venetian-ruled Nafplio"), *Paroussia*, VII (1991), 433-481; Oikonomou, "Opseis tis ellinikis emporikis naftilias kata to 17o ke 18o aiona. O thesmos tou emporikou proxenou ke to proxeneio ton Ellinon emporon Othomanon ypikoon ston Chandaka" ("Aspects of Greek Commercial Shipping in the Seventeenth and Eighteenth Century. The Office of the Commercial Consul and the Consulate of Greek Merchants of Ottoman Citizenship in Candia"), *Paroussia*, X (1994), 363-438; and Gerassimos D. Pagratis, "To *Consulaton ton Mitilineon* sti venetokratoumeni Kerkyra, 1548-1549" ("The Consulate of Mytiliners in Venetian-ruled Corfu"), *Eoa ke Esperia*, IV (2000), 22-45.

[27]See Ploumidis, *Oi venetokratoumenes Ellinikes chores*, 113-114 and 117-121; and Christa Panayotopoulou, "Ellines ploioktites ke naftikoi apo ta paleotera oikonomika vivlia tis Ellinikis Adelfotitas Venetias" ("Greek Shipowners and Seamen Recorded in the Oldest Financial Registers of the Greek Confraternity of Venice"), *Thisavrismata*, XI (1974), 308-328.

[28]MCV, DDR, b. 217, f. 278r. See Alberto Tenenti, *Naufrages, Corsaires et Assurances maritimes à Venise 1592-1609* (Paris, 1959), 563-567.

[29]Angheliki Panopoulou, "Opseis tis naftiliakis kinissis tou Chandaka to 17o aiona" ("Aspects of Shipping Activities in Candia in the Seventeenth Century"), *Kritiki Estia*, II (1988), 152-210. For the relevant archival material, see Maria Francesca

These declarations are also found in the State Archives of Cephalonia and are as interesting as those of Crete. In them we find series of books and records, such as sailing licences, passports, cargo registers and sanitary regulations covering the late seventeenth to the early twentieth centuries. Only the "books of licences for loading and unloading" have been published so far, but they contain some references to monies deposited as guarantees against participation in illicit trade. These kinds of records contain the name of the trader or his proxy; the trademark of his company; the type of vessel; the name of the captain or owner; the point of origin and final destination; and the goods carried and their weight.[30]

Records of port sanitary services set out in detail the inspections made of arriving vessels and the processes of disinfection and cleansing of crew and cargo before the granting of a "free *pratique*," or clean bill of health, that would permit them to proceed. The thoroughness of quarantine records also enables the researcher to derive quantitative data on Greek commercial shipping. The regulations of the Venetian Commissioners (*Provveditori*) of Health, their correspondence and other quarantine documents relating to the movement of passengers and crews, the crew registers and other records are kept in a 240-file archival series at the State Archives of Corfu. Only its seventeenth-century records have so far been researched, and these include reports by merchants dealing with the Ottoman-ruled mainland. They provide the name and usually the origin of the shipowner. They identify the cargo, the port from which the ship sailed, the duration of its journey, the ports where it called, reports on its encounters with other ships, cases of epidemic diseases and deaths of members of its crew and passengers, as well as pirate attacks or shipwrecks witnessed during the voyage.[31]

Few historians have researched these quarantine records but fewer still are the records which have survived in places other than Corfu. Since the

---

Tiepolo, "Note sul riordino degli Archivi del Duca e dei Notai di Candia nell'Archivio di Stato di Venezia," *Thisavrismata*, X (1973), 94.

[30]Nikos Moschonas, "Naftiliaki drastiriotita sto Ionio sta teli tou 17ou aiona" ("Maritime Activities in the Ionian Sea in the Late Seventeenth Century"), in *6o Diethne Panionio Synedrio* (*Proceedings of the Sixth International Ionian Conference*) (2 vols., Athens, 2001), II, 199-210; and Mosschonas, "Navigation and Trade in the Ionian and Lower Adriatic Seas from the Eighteenth Century to 1914," in Apostolos E. Vacalopoulos, Constantinos D. Svolopoulos and Béla K. Király (eds.), *Southeast European Maritime Commerce and Naval Policies from the Mid-Eighteenth Century to 1914* (Highland Lakes, NJ, 1988), 189-196.

[31]Aliki Nikiforou's study on the maritime trade of Corfu during the seventeenth century ("I diakinissi tou emporiou sto limani tis Kerkyras kata ton 17o aiona," in Nikiforou [ed.], *Kerkyra, mia mesoyiaki synthessi* [Corfu, 1998], 81-100) was based on archival sources found at the local State Archives.

archives of Zakynthos were destroyed during the 1953 earthquake, the most promising surviving documentation is in Venice in the archival series of the Duke of Crete (Duca di Candia). There are also a few surviving documents of the sanitary and customs offices (*Magistrato di Sanità, Dogana da Mar*) which recorded the arrivals and departures of vessels from Venice; the quantities of cargo imported and exported; and other details that could provide us with numeric data. Archives of other port cities significant for Greek maritime commerce, such as Dubrovnik, Ancona, Bari, Messina, Leghorn and Genoa, also need to be consulted.

Important historical data concerning maritime and mercantile issues are also provided in legal papers, such as the *stampe*, printed judicial records relating to commercial court cases. They shed light on the establishment and operation of commercial companies, the correspondence between members, financial records, etc. Most *stampe* were printed in the eighteenth century, but there is also documentation from previous periods.[32]

The prize courts were a special category of justice in countries which were centres for corsairing or were plagued by frequent pirate raids at sea or incursions by land. They dealt, among other things, with litigation arising from the unlawful seizure of persons or property. To date these have only been studied in the two-volume work by D. Themeli-Katiphori on the "Maritime Court" during the governorship of Ioannis Kapodistrias (1828-1831).[33] In addition to Greece, similar courts functioned in other parts of the Mediterranean. The two prize courts of Malta (*Tribunale degli Armamenti* and *Consolato di Mare*) have been identified by Gelina Harlaftis as important sources for the history of Greek shipping in the seventeenth and eighteenth centuries.[34]

The jurisdiction of port officials also extended to judicial matters. In the case of a mishap at sea, the captain or owner of the vessel involved had to report the incident within twenty-four hours of arrival in port to the principal port or political official (to the *provveditore* in Venetian domains and to the *Assemblee e Consolato di Mare* in Dubrovnik) or consular authority (when abroad) giving all the details, especially about damage to the ship or cargo in order to be entitled to compensation. State officials recorded what was re-

---

[32]Panayotis Michailaris, "I emporiki synergassia tou venetikou oikou Taroniti-Theotoky ke ton adelfon G. kai Th. Georgivalon (1732-1737)" ("The Commercial Cooperation between the Venetian Firm of Taroniti-Theotoki and the Brothers G. and Th. Georgivalos"), *Mnimon*, VIII (1980), 226-302.

[33]Despina Themeli-Katiphori, *I dioxis tis Pirateias ke to Thalassio Dikastirion kata tin protin kapodistriakin periodon, 1828-1829 (The Prosecution of Piracy and the Maritime Court during the First Kapodistrias Period)* (2 vols., Athens, 1973).

[34]Gelina Harlaftis, *Istoria tis Ellinoktitis Naftilias, 19os-20os aionas (A History of Greek-Owned Shipping, 19th-20th Century)* (Athens, 2001), 61-63.

ported by the captain and members of the crew in the form of questionnaires (*prove di fortuna*) following the model used in quarantine records. They recorded the name, type, flag, port of origin and destination, tonnage and ownership of the ship; the expenses incurred in its anchoring and/or hauling up at the port; the composition, geographic origin and, on occasion, age of the crew; and the causes of the incident (shipwreck, fire or pirate raid).[35]

Such reports have been found and systematically researched in many Mediterranean archives. In Greece, the *prove di fortuna* preserved in the State Archives of Cephalonia, Corfu and Kithyra have been classified and/or researched.[36] A large number of such records, classified into fifteen files dating between 1770 and 1797, are kept in the State Archives of Venice.[37] Around one thousand cases involving Venetian, English, French, Ottoman, Austrian and Ragusan ships between 1629 and 1811 are recorded in a series of registers, now held by the archives of Dubrovnik.[38] Dozens of files containing papers relating to similar issues from the mid-eighteenth century to the 1810s are found at the State Archives of Trieste.[39]

---

[35]Angeliki Panopoulou, "Peripeteies Kranidioton naftikon sti thalassa ton Kythiron (teli 18ou aiona)" ("Vicissitudes of Kranidi Sailors in the Sea of Kithyra in the Late Eighteenth Century"), *Peloponnissiaka*, XXI (1995), 289-290.

[36]Gilberto Zacché, "*Prove di fortuna*: Una inedita fonte per lo studio della navigazione commerciale nelle acque di Cefalonia nel XVIII secolo," in *Praktika tou 5ou Diethnous Panioniou Synedriou (Proceedings of the Fifth International Pan-Ionian Conference)* (2 vols., Argostoli, 1989), I, 155-179; and Zacché, "*Prove di fortuna*, fonti inedite per lo studio dei rischi della navigazione mercantile (XVI-XVIII secolo): il caso di Cefalonia," *Studi Veneziani*, XV (1988), 253-270, where a list of relevant titles is provided. The *prove di fortuna* preserved at the State Archives of Kithyra date back to the second half of the eighteenth century; see Panopoulou, "Peripeteies Kranidioton," 289-296. I have identified records of seventy shipwrecks which occurred between 1661 and 1795 at the State Archives of Corfu. The results of this research will be presented at the XXXVII Settimana di Studi of the Datini Institute of Economic History in Prato, 11-16 April 2005, under the title "'Le fortune di mare:' accidenti della navigazione mercantile nei mari Ionio e Adriatico (dalle *prove di fortuna* degli Archivi di Stato di Corfù: 1611-1795)."

[37]These files are part of the *Cinque Savi alla Mercanzia* series; see Tiepolo, "Archivio di stato di Venezia," 981.

[38]J. Luetić, "*Prove di fortuna* di navi veneziane a Ragusa," *Bollettino dell' Istituto di Storia della Società e dello Stato Veneziano*, II (1960), 215-221.

[39]Grazia Tatò, "Le prove di fortuna nel XVIII e XIX secolo negli atti dell' Archivio di Stato di Trieste," in Mario Marzari (ed.), *Navi di Legno. Evoluzione tecnica e sviluppo della cantieristica nel Mediterraneo dal XVI secolo à oggi* (Trieste, 1998), 205-216.

Particularly informative are the decisions or sentences of the Venetian Judges of Foreigners (*Giudici al Forestier*) and Consuls of Merchants (*Consoli di Mercanti*). The first comprised junior magistrates entrusted with the settlement of disputes between foreigners and between them and Venetian subjects (which were resolved either by vote or in accordance with law). They also litigated on freight rates, mariners' wages and the leasing or purchase of property by foreigners. From the fourteenth century onwards, cases of minor damage involving ships and charters also came under their jurisdiction.[40]

The Consuls of Merchants, on the other hand, settled differences between traders. Established in the thirteenth century, they regulated the Republic's maritime trade. They monitored it and penalised those who hindered it in any way. They were also responsible for estimating the tonnage of departing vessels and the weight of their cargos. Most of the records relating to this institution to have survived date from the seventeenth century.[41]

The demand for Mediterranean agricultural products from European countries, combined with food shortages in the Levant, enticed a large number of Greek capitalists into maritime trade. Indeed, few places in Greece or other parts of the Mediterranean were self-sufficient in food in this period. The danger of famine was constant from the early sixteenth century onwards, when the sharp increase of the Mediterranean population coincided with a crisis in Italian grain production. Much information on this matter, even concerning Ottoman-ruled territories, may be obtained from Venetian sources. In Venetian domains the public services entrusted with provisioning were manned by members of the privileged classes and were under the supervision of local Venetian authorities. Copies of relevant documentation can be found in the minutes of the "Council of Communities," which provide evidence on imports, ships, countries of origin and other matters. In some cases, sources provide concentrated data which facilitate the work of the researcher.[42] Many relevant sources are also in Venice, where the *Provveditori alle Biave* managed the town's grain reserves and secured the services of Venetian and foreign shpowners to replenish the warehouses of the Rialto and to furnish the navy with grain when at war. Valuable information on Greek merchant shipping can be obtained from the correspondence between the *Capi del Consiglio de' Dieci*

---

[40]Roberto Cessi, "La *Curia Forinsecorum* e la sua prima costituzione," *Nuovo Archivio Veneto*, XXVIII (1914), 202-207; Marco Ferro, *Dizionario di diritto comune e veneto* (2 vols., Venice, 1845-1847), II, 762-764; Andrea Da Mosto, *L' Archivio di Stato di Venezia* (Rome, 1940), 91; and Tiepolo, "Archivio di Stato di Venezia," 989.

[41]Da Mosto, *L' Archivio di Stato di Venezia*, 99-100; and Tiepolo, "Archivio di Stato di Venezia," 979-980.

[42]See, for instance, the series *Enetokratia* in the State Archives of Corfu.

in Venice and the regional Venetian officials stationed in the Levantine domains about the import of Ottoman cereals into Venice or its dependencies.[43]

Thanks to their access to the Rumelia sources and their presence in every significant port city of the Levant, Greeks played a prominent role in the transportation of Ottoman wheat and maintained an information network to support it.[44] In addition to Volos and Salonica, a share in the storage and trade of cereals was also held by the Aegean islands, either because they produced a limited quantity, such as Patmos, or because they collected it from the nearby mainland. Following the Sultan's first prohibition of the export of cereals from the Ottoman Empire (issued in 1555), the illicit trade in Ottoman wheat, with its epicentre in the Aegean, boomed; wheat was carried to the port of Chania and then on to Venice. The transport of Ottoman grain to Italy constituted the basis for the development of Greek commercial shipping two centuries earlier than previously thought. The business was supported by the Venetian state through reductions in the duty on grain imports to the capital and its domains.

Maurice Aymard has compiled a list of ships leased by the Venetian authorities for the import of grain from Anatolia to the Republic on the basis of information in *Officio delle Biavi* records dating back to 1551-1552 and 1560-1561. At least two Greek vessels of 360 and 720 tonnes are included in the list.[45]

The illicit trade in cereals constituted a promising field for investment. Records relating to this business, especially correspondence between Greek informers and Venetian authorities about the measures taken by the Ottomans to impede smuggling, shed light on early modern Greek merchant

---

[43]See, for example, Archivo di Stato di Venezia (ASV), Capi del Consiglio de' Dieci, Lettere di rettori ed altre cariche, b. 290-293.

[44]For the grain trade, see the "classical" study by Maurice Aymard, *Venice, Raguse et le commerce du blé* (Paris, 1966). For the grain policies of Venice in its dominions, see Aymard, *Venise, Raguse*, 72, *passim*; Dimitrios Tsougarakis, "I sitiki politiki tis Venetias stin Kriti ton 13o kai 14o aiona. Parayoyi, diakinissi ke times tou sitariou" ("The Grain Policies of Venice in Crete in the Thirteenth and Fourteenth Century. Production, Trade and Prices of Wheat"), *Messaionika ke Nea Ellinika*, III (1990), 39-72; Marianna Kolyva-Karaleka, "Yia to *Fondego* tis Zakynthou (1600s-1700s ai.). To provlima tou epissitismou" ("About the *Fondego* of Zakynthos [Sixteen to Seventeen Century]. The Issue of Provisions"), in *O artos imon. Apo to sitari sto psomi* (Athens, 1994), 200-204; and Despina Vlassi, "La politica annonaria di Venezia a Cefalonia: Il fondaco delle biade (secc. XVI-XVIII)," *Thisavrismata*, XXV (1995), 274-316.

[45]See Aymard, *Venise, Raguse*, 58-59. On pages 173-176 the author annotates sources found in the archives of Venice, Florence, Modena and Dubrovnik pertaining to the trade of cereals that contain significant information on Greek shipping.

shipping (ships, traffic networks).[46] Research in the records of Venetian, Cretan or Corfiot notaries specialising in maritime affairs shows that the trading and seafaring classes of the Venetian dominions were by and large engaged in the trade of grain not only for the provision of the local population but also for export to Venice or elsewhere.

Another incentive for the development of Greek commercial shipping was the trade in salt, the second most important Mediterranean product traded. Starting in 1533 the Venetians sought to promote the development of shipping by subsidizing the building of large ships and the transport of salt from the salt beds of Cyprus and Ibiza. The studies of Gino Luzzatto, Jean-Claude Hocquet and other researchers have revealed that Greeks took advantage of these measures.[47] In 1589 the Corfiot Antonio Burlion spent 12,000 Venetian *ducats*, an immense amount at the time, to build a ship of 480 tonnes (800 *botti*).[48] Another Corfiot, Mathew Vergis, spent 15,018 *ducats* from a state loan to build the ship *Vergi* with a capacity of 540 tonnes (900 *botti*). In order to pay back his credit to the Venetian treasury, the ship transported salt to Venice: between 1560 and 1569 he undertook nine trips to Cyprus and one to Ibiza.[49]

The amount of salt shipped from the dominions to Venice or elsewhere was recorded by officials. In addition to the amount of salt carried, a record was also kept of the name and type of the ship; the names of its captain and owner; the duration of its voyage; the quantity of salt; as well as other details.[50] Much information on the shipping of salt is provided in Hocquet's remarkable work.[51]

---

[46]Much information is found in the relevant series at the ASV, such as Provveditori alle Biave, Capi del Consiglio di X-Lettere di Rettori e di altre cariche, Consiglio X-Comuni. See Tiepolo, "Archivio di Stato di Venezia," 898-902 and 927-928.

[47]Gino Luzzatto, "Per la storia delle costruzioni navali à Venezia nei secoli XV e XVI," *Scritti storici in onore di Camillo Manfroni* (Padus, 1925), 383-400; Jean-Claude Hocquet, "Il libro *Creditorum Conducentium sale Cypro* dell' Archivio di Stato di Venezia," *Archivio Veneto*, CVIII (1977), 43-81; and Hocquet, *Le sel et la fortune de Venise* (2 vols., Lille, 1982).

[48]Luzzatto, "Per la storia delle construzioni navali," 397, note 3.

[49]Jean-Claude Hocquet, *Voiliers et Commerce en Méditerranée 1200-1650* (2 vols., Paris, 1979), II, 454 and 580; and Hocquet, "Il libro *Creditorum Conducentium sale Cypro*," 43-81.

[50]See ASV, Provveditori al Sal. See also Tiepolo, "Archivio di Stato di Venezia," 925-927.

[51]Hocquet, *Voiliers et Commerce*. The list of archival sources used by Hocquet constitutes a useful guide for the researcher.

No quantitative data on shipping in the period under consideration have survived for certain parts of Greece. In these cases, personal records and especially notarial registers, if they exist, constitute the only sources for maritime history. Notaries were commonplace in Latin- and especially Venetian-ruled regions, such as the Seven Ionian Islands, Chios, Cyclades and Crete. The biggest collection of notarial papers is in the Ionian Islands. In Corfu in particular there are 1262 files dating from as early as the mid-fifteenth century, although most are from 1540 onwards. The notarial records in the archives of Cephalonia, Lefkas, as well as on the smaller Ionian islands of Paxos, Ithaca and Kithyra, are also important.[52] The rich collections of notarial deeds in Venice and other Italian port cities which traded in the Levant at the time (Genoa, Leghorn, Palermo and Ancona) should also be consulted.

The number of Greek historians who understand the value of notarial sources has increased recently. These records facilitate the writing of a *long-durée* social history and provide details that cannot be found in the files of state institutions. The documents of the public administration and state offices are poor in details and do not usually identify the reasons why a certain decision was taken by the authorities; moreover, their language is "cold" and "in-

---

[52]For the notarial material preserved in Corfu, see Georgios E. Rodolakis, "To Notariako Archeio tis Kerkyras" ("The Notarial Archive of Corfu"), *Epetiris tou Kentrou Erevnis tis Istorias tou Dikaiou*, XXXII (1996), 9-137; and Aliki Nikiforou, "L'Archivio di Stato di Corfu da ieri ad oggi," in Constantini and Nikiforou (eds.), *Quaderni di Cheiron*, II, 223-225. In Lefkas, there are seventy-nine codices dating back to the period 1692-1864; see Raoul Guêze, "L'archivio di Stato di S. Maura (Leucade)," *Studi Veneziani*, X (1968), 705-720; and Spyridon Flogaitis, "To notariako archeio tis Lefkadas" ("The Notarial Archive of Lefkas"), *Epetiris tou Kentrou Erevnis tis Istorias tou Ellinikou Dikaiou*, XXII (1975), 146-170. In Ithaca there are forty codices dating back to the years 1624-1864; see Raoul Guêze, *Note sugli Archivi di Stato della Grecia* (Rome, 1970), 40. The notarial material of Cephalonia consists of 739 registers dating back to the years 1536-1900 and is the largest such collection found in the Seven Islands except Corfu's; Anastassia Sifoniou-Karapa, Menelaos Tourtoglou and Spyridon Troianos, "To Notariakon Archeion Kefallinias" ("The Notarial Archive of Cephalonia"), *Epetiris tou Kentrou Erevnis tis Istorias tou Ellinikou Dikaiou*, XVI-XVII (1969-1970), 41-231; and Nikolaos Moschonas, "Topikon Istorikon Archeion Kefallinias. Ergassiai taxinomisseos ke archeiothetisseos" ("The Local Historical Archive of Cephalonia. Report on Classification Work Carried Out"), *Symmeikta*, II (1970), 480-483. For Zakynthos, see Fedon Bouboulidis, "Notarioi Zakynthou" ("Notaries of Zakynthos"), *Epetiris tou Archeiou tis Istorias tou Ellinikou Dikaiou tis Akadimias Athinon*, VIII (1958), 112-133. For the archival material that survived the fire following the earthquake of 1953, see Marianna Kolyva-Karaleka, "Katalogos Istorikou Archeiou Zakynthou-A" ("Catalogue of the Historical Archive of Zakynthos, Part A"), *Mnimon*, X (1985), 17-76. For Kithyra, see Chryssa Maltezou, "To Notariako Archeio Kythiron" ("The Notarial Archive of Kithyra"), *Deltion tis Ioniou Akadimias*, I (1977), 15-84; and Maltezou, "Les archives vénitiennes de Cythére. Un fonds historique négligé," *Byzantinische Forschungen*, V (1977), 249-252.

flexible." On the contrary, an increasing number of studies on economic and social history, and on the history of mentalities and law, are based on notarial sources. The deciphering of notarial rubrics and their statistical evaluation enlightens the researcher about social norms. Notarial records are also a source for the study of commerce and can yield information on topics, such as the social position of merchants, shipowners, captains and sailors; types of ships; fiscal laws and the like. The vast majority of such notarial deeds concern partnerships, in which the participants pooled their capital for greater effect and spread their risks, eventually sharing the profit or loss.[53]

As Alberto Tenenti has pointed out, the systematic or chance specialisation of notaries on certain social groups greatly assists the historian and facilitates statistical analysis.[54] Tenenti has studied the deeds of two notaries over a period of two decades. These notarial acts were drafted for merchants and shipowners who, as soon as they were informed of damage, wreck or loss affecting a ship or its cargo, immediately informed their insurers so that the latter might take the necessary steps to compensate them. The documents used by Tenenti contain detailed information on about 1000 ships: their insurers; the ship or cargo owners insured; the type of damage; the place where it occurred; the nature and quantity of the goods being transported (in a variety of units of measurement); and the ports of origin and destination. The author admits, however, that even had he studied all the notarial archives of the period he would not have been able to reconstruct completely the movements of the port of Venice. It is common knowledge that every source provides information reflecting the purpose for which it was created and is thus limited in its application to wider issues. Nevertheless, the information in his study and its index are useful tools for other researchers. Certain Greek and non-Greek historians have used Tenenti's findings for a variety of purposes, including the study of Greek insurers and insurance brokers in Venice, the extent of the use of insurance contracts by Greeks, Greek merchants/shipowners, and so on.[55]

---

[53]Gerassimos D. Pagratis, "Thalassio Emporio sti venetokratoumeni Kerkyra, 1496-1538" ("Maritime Trade in Venetian-ruled Corfu") (Unpublished PhD thesis, Ionian University, 2001).

[54]Tenenti, *Naufrages, Corsaires et Assurances maritimes*.

[55]Dimitrios Gofas, "Asfalistiria tou 16ou aionos ek tou archeiou tou en Venetia Ellinikou Institoutou" ("Sixteenth-Century Insurance Contracts from the Archive of the Hellenic Institute in Venice"), *Thisavrismata*, XVI (1979), 54-88; Gofas, "Asfalisseis ploion ke thalassion metaforon apo Ellines giro sta teli tou 16ou aiona" ("Insurance of Ships and Maritime Transport by Greeks around the Late Sixteenth Century"), *Pepragmena tou 7ou Diethnous Kritoloyikou Synedriou* (2 vols., Rethymno, 1995), I, 193-219; Fani Mavroidi, *Simvoli stin Historia tis Hellinikis Adelfotitas Venetias sto 16o aiona. Ekdossi tou Defterou Mitroou Egrafon, 1533-1562 (Contribution to the History of the Greek Confraternity of Venice. Publication of its Second Register)* (Athens,

The analysis by Benjamin Arbel of insurance claims following ship-wreck has also shed light on shipping in the Levant at the time. Candia was cited most often (seventy-one cases) as the place of origin of shipowners sub-mitting insurance claims, as the point of departure or destination of ships in-volved in accidents or as the place where the accident occurred. It was fol-lowed by Zakynthos (fifty-nine), Constantinople (thirty-nine), Dubrovnik (thirty-nine), Corfu (thirty-eight), Cephalonia (twenty) and Kithyra (two).[56]

Findings based on notarial deeds can sometimes be confirmed by cross-checking with other sources. But few such sources relating to the eco-nomic life of Greek lands and the Greek diaspora overseas have survived. One exception is the commercial correspondence between members of a shipping partnership based on Crete in 1539.[57] It includes part of the correspondence of the Igoumenos company, a Venice-based trading firm, the owners of which originated from Ioannina. It operated in the years 1556-1685 and was involved in the shipping of merchandise from Ioannina to Venice via Sagiada, where it had an agent.[58] It also had representation in Corfu. An account book belonging

---

1976); and Mavroidi, "Prossopa ke drastiriotites sto deftero misso tou 16ou aiona" ("Prominent Individuals and Their Acts in the Second Half of the Sixteenth Century"), *Dodoni*, XVII (1998), 57-161.

[56]Benjamin Arbel, "Riflessioni sul ruolo di Creta nel Commercio Mediterraneo del Cinquecento," in Gherardo Ortelli (ed.), *Proceedings of the International Conference: Venezia e Creta* (Venice, 1998), 245-259; and Arbel, "The Ionian Islands and Venice's Trading System during the Sixteenth Century," in *Proceedings of the Sixth Pan-Ionian Conference* (2 vols., Athens, 2001), II, 155.

[57]Kaklamanis, "Markos Defaranas," 224-225 and 265-274. The long corre-spondence of Andrea Berengo comprises 292 letters, which unfortunately are of little interest for a historian of Greece. See Ugo Tucci, *Lettres d'un marchand venitien, Andrea Berengo, 1533-1556* (Paris, 1957).

[58]The records of the Igoumenos company are classified into fifteen files to-gether with the *libro maestro* and are preserved in the archive of the Hellenic Institute of Venice (Old Archive). For Epiphanios Igoumenos and his family, see Konstantinos Mertzios, "To en Venetia *Ipeirotikon Archeion*" ("The Epirote Archive in Venice"), *Ipeirotika Cronika*, XI (1936), 29-64. Records of two other Greek commercial compa-nies based in Venice in the eighteenth century are also at the Hellenic Institute: the Selekis-Sarros and Melos archives. On the former, see Vassilis Kremmydas, "Istoria tou ellinikou emporikou oikou tis Venetias Selekis ke Sarou. Mia statistiki prosseghissi" ("History of the Venice-based Greek Company of Selekis and Saros. A Statistical Ap-proach"), *Thissavrismata*, XII (1975), 171-199; on the latter, see Eftychia Liata, "Enas Ellinas emporos sti Dyssi. Poreia mias zois apo ton 17o ston 18o ai." ("A Greek Mer-chant in the West. His Career in the Seventeenth and Eighteenth Century"), *Rodonia. Timi ston M. I. Manoussaca* (2 vols., Rethymno, 1994), II, 279-297.

to the Venetian merchant Giacomo Badoer also reflects his transactions with Greek traders in the mid-fifteenth century.[59]

Personal letters and petitions can also be considered as "private" sources for Greek maritime history. In 1623, for instance, Stathis Marinos from Lefkas wrote to the Duke of Never describing the situation in the Greek lands and urging him to liberate them. In an effort to convince him, Marinos assured the Duke that the local population would come to his assistance and mentioned that in Lefkas there were forty vessels (*vascelli*) which travelled to Barbary, Tunis, Turkey, Venice and other countries. He further claimed that the island had another 500 boats which carried wheat and wine to Corfu, Zakynthos and elsewhere.[60] The claim concerning the number of craft seems somewhat inflated.

Contemporary historians make considerable use of travelogues as a source for maritime history. Travel books relevant to Greek history have already been studied systematically.[61] They describe eloquently, directly and vividly the everyday social and economic life at the time and provide details that cannot be found in official sources. Yet there are shortcomings (subjectivity, platitude, repetition) which can be overcome if we combine the study of different travel books and cross-check with other kinds of sources. Only if it is considered as first-hand material for further research can the data on commerce and shipping provided by travel books be used correctly. It often sheds light on the products of a certain region, the routes followed by traders, the duration of journeys, piracy and its consequences on coastal areas, types of ships, shipbuilding, living conditions on board ships, ship management, crew composition and freight rates. In the eighteenth and nineteenth centuries there were travellers, such as F. Beaujour and X. Scrofani, who provided statistical

---

[59]U. Dorini and T. Bertelè (eds.), *Il "libro di conti" di Giacomo Badoer (Costantinopoli 1436-1440)* (Rome, 1956).

[60]Panayotis Chiotis, *Istoria tis Eptanissou ke idios tis Zakynthou, 3* (Corfu, 1863), 158-159. Cf. Vassileios Sfyroeras, "I emporiki naftilia sta venetokratoumena Eptanissa. Provlimata erevnas ke diapistosseis" ("Commercial Shipping in the Venetian-ruled Seven Islands. Research Issues and Conclusions"), *Praktika Iou Synedriou Eptanissiakou Politismou (Proceedings of the First Conference in Septinsular Culture)* (Thessaloniki, 1991), 43-44.

[61]See the special issue of *Tetradia Ergassias*, XVII (1993), on travel literature and its use as a historical source. See also Eleni Aghelomati-Tsougaraki, "Ellinika Periiyitika Keimena (16os-19os ai.)" ("Greek Travel Literature, Sixteenth to Nineteenth Century"), *Messaionika ke Nea Ellinika*, VI (2000), 155-180, where an updated list of titles is provided.

data on maritime trade.[62] The area covered by travel books usually coincides with the most frequented land and sea routes.[63]

Chronicles and diaries constitute another category of "private" primary source, and despite their shortcomings, they are the only source available on certain issues. The diary of Marino Sanudo is the best known and provides rich information. Thanks to his office in the Great Council of Venice, Sanudo was well-placed to receive first-hand, detailed information on the Republic's public life. His diary has been used to compile the first list of merchants and sailors and to study pirate attacks on Venetian dominions in the first half of the sixteenth century.[64] He provides detailed information on the fleets of the Venetian dependencies, the types of ships used, the strength of their crews, social aspects of shipownership and other matters. Particularly useful are two lists of Venetian ships that he provides.[65] His diary is also informative on the mercantile fleet of Corfu. He notes, for instance, that in 1499 the Corfiots offered twenty-three ships to the Venetian navy,[66] and in 1513, fifty-three Corfiots, mainly feudal lords and shipowners, offered and financed the manning of an equal number of *gripi* for the Venetian campaign in Apulia, from which, according to Sanudo, they expected to profit.[67]

---

[62]Felix Beaujour, *Tableau du commerce de la Grèce formé d' après une annèe moyenne depuis 1787 jusqu' à 1797* (2 vols., Paris, 1800); Xavier Scrofani, *Voyage en Grèce, fait en 1794 et 1795* (3 vols., Paris, 1801); and François Pouqueville, *Voyage de la Grèce* (6 vols., Paris, 1826-1827).

[63]For travel books researched by Greek historians, see Konstantina Filopoulou-Dessylla, *Taxidiotes tis Dyssis, piyi ghia tin ikonomiki zoi tis othomanikis aftokratorias stous chronous tou Souleiman tou Megaloprepous, 1520-1566 (Western Travellers as a Source for the Economic Life of the Ottoman Empire at the Time of Süleyman the Magnificent)* (Athens, 1984). Excerpts from Western travellers, classified according to subject, are published by Kyriakos Simopoulos, *Xenoi taxidiotes stin Ellada (333 A.D.-1800) (Foreign Travellers to Greece, 333 AD to 1800)* (2 vols., Athens, 1970-1973). Excerpts from travel books on Crete are published by Democratia Hemmerdigner-Iliadou, "La Crète sous la domination vénitienne et lors de la conquête turque (1322-1684)," *Studi Veneziani*, IX (1985), 535-623.

[64]Ploumidis, *Oi venetokratoumenes Ellinikes chores*, 117-21; and Alexandra Krantonelli, *Istoria tis Peirateias stous protous chronous tis Tourkokratias, 1390-1538 (History of Piracy in the First Centuries of Ottoman Rule)* (Athens, 1985).

[65]See Lane, *Navires et Constructeur*, 253-256.

[66]Marino Sanudo, Diarii (1496-1533), 2, columns 1243 and 1247.

[67]*Ibid.*, 16, coll. 606, 610-613. Cf. Nikos Karapidakis, "I Kerkyra ke oi Venetoi: Anagnossi ke dynamiki tou astikou chorou" ("Corfu and the Venetians. Reading and Dynamics of the Urban Space"), in Ennio Concina and Aliki Nikiforou-Testone

Lane has highlighted the value of Sanudo's diary as a source on Venetian maritime trade. He has also compiled a list of ship departures from Venice in the years 1404-1433 on the basis of Antonio Morosini's diary. He has, nevertheless, highlighted the unreliability of chronicles, as their writers, intent on impressing the reader, focussed on large vessels and disregarded smaller ones.[68] Other Venetian diaries, such as those of Girolamo Priuli and Domenico Malipiero, are equally useful for maritime history but have not yet been used by Greek historians.[69]

Different commercial countries used different weights and measures. Commercial manuals which provided conversion tables were particularly useful in this chaos. The presence of certain weights and measures in a manual produced for use in a particular commercial centre must have reflected that centre's commercial networks. These manuals, though, are not authoritative since they were compiled on the basis of second-hand data accumulated by a small circle of traders; they can only be used to complement other primary sources. Despite the shortcomings of commercial manuals, a first attempt to identify a commercial network can be based on them. Although a few such endeavours have already been undertaken, we still await others.[70]

What can we expect from an examination of the aforementioned archival sources? A wealth of quantitative data, direct information on Greek commercial shipping, or just hints useful for a general synthesis? The possibility that they might provide the researcher with quantitative data on local fleets,

---

(eds.), *Kerkyra: Istoria, Astiki zoi ke Architektoniki, 14th-19th ai. (Corfu: History, Bourgeois Life and Architecture, Fourteenth to Nineteenth Century)* (Corfu, 1994), 41-48.

[68]Lane, "La marine marchande," 10 and 18-19.

[69]Girolamo Priuli, *I Diarii* (Bologna, 1973); and Domenico Malipiero, "Annali veneti dell'anno 1457 al 1500," in T. Gar and A. Sagredo (eds.), *Archivio Storico Italiano*, series I, VIII (Florence, 1843-1844).

[70]An attempt to use data on weights and measures from commercial manuals to draw general conclusions about the economic structure of the Seven Islands and their role in Mediterranean trade networks has been undertaken by Ugo Tucci, "Le Isole Ionie e la metrologia commerciale del Mediterraneo Centro-Orientale," in Massimo Costantini (ed.), *Il Mediterraneo Centro-Orientale tra Vecchie e Nuove Egemonie* (Rome, 1998), 187-194. The significant table of commercial weights and measures drawn by B. Paxi, *Tarifa la qual val tratta de ogni sorte de pexi e misure* (Venice, 1503), has been published and annotated by Agathaghelos Xirouchakis, "To emporion tis Venetias meta tis Anatolis kata ton Messaiona epi ti vassei ton emporikon katalogon tou Vartol. Paxi" ("The Commerce of Venice with the Levant in the Middle Ages on the Basis of the Commercial Lists of Vartol. Paxi"), *Epetiris Etaireias Kritikon Spoudon*, I (1938), 17-61; and III (1940), 241-296. The manual by Balducci Pegolotti, *La pratica della mercatura* (Cambridge, 1936), is also of interest to historians of Greece.

such as the register of Corfiot shipowners by Sanudo, or on the presence of Greek ships in foreign ports, should not be excluded. The inferior political position of Greeks and the small tonnage of their ships probably explain why their vessels were not always registered by the political and administrative authorities of European metropolises. More reliable conclusions can be expected from patient research and a continually updated database.

The research carried out so far can identify the parameters and fields of such a database. The latter could include quantitative data pertaining to Greek maritime trade at the time, to the shipping of merchandise and to the circulation of capital. A qualitative examination of quantitative primary sources in conjunction with conclusions drawn from parallel studies might help us to find reliable answers to several historical questions, such as the conditions for the creation and development of a local fleet, its average tonnage in different periods, the accumulation of capital, the planning of voyages, the "take off" from local transactions to the export trade, the impact of maritime trade on local societies, the extent of the co-operation between Greeks and foreign maritime powers, and so on.

Researchers of the history of Greek merchant shipping face certain methodological problems. First, the identification of Greeks is difficult since they were blurred with other Venetian or Ottoman subjects and were incorporated in the maritime networks of various European countries which traded in the Levant at the time. Moreover, supposedly "suitable" sources do not provide the tonnage of ships, which has to be estimated using indirect methods. The practice of dividing the ownership of a ship into shares further complicates research. The identification of ships owned by shareholders is rendered even more difficult by the absence of adequate ship registers.

Sources on Greek commercial shipping must therefore be complementary and have to be cross-referenced for the construction of an extensive database. The close and concerted co-operation of historians is therefore necessary if they are to overcome the problem of the small amount and dispersion of archival material.

An Outline of Ottoman Maritime History

Eyüp Özveren and Onur Yildirim

Introduction

Had the Ottomans not contested the Venetians and the Spaniards in the Mediterranean and the Portuguese in the Indian Ocean, they would have gone unnoticed in the annals of maritime history, and the question of whether or not the Ottoman Empire constituted a maritime power would not have appeared on the agenda in the first place.[1] Because they played big and bid for supremacy twice, once in the Mediterranean and the second time in the Indian Ocean, the Ottomans earned themselves a big question mark as far as their maritime legacy is concerned. In our opinion, a state does not have to fight major naval wars and win them, as the Ottomans quite often did, to become a maritime power. The Ottoman Empire was *also* a maritime power because it stretched along the shores of the eastern Mediterranean; because communications between its various constituent parts required regular sea borne traffic; and because the imperative to prevent foreign intrusion into the eastern Mediterranean was of vital importance to the survival of the territorial integrity of the empire. We say "also" because it was first and foremost a land-based empire. This had nothing to do with religious or cultural factors. It was just a dictate of circumstances to which its two predecessors, the Byzantine and Roman empires, had also been subject. All three empires controlled a good part of the Mediterranean by dominating considerable stretches of its coast. The Roman and Byzantine empires patrolled their coasts and major routes and instituted law and order just as the Ottomans would subsequently do. Their naval strategy was on the whole defensive. In this respect, the "long sixteenth century" is an exception in early modern times insofar as naval warfare came to constitute a means and mechanism of further conquest. In view of these considerations, we believe the Ottoman Empire can rightfully claim its own maritime history.

A maritime history in general rests on the histories and interactions of two components, namely the navy and the merchant marine. At any one time one typically stands above the other. There are also intermediate cases where there exists a balance between the two with a strong level of interaction. In the case of the Ottoman Empire, naval history dominates maritime history. This

---

[1]We would like to thank Carmel Vassallo and Sheila Pelizzon for their comments and Burak Beyhan for the preparation of the maps.

147

has to do with two major factors. First, the state played a major role by way of its strategic priorities in tilting the balance in favour of the navy. Second, records of the navy as a centralized institution by far outweigh those of the highly dispersed and largely taken-for-granted merchant marine. In other words, archival sources as well as secondary literature have biased scholarship in favour of the navy. In addition, the Ottomans did not see and treat the merchant marine as a precondition for the development of the navy. The navigational circumstances of the Mediterranean also encouraged this position. The Mediterranean is known for its irregular and unreliable winds. This necessitated a longer than usual dependence on oar-propelled vessels for warfare and sailing ships for commerce. The consequence was a rigid specialization between the navy and the merchant marine. There was thus a rift between the Ottoman navy and Ottoman merchant shipping. In this respect, the Ottomans shared with the Venetians the same comparative disadvantage *vis-à-vis* the Dutch. The life span of naval ships meant that in times of extended peace, Ottoman and Venetian naval units would simply rot at their moorings while Dutch ships could revert to commercial use. It was not feasible for the Ottomans to maintain a sizeable navy when warfare was not regular, as was the case during the sixteenth century, or when major conflict was not imminent.

Having put forward the idea that the navy is at the centre of Ottoman maritime history, we are obliged to survey naval affairs in order to identify the crucial turning points and how things were perceived from above at those critical junctures. Cartography is a good reflection of how a maritime power perceives its maritime environment and operational range. To this effect, we shall take a brief look at Ottoman cartographic accomplishments.

We shall subsequently identify the basic types of Ottoman ships and how they changed over time. This is important for two reasons. First, ship types are dictated to a great extent by the realities of the sea. Therefore, countries that share the same maritime environment learn from one another about the vessels best suited for the sea in question. In this way, we can know to what extent the Ottomans shared with their rivals a certain expertise characteristic of the Mediterranean. Second, trends in the evolution of ship typology over time are indicative of technological advance. This clearly had consequences for the organization of shipbuilding and acquisition procedures, repair and maintenance, as well as labour skills, although once a navy already existed there was a tendency to do more of the same rather than shift to a new paradigm as long as the immediate consequences could be tolerated. In the fashionable contemporary parlance, a "path-dependence" is likely to be self-reinforcing. Major wars or extended periods of peace that destroy the navy in one way or another prepare the ground for a wholesale paradigm shift. During the period under review, there were at least two such major changes. The first came with the transition from oars to sails towards the end of the seventeenth century, and the second with the advent of steam in the nineteenth century.

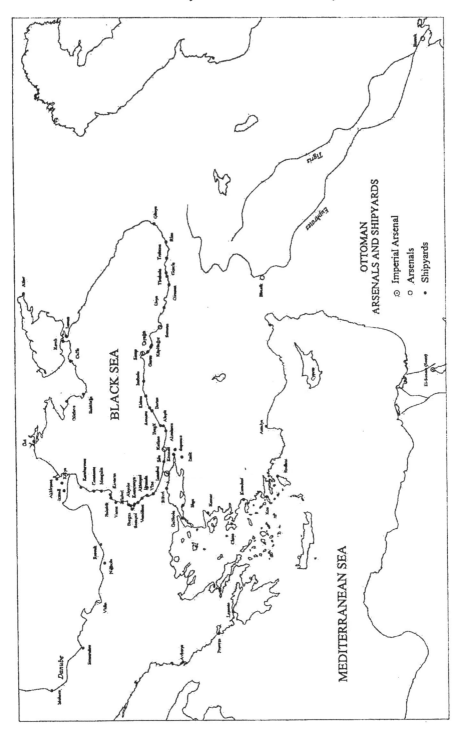

OTTOMAN
ARSENALS AND SHIPYARDS

⊙ Imperial Arsenal
○ Arsenals
• Shipyards

BLACK SEA

MEDITERRANEAN SEA

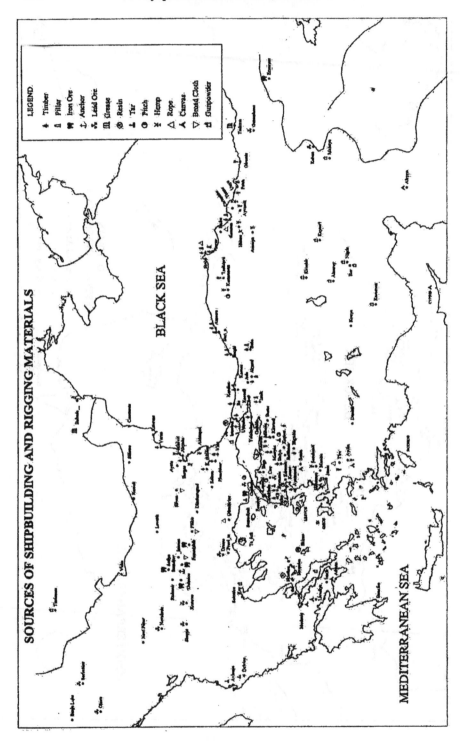

In general, naval units can originate from three different sources. They can be built, bought or seized as prizes. During the "long sixteenth century," a substantial number changed hands among the contesting powers of the Mediterranean. Corsairs were largely responsible for the seizure of foreign ships on behalf of the Ottoman navy. This was one channel through which technology was actually transferred from the western to the eastern half of the Sea. To keep these vessels operational, repair and maintenance facilities were needed, which constituted the foundations of a shipbuilding industry. This factor notwithstanding, in order to have ships at a time when large-scale purchases abroad were well-nigh impossible, a country had to have a shipbuilding sector, but while the navy had centralized and permanent shipyards, merchant vessels often were built in somewhat makeshift facilities. On the whole, the location of shipyards was determined mostly by ease of access to shipbuilding materials, especially timber. Depletion of such resources often resulted in the closure of smaller shipyards. In the case of naval shipyards, on the other hand, the choice of site was dependent on strategic concerns. In this case, the scale and polices relating to the procurement of materials helped compensate for the disadvantages arising from distance from supply. The Imperial Arsenal in Istanbul, first in the hierarchy of Ottoman shipyards, was the Turkish counterpart of the famous Venetian *Arsenale*. A facility of massive proportions, it relied on the mobilization of a range of inputs, including timber for masts and the hull, sailcloth, ropes, pitch and tar, as well as iron and other metals. Some of these were basic construction materials, while others were essential for the fitting and rigging of ships. Without a regular supply it was impossible to maintain existing naval vessels, let alone construct new ones.

An organized production process like the one at the Imperial Arsenal resulted in a massive concentration of workers with various levels of skill. Labourers were not only an essential part of shipbuilding but were also a *sine qua non* for the operation of the navy and the merchant marine. We thus need to know the kind of people who built and manned the Ottoman ships of various sorts. Maritime history, in our view, is also *social* history – it has as much to do with people as with the sea.

The Navy from the Fifteenth to the Nineteenth Centuries

For most of the fifteenth century the size and strength of the Ottoman navy was not comparable to its contemporaries (e.g., Venice, Genoa, Spain). The vessels of the Ottoman fleet mostly served a two-fold purpose: the transport of men and material, and the monitoring of coastal borders. The rise of the Ottomans as a major naval power dates from the time of Mehmed II, who felt that:

> sea-power was a great thing, that the navy of the Italians was
> large and that they dominated the sea and ruled all the islands

in the Aegean, and that to no small extent they injured his own coastlands, both Asiatic and European, especially the navy of the Venetians. Hence he [was] determined to prevent this by every means and to be the powerful master of the entire sea if he could, or at least to prevent them from harming his possessions.[2]

The Ottoman fleet, excluding transport and service vessels, comprised around 350 units at the time of the conquest of Constantinople under Mehmed II.[3] It increased immensely during the reign of his son, Beyazıd II.[4] During the reign of Beyazıd II (1481-1512), the Ottoman fleet expelled the Genoese, from whom his grandfather Murad II (1421-1451) had leased ships to transport Ottoman troops across the Dardanelles to Europe.[5] By the end of the fifteenth century, the Ottomans had not only seriously reduced the Venetian and Genoese presence in the Aegean and eastern Mediterranean but had also started to patrol the Black Sea and the Aegean shores. The continuous struggle with the Genoese and Venetians played a crucial role in building a strong naval force which brought under control some strategic islands around the Dardanelles and the Aegean. Beyazıd II's comprehensive reform programme played a decisive role in improving the fortunes of Ottoman seafaring. Apart from increasing the number of ships, he adopted a policy of employing experienced ships' captains.[6] In this regard he integrated certain corsair captains, such as Kemal Reis, Burak Reis and Piri Reis, into the Ottoman navy.[7] The degree to which the knowledge of these captains and their experience in combat on the high seas benefited the Ottomans and increased the technical competence of their navy is hard to assess. What is definite is that towards the end of Beyazid II's

---

[2]Kritovoulos, *History of Mehmed the Conqueror* (Princeton, 1954), 185.

[3]*Ibid.*, 186-187.

[4]H.J. Kissling, "İkinci Sultan Bayezid'in Deniz Politikası Üzerine Düşünceler: (1481-1512)" ("Reflections on the Naval Policy of Bayezid II"), *Türk Kültürü*, No. 84 (1969), 894-906.

[5]Kate Fleet, "Early Turkish Naval Activities," *Oriente Moderno*, XX, No. 1 (2001), 138.

[6]Kissling, "İkinci Sultan," 900-905.

[7]Under the command of Kemal Reis, the Ottoman navy sailed c. 1487 as far as the western Mediterranean to help the Moors in Andalusia. Thomas Goodrich, *The Ottoman Turks and the New World: A Study of Tarih-i Hind-i Garbi and Sixteenth Century Ottoman Americana* (Wiesbaden, 1990), 5.

reign, the Ottoman fleet could compete effectively with the galleys of its contemporaries, particularly those of Italian republics such as Venice and Genoa.[8]

Beyazıd II's legacy to his successors in terms of naval strength was considerable. It would not be much of an exaggeration to state that under his reign the sea became the channel through which the Ottomans combined economies of conquest with economies of trade.[9] The rise of the Ottomans to the position of a world power was underscored by the establishment of a strong infrastructure for the navy, which came about after securing permanent access to the resources for shipbuilding, cannon founding, crew mobilization and provisioning. These were accomplished largely by Selim I (1512-1520), who inherited the Ottoman throne from his father, Beyazıd II. Under the latter's leadership, the Ottomans had captured the major ports of Caffa (1475), Killia (1484) and Akkerman (1484) in the Black Sea, thereby seizing all the major points of trade between the north and the south. Control of these ports turned them into major entrepots in the trade between Istanbul and eastern Europe. On the eve of the new century, a series of naval victories reinforced the Ottoman presence in the eastern Mediterranean. The Ottoman navy captured Lepanto (1499), Modon (1500), Koron (1500), Navarino and Durazza off the southwest portion of the Morea.[10]

The beginning of the new century marked the start of a major rivalry between the Ottomans and the rising naval power of the period, the Portuguese, who had recently rounded the Cape of Good Hope and had thus found an alternative to the traditional commercial route between Asia and Europe. The Portuguese merchants began their exploitation of India while their patrons directed their energies to the capture of the Red Sea with a view to cutting the Egyptian transit route in the traditional spice trade.[11] The period 1503-1513 was marked by increasing efforts by the Portuguese to control the Red Sea and to establish stations along the Arabian Peninsula and Africa. The Mamelukes resisted Portuguese pressure until 1509 and eventually appealed to the Ottomans for help. Ottoman assistance came in the form of the provision of guns, iron and timber, followed by the construction of a navy in the Suez Arsenal

---

[8]Kissling, "İkinci Sultan," 894.

[9]Palmira Brummett, *Ottoman Sea Power and Levantine Diplomacy in the Age of Discovery* (Albany, NY, 1994), 89-121.

[10]Andrew Hess, "The Evolution of the Ottoman Seaborne Empire in the Age of Oceanic Discoveries, 1453-1525," *American Historical Review*, LXXV, No. 7 (1970), 1906.

[11]Salih Özbaran, "Ottoman Naval Policy in the South," in İ.M. Kunt and C. Woodhead (eds.), *Süleyman the Magnificent and His Age: The Ottoman Empire in the Early Modern World* (London, 1995), 55-70.

and finally by the supply of manpower (e.g., janissaries, levends,[12] Turcoman mercenaries, etc.) to man these ships. The close naval cooperation between the Ottomans and the Mamelukes resulted in the political domination of the latter by the former after the accession of Selim I to the throne.[13]

The golden age of the Ottoman navy began under the reign of Selim I, who was involved in a vigorous campaign to extend the eastern frontiers of the empire. Ottoman expansion faced no concerted resistance on either sea or land during Selim I's reign. Under his leadership the Ottomans captured Egypt, Syria and the Hedjaz and extended their control to all the Levantine outlets of eastern trade. The development of sea power enabled the Ottomans not only to do away with Venetian and Mameluke dominance in the Mediterranean but also to challenge the stranglehold of the Portuguese over the Indian Ocean. The conquest of Egypt in 1517 was particularly important because it gave the Ottomans their first outlet to the Red Sea and the Indian Ocean. This position brought them into direct confrontation with the Portuguese in the Red Sea, the Gulf of Basra and the Indian Ocean.[14]

By the time Süleyman (1520-1566) came to power, the Ottomans had already turned the Black Sea into an Ottoman lake and had taken major steps to make the eastern Mediterranean another exclusive domain of Ottoman seafaring. Süleyman pursued the latter project by capturing the island of Rhodes (1522) from the Knights of St. John and completed it with the capture of Preveza (1538) under the leadership of the renowned Ottoman Kapudan Paşa, Barbarossa.[15] The Ottoman navy consisted of 300 ships (*kadırga*), most of which were oar-propelled and which participated in the conquest of Rhodes. But the naval initiatives of Beyazıd II and Selim I came largely to a halt under Süleyman, who concentrated his efforts on the defence and consolidation of the imperial territories, particularly along the Safavid frontiers. Nevertheless, the conquest of Iraq in 1534 gave the Ottomans their second outlet to the Indian Ocean and the East at the port of Basra. The Ottomans used this port to patrol the Persian Gulf and successfully kept the Portuguese away from their own

---

[12]Levends were Ottoman privateers who joined the Ottoman navy with their ships when their services were needed.

[13]Brummett, *Ottoman Sea Power*, 120, states that "Ottoman naval aid to the Mamelukes was a calculated move to expand the Ottoman sphere of influence into the Mameluke territories, thus paving the way for their conquest."

[14]Cengiz Orhunlu, "Seydi Ali Reis," *İstanbul Üniversitesi Edebiyat Fakültesi Tarih Enstitüsü Dergisi*, No. 1 (1970), 39-56.

[15]Colin Imber, "The Navy of Süleiman the Magnificent," *Archivum Ottomanicum*, VI (1980), 211-282.

waters.[16] Yet the Ottoman galleys, more suited to coastal warfare, never pre-
vailed over Portuguese sailing vessels geared to open-sea warfare when it came
to encounters on the high seas. Not surprisingly, the two renowned Ottoman
admirals and cartographers, Piri Reis and Seydi Ali Reis, both failed in suc-
cessive engagements with the Portuguese fleet in the Indian Ocean. Piri Reis
lost his head for his alleged responsibility in the defeat, while the life of Seydi
Ali Reis was probably spared due to his good connections at the palace.[17]

Perhaps a parenthesis should be opened here to mention the contributions of the aforementioned Ottoman seamen, as well as those of scholars and
administrators such as Katip Çelebi (Haji Khalifeh), to Ottoman and world
cartography. In 1520, Piri Reis completed a pioneering work of cartography,
Kitab-ı Bahriyye (*The Book of the Seas*), based on his seafaring in the Atlantic
and Indian oceans, in which he illustrated with rich details all the physical features of "the entire Mediterranean coastline and the maritime regions visited
by Iberian sailors in both the New World and the East."[18] A more elegant second edition was prepared in 1526 to be presented to the Sultan.[19] We can only
speculate as to whether this information was subsequently incorporated into
Ottoman naval plans. It can be safely assumed, however, that his work established a precedent for others to follow. Seydi Ali Reis, after his return to İs-
tanbul from the ill-fated Indian Ocean expedition of 1554, set out to recount
his experiences in a book entitled *Mir'at-ı Memalik* (*Mirror of Countries*) in
which he dealt with the Red Sea, Persian Gulf and Indian Ocean, and also included a couple of pages of information on the New World and the Pacific.[20]

---

[16]Başbakanlık Osmanlı Arşivi (BOA), Mühimme Defterleri (MD) 3/550 and
6/257. These two documents are undated, but their contents suggest that they were
issued c. 1530.

[17]Orhunlu, "Seydi Ali Reis," 52.

[18]Andrew Hess, "The Battle of Lepanto and Its Place in Mediterranean History," *Past and Present*, LXXVII (1972), 57.

[19]Svat Soucek, "Tunisia in the *Kitab-i Bahriye* by Piri Reis," *Archivum Ottomanicum*, V (1973), 131.

[20]The third well-known Ottoman cartographer-geographer, Katip Çelebi
(1609-1658), represented a distinct line of cartographic tradition in that he was neither
affiliated with the Ottoman navy nor did he ever participate in a maritime campaign.
His well-known work *Tuhfetü'l-Kibar fi Esfari'l-Bihar* provided a history of Ottoman
maritime wars from the beginning of the fifteenth century to 1656, gave the biographies
of Ottoman admirals and offered details of the Empire's maritime institutions and practices. His later work, *Cihannüma*, demonstrated familiarity with a large corpus of
available Eastern and Western literature on geography, provided a comprehensive survey of Ottoman and world geography, and recounted the voyages and discoveries of

For a period of nearly forty years after the victory at Preveza, the Ottomans were not involved in any major naval confrontation in the Mediterranean or elsewhere, if we exclude the recapture of Aden in 1548. But this does not mean that naval activity came to a complete halt. As mentioned above, in 1552 an Ottoman fleet under the command of Piri Reis sacked Muscat and attempted unsuccessfully to capture the port of Hormuz from which the Portuguese controlled maritime traffic to and from the Gulf.[21] In a subsequent effort to bring back the shattered fleet of Piri Reis, Seydi Ali Reis engaged the Portuguese forces in the Indian Ocean but again to no avail. In 1565 the Ottomans undertook an ambitious amphibious operation that required the mobilization of vast resources and the organization of a hitherto unparalleled logistics operation in an ultimately unsuccessful effort to seize Malta, an objective halfway across the Mediterranean. Despite the setback, the Ottoman fleet was swiftly reorganized, and five years later set out on another major undertaking, the capture of Cyprus from the Venetians. The conquest of the island was successfully brought to an end when Famagusta (Magosa) was taken on 1 August 1571, prompting the Europeans to unite their naval forces against the Ottoman threat at the behest of Pope Pius V. The engagement of the Ottoman fleet with the fleet of the Holy League off the coast of Lepanto on 7 October 1571 gave the Ottoman imperial fleet its first major defeat at sea in the Mediterranean, an event that marked a turning point in the history of the region.[22] For many historians this event denoted the beginning of "an epoch in which the Mediterranean no longer occupied a central place in the events that would mould Europe's future."[23] While it became the epic event marking the end of Ottoman power, it also signalled the beginning of Europe's shifting of "the centre of her creative activity north and east, relegating the Christian states of the Mediterranean to the periphery of a new European and global order."[24] For some historians the significance of this event lies in its settlement of the old struggle between Muslims and Christians. What is relevant for our purpose is that at Lepanto the Ottoman galleys were pitted against those of their European rivals and found wanting, especially as regards firepower, and as a conse-

---

Magellan and Columbus. Katip Çelebi, *Tuhfetü'l Kibar fi Esfari'l Bihar (A Gift to the Nobles on Naval Wars)* (2 vols., Istanbul, 1980).

[21]Özbaran, "Ottoman Naval Policy in the South," 63.

[22]Fernand Braudel, *The Mediterranean and the Mediterranean World in the Age of Philip II* (2 vols., New York, 1972), II, 1088-1142.

[23]Hess, "Battle of Lepanto," 53.

[24]Michael Murrin, *History and Warfare in Renaissance Epic* (Chicago, 1994), 141-148; and Hess, "Battle of Lepanto," 53.

quence the Ottoman navy immediately embarked on a measure of restructuring in an effort to retain control of its possessions in the Mediterranean. The Ottoman Imperial Arsenal worked to its full capacity and within a year rebuilt the imperial fleet along improved lines. The eventual success of the Tunis campaign (1569-1574) testifies to the rapid recovery of the Ottoman navy. The declining power of their traditional foe at sea, Venice, during the same period helped the Ottomans retain their position in the eastern Mediterranean. But Ottoman naval affairs entered another quiet period in the latter years of the sixteenth century when state authorities decided to focus on the internal problems of the Empire (growing rural unrest, the rise of the local notables, etc.) and the expansion of the western frontiers, rather than pursuing further naval conflict in the Mediterranean. The conquest of Crete, the largest eastern Mediterranean island still in Venetian hands, took place half a century later and constituted the one major naval action of the seventeenth century.

Ottoman naval history records the assault on Crete as the longest of all naval battles. It was a move calculated to restore the Empire's eroding hold over the eastern Mediterranean in general, and to eliminate the Venetian threat to the route to Egypt in particular. Preparations got underway in the 1640s, and the Ottoman navy embarked on its expedition in 1645. Ottoman forces seized the greater part of the island in 1645-1646, but the fortress of Candia resisted its assault until 1669. The conquest of Crete was the last of the sea ventures that the Ottomans had been vigorously pursuing in the eastern Mediterranean since the late fifteenth century. It was not until 1707 that Ottoman ships once again ventured beyond home waters to besiege Messina with a small fleet and to go as far as the coast of Spain.

The first half of the eighteenth century was a period of peace during which the Ottoman navy remained idle. While European arsenals were the scene of major technological innovations, Ottoman shipbuilding made no substantial alterations from the traditional forms and methods of the previous century. Furthermore, "neglect and corruption, incapable officers and men, poorly designed and built ships, and disorder and anarchy aboard them caused the Ottoman fleet in every way to mirror the internal condition of the Empire on which it was based."[25] To this picture was added a series of changes in the financial policies of the state (e.g., spread of life-long tax-farming, the conversion of extraordinary taxes into regular ones, etc.) which triggered a movement among the provincial elite (*ayan*) towards decentralization, resulting in the disruption of the traditional provisioning institutions and practices of the state. The effects of growing impediments to the procurement of necessary supplies from the provinces through the traditional provisioning system, coupled with the mounting problems of negligence and corruption in the admini-

---

[25]Stanford Shaw, "Selim III and the Ottoman Navy," *Turcica*, I (1969), 215.

stration, put the Ottoman navy at a disadvantage compared to its rivals. During the Russo-Ottoman war, the confrontation of the Ottoman and Russian fleets off the coast of Çeşme in 1770 resulted in the complete annihilation of Ottoman naval forces. Like the previous defeat at Lepanto, the rout at Çeşme prompted the Ottomans to reconsider their naval policies. A prominent Ottoman admiral, Cezayirli Gazi Hasan Paşa, was put in charge of the reorganization of the naval forces, and to this end he invited European experts to help train the necessary personnel and to establish educational institutions. The first educational institution entrusted with the training of personnel for the navy was established in 1784. It was called *Mühendishane-i Bahri-i Hümayun* (Engineering School of the Imperial Navy). Certain European engineers and nautical experts, particularly French, Swedish and British, were brought in to teach. Some of these experts (e.g., M. Bonneval, Le Brun, etc.) prepared reports about the conditions of the navy and made suggestions, particularly on the modernization and enlargement of construction and repair facilities at the Imperial Arsenal.[26] The modernization of the Ottoman navy was the first step towards the modernization of the armed forces, a development that was concurrently to be implemented in the North African regencies.[27] It formed part of the reform agenda of Selim III and included the 1804 promulgation of a decree (*kanunname*) establishing the Ministry of Naval Affairs (*Umur-ı Bahriye Nezareti*).[28] The Ministry was entrusted with the task of implementing naval reform, and the first step in this direction was the establishment of an independent naval treasury department (*Tersane Hazinesi*). All these attempts proved inconclusive, as the reformist Sultan Selim III was dethroned in 1807 and the Ministry of Naval Affairs abolished. Although Selim's successor, Mahmud II, launched yet another comprehensive reform programme, naval affairs were largely neglected, resulting in the gradual deterioration of the existing fleet and the paving of the way for the third major defeat in Ottoman maritime history. The humiliating destruction of the poorly built and designed Ottoman ships by the Anglo-French-Russian alliance at Navarino in 1827 brought down the curtain on a navy that had been an important handmaiden to a now ailing Empire.

---

[26]*Ibid.*, 222-226, provides a full list of the foreign engineers and nautical experts who served the Ottoman government during the reign of Selim III.

[27]Daniel Panzac, *Les corsaires barbaresques: La fin d'une épopée 1800-1820* (Paris, 1999).

[28]Ali İhsan Gencer, *Bahriye'de Yapılan Islahat Hareketleri ve Bahriye Nezareti'nin Kuruluşu (1789-1867)* (*Reform Activities in the Ottoman Navy and the Establishment of the Ministry of Naval Affairs*) (Istanbul, 1985), 63-69.

Ottoman Shipping and Ship Types

The fifteenth century was an age of far-reaching innovations as far as naval technology was concerned.[29] Carlo Cipolla argues, perhaps in a technologically deterministic way, that without the fifteenth-century developments in naval technology, the overseas expansion of Europe would have been impossible.[30] The Ottomans closely followed these developments as they observed them in action during their encounters with the naval powers of the age, particularly the two Italian maritime republics, Venice and Genoa. Large round ships known as *bargias* used as warships by the Venetians were the technological wonder of the age with their fully-armed decks. The Ottoman navy, similar to the Venetian, Genoese and Spanish navies, followed the traditional maritime technology of the Mediterranean, consisting of heavy "round ships" used as merchantmen and long galleys used as men-of-war. These two types remained in use for a long time but underwent some modifications along the way. Until the end of the seventeenth century, the Ottoman fleet was dominated by armed galleys propelled by oars and sails. These galleys, or *kadırga*, had elongated hulls, varied in size, and ordinarily had two or three banks of oars (twenty-five to thirty benches per side). Besides their function as warships, they were also used to carry goods when the need arose.

Ottoman oar-propelled vessels were classified into four major types: *kalita, kadırga, mavna* and *baştarda*.[31] The *kalita*, which was smaller than the average galley and had nineteen to twenty-four oar benches, was a favourite of Mediterranean corsairs, while the *kadırga,* or galley, which had twenty-five or twenty-six oar-benches and had been used by the Byzantines, became the principal vessel of the Ottoman fleet. The Ottomans used the term *mavna* to describe the larger galleys used by the Italian republics for commercial transport, particularly in their long-distance trade. The *baştarda,* on the other hand, was larger than the galley but had a somewhat lower structure. The Ottomans gave up on attempts at the adoption of state-of-the art technology in shipbuilding, and receptiveness to European naval technology innovation diminished after a series of defeats by the Portuguese in the Indian Ocean and the Christian alliance at Lepanto during the sixteenth century. Hence, the types of vessels re-

---

[29]Carlo Cipolla, *Guns, Sails and Empires: Technological Innovation and the Early Phases of European Expansion, 1400-1700* (New York, 1965), 78-81; and John H. Pryor, *Geography, Technology, and War: Studies in the Maritime History of the Mediterranean, 649-1571* (Cambridge, 1992), 25-86.

[30]Cipolla, *Guns, Sails and* Empires, 137.

[31]Svat Soucek, "Certain Types of Ships in Ottoman-Turkish Terminology," *Turcica*, VII (1975), 234-238.

ferred to above continued to comprise the mainstay of the Ottoman navy until the mid-seventeenth century.

A partial explanation for the belated adoption of sailing ships by the Ottomans may be that having no maritime trade comparable to that of the Italian republics or other European states, they had no vested interest in the creation of a specialized merchant marine. In long-distance transport, the state relied heavily on ships run by two different types of operators. While the first type did their business exclusively with the state at fixed rates of remuneration, the second chartered their ships at market rates. During the sixteenth and seventeenth centuries, the low cost and relatively secure nature of sea transport led to increased dependence on merchant ships. The evidence suggests that the transportation of cereals from one location to another over a period of thirteen to fifteen days was nearly two-thirds cheaper by sea than by land.[32] Merchant ships used in long-distance transportation were usually sailing ships, such as the *barça* (*barza* or galleon), *karaka* (carrack) and *polika*, which operated from April to November on the high seas. The state only used its own galleys, or *kadırga*, for the transport of cereals in case of emergency.

The first time galleons appeared in the Ottoman navy was shortly before the beginning of the Cretan campaign in 1645. These were mainly small craft known as *burtun* or *borton*. The efficiency of these ships having been proven, Mehmed IV (1648-1687) ordered the construction of large galleons, but those attempts failed due to the lack of technological expertise, labour and, most important in the short run, fiscal resources. It was only after 1682 that the large galleon became the principal vessel of the Ottoman fleet. But by then galleons had already evolved into warships that became the ships-of-the-line of the French, Dutch and English navies. Although the transition to galleons helped the Ottomans restore and maintain their dominance in the eastern Mediterranean until the second quarter of the eighteenth century, the absence of any serious naval action over the next fifty years led to a neglect of naval affairs. As a consequence, the Ottoman navy gradually lagged behind its European contemporaries in terms of both technology and numerical strength. In contrast to the fast and efficient warships of rival navies, the archaic ships of the Ottoman navy were massive and bulky. As Stanford Shaw put it:

> these ships were extremely difficult to manoeuvre in the ordinary course of sailing, let alone in battle, and were prone to capsize as the result of sudden movements by inexperienced hands during storms or battles. In addition to this, the ships

---

[32]Lütfi Güçer, *XVI-XVII. Asırlarda Osmanlı İmparatorluğu'nda Hububat Meselesi ve Hububattan Alınan Vergiler* (*The Grain Problem and the Taxes on Grain in the Ottoman Empire during the Sixteenth and Seventeenth Centuries*) (Istanbul, 1964), 32-36.

were structurally unsound; excessive distances between their principal beams caused them to break up entirely during violent storms; the use of soft wood, because of its finer appearance, and the failure to apply caulking regularly between the underwater planks caused them to be unusually porous and to take on water almost continuously.[33]

The shortcomings recounted above offer a partial explanation for the disastrous confrontation of the Ottoman fleet with a small Russian squadron at Çeşme in 1770, a debacle that galvanized the Ottomans into modernizing their fleet. Although forty-five major fighting ships were built along modern lines, and all the older vessels remodelled during the naval reforms of the late eighteenth century, they were never seriously put to the test against the modern fleets of Europe in the next three decades. In its few engagements against French naval forces at the turn of the century, the Ottoman fleet showed some vitality but this was nowhere close to the performance of earlier times. Indeed, the entire Ottoman fleet was burned by the Anglo-French-Russian fleet at Navarino on 20 October 1827 before it had a chance to show its mettle. This incident not only marked the end of reform but for the first time left the Empire without a proper fleet. That same year the Ottomans purchased their first steamship from the British, to which another was added two years later.[34] The incorporation of steamships into the Ottoman navy and the purchase of steam engines from the United States to upgrade the existing vessels opened a new era in Ottoman naval history in which the navy became increasingly dependent on Western technology and proved far from efficient in competing with the navies of neighbouring countries, such as Russia or a resurgent Greece, let alone with the Europeans. On the eve of its dismemberment, the Ottoman state acquired its first submarines from the Nordenfelt Guns and Ammunition Company in England, but the opportunity for their use never arose.[35]

Ottoman Shipbuilding: The Establishment of the Imperial Arsenal

In the late fourteenth century, the first large Ottoman arsenal was built over the former Byzantine arsenal in Gallipoli, a strategic point commanding the entrance to the Dardanelles from the Sea of Marmara. The facility was rebuilt by Saruca Paşa during the reign of Yıldırım Beyazıd, and the city became a residence for Ottoman sea captains and, at the time of Süleyman, the centre of

---

[33]Shaw, "Selim III and the Ottoman Navy," 213.

[34]Gencer, *Bahriye'de Yapılan Islahat Hareketleri*, 109-110.

[35]Konstantin Zhukov and A. Vitol, "The Origins of the Ottoman Submarine Fleet," *Oriente Moderno*, XX, No. 1 (2001), 221-232.

a newly-created maritime province called Cezair-i Bahr-i Sefid. Revenues from the province were used to pay various naval expenses, including the salary of the grand admiral (*Kapudan Paşa*) and other maritime officials. Not much is known about the capacity of the Gallipoli arsenal apart from that it took over the functions of the existing small arsenals located in different parts of the Empire (e.g., İznikmid, Karamürsel and Edincik).[36] During the reigns of Mehmed II and Beyazıd II, its capacity must have increased substantially since both were engaged in a fierce struggle against the naval giant of the period, the Venetian Republic. Although Mehmed II set out to construct a new arsenal in Galata following the conquest of Constantinople, the Gallipoli Arsenal remained the principal Ottoman naval base until the second decade of the sixteenth century.

Our information on Ottoman shipbuilding comes from the reign of Selim I, who completed the expansion of the arsenal in Galata. This facility was designed to build and repair ships and was completed in 1515. When the arsenal was working at maximum capacity, as in 1530, it could build twenty-four galleys and repair eight; the number of ships built over the five-year period 1527-1531 was forty-four.[37] The evidence would seem to indicate that in 1515 the Ottomans had a navy of 400 ships participating in the campaign against the Mamelukes.[38] The number of ships in the campaign of Herceg Novi (Castelnuovo) in 1539 was 155.[39] The Galata Arsenal was designated as the Imperial Arsenal (*Tersane-i Amire*), where most of the ships were to be built; it functioned as the military, financial and administrative centre of the Ottoman navy well into the late nineteenth century. Concurrently, arsenals such as the ones in Gallipoli, Suez, Sinop, Samsun, Basra, Rusçuk and Kefken worked to supplement the activities of the Imperial Arsenal.

During the late eighteenth century, the Imperial Arsenal underwent a major modernization programme under the guidance of European engineers and nautical experts. The initial efforts focussed on a reconstruction and reno-

---

[36]İsmail H. Uzunçarşılı, *Osmanlı Devleti'nin Merkez ve Bahriye Teşkilatı* (*Central and Naval Administration in the Ottoman Empire*) (Ankara, 1988), 396-399; Halil İnalcık, "The Ottoman State: Economy and Society, 1300-1600," in Halil İnalcık and D. Quataert (eds.), *An Economic and Social History of the Ottoman Empire, 1300-1914* (Cambridge, 1993), 93-94.

[37]İdris Bostan, *Osmanlı Bahriye Teşkilatı: XVII. Yüzyılda Tersane-i Amire* (*Ottoman Naval Organization: The Imperial Arsenal during the Seventeenth Century*) (Ankara, 1992), 6.

[38]Hess, "Evolution of the Ottoman Seaborne Empire," 1909.

[39]Colin Imber, "The Costs of Naval Warfare: The Accounts of Hayreddin Barbarossa's Herceg Novi Campaign in 1539," *Archivum Ottomanicum*, IV (1972), 203-216.

vation of the facilities with a view to the building of new ships for the fleet. In the first instance the Ottomans replaced the two old wooden dry docks, which were almost constantly in need of repair and rebuilding, with three permanent stone ones. The latter were far superior in capacity, efficiency and durability. Then they proceeded with the construction of five new shipbuilding forms, as well as a new dry dock, which they modelled after the one at Toulon.[40] The modernization of the Arsenal continued with the building of two new mast machines which greatly increased the speed and efficiency of the operations by which masts were prepared for ships. As was mentioned above, these changes enabled the Ottomans to build new warships along European standards. The size of the fleet increased from seventeen ships-of-the-line and twenty frigates and corvettes in 1796 to a total of forty-two vessels in 1811.[41] The establishment of the Ministry of Naval Affairs with an independent treasury in 1804 brought about major changes in the administration of an Imperial Arsenal whose conditions had worsened over the previous century. Gencer and Shaw provide detailed surveys of the administrative, fiscal and other reforms accompanying the changes that took place in the Imperial Arsenal. With the dethronement of Selim III, however, the reforms were halted.

Construction Material[42]

Ship construction required a continuous flow of a wide range of different raw materials. To ensure a constant supply the Ottoman state instituted a complex network of provisioning throughout the imperial territories during the early sixteenth century. Timber topped the list of these materials, and most of the timber used in the construction of ships in the Imperial Arsenal came from the mountainous areas along the Sea of Marmara (Propontus) and the Black Sea. The neighbouring province (*liva*) of Kocaeli, which included settlements with abundant forests, such as İznikmid, İznik, Yalakabad and Sapanca, was particularly important. For highly specialized items such as masts, the Ottomans occasionally exploited distant and diverse sources of supply such as Albania, the Carpathian Mountains and the Taurus Mountains in southern Anatolia. The subject populations (*reaya*) of the designated districts were obliged to provide the state with sufficient timber to construct the number of ships planned for a particular year. The number envisioned for a specific year varied according to military circumstances. It could be as high as ten, as in 1682. But the *Porte*

---

[40]Shaw, "Selim III and the Ottoman Navy," 224.

[41]*Ibid.*, 226; and Gencer, *Bahriye'de Yapılan Islahat Hareketleri*, 100.

[42]Most of the information in this section was obtained from Hezarfen Hüseyin Efendi, *Telhisü'l-Beyan fi Kavanin-i Al-i Osman (Report of Declaration on Ottoman Laws)* (Ankara, 1998), 162-169.

retained the right to order the governors and judges of other districts to supply timber for the Arsenal. The registers of important affairs (*mühimme defterleri*) are full of orders issued to the governors or judges of districts as far as Caffa and Tat to provide timber for the construction of ships in Istanbul.[43] For nearly two centuries the areas along the Sea of Marmara supplied most of the timber for the Imperial Arsenal, leading to the gradual deforestation of that region. In the second half of the seventeenth century state officials in charge of extracting timber from this region began to ask the *Porte* to waive a certain portion of the timber demanded. Whether or not this request was acceded to by the *Porte* is not known. What is known, however, is that the reduction of the forested areas around the Marmara Sea led the state to look into the possibility of procuring timber for the Imperial Arsenal from around Bolu, several hundred kilometres to the east of Istanbul, at the end of the seventeenth century.

Although it was easy to find timber, it was quite difficult to find wood suitable for masts. The pine trees used to make masts were obtained from the area of İznikmid, around one hundred kilometres to the east of Istanbul, more specifically in the areas of Ada, Akyazı, Sarıçayır, Akhisar and Geyve. The declining size of forests in the İznikmid region prompted state officials to divert their attention not only to Bolu but also to the other forested areas of the Black Sea, such as Samsun, Sinop, Çayağzı, Kitros and Alaçam, during the seventeenth century. For the small arsenals, wood was less of a problem. The high cost of transportation led small arsenals, such as the ones in Basra and Sinop, to rely exclusively on timber from the neighbouring areas. While the Basra Arsenal secured its wood supplies from the mountains of Maraş,[44] the arsenal at Sinop relied on the supply of timber from its own hinterland, as well as the Black Sea forests further away.

Another important raw material for the construction of ships was tar. The *Porte* secured some of the tar it needed from *Kal'a-i Sultaniye* (Çanak-kale), Albania, Walachia and the coastal settlements of the Black Sea, such as Sinop, Samsun, Bartın and Bafra. As for pitch, the Imperial Arsenal exploited the region of Avlona.[45] This was supplemented with pitch from Mythilene, Gallipoli and Lapseki. The iron used to make anchors and other metal accessories for ships was obtained from the Bulgarian town of Samakov.

Different types of cloth were used for the sailing ships. A raw cloth known as *kirpas* was used for sails and tents. The principal sources of supply were Gallipoli, Egypt and Cyprus, supplemented with material from certain Aegean settlements, such as Menemen and Eğriboz. During the sixteenth century, Aleppo supplied some of the cloth for the Imperial Arsenal via Adana.

---

[43]BOA, MD 6/1103.

[44]*Ibid.*, 3/463, 28 Muharrem 967, 30 October 1559.

[45]*Ibid.*, 3/272 26 Zilkade 966, 30 August 1559.

Towards the end of the seventeenth century, the *Porte* resorted to foreign merchants, particularly French, for raw cloth to be used in the making of sails. The silk cloth used in fitting out the ships came from Bursa. Another kind of textile, broadcloth (*çuka*), was usually obtained from Salonica.

As for the material used in shipboard armament, the principal item was gunpowder. Various minerals used in the making of gunpowder came from different regions. Saltpetre (potassium nitrate) came from Egypt, Karaman, Kayseri, Niğde, Bor, Kırşehir, Aksaray, Malatya, Syria, Lebanon, Baghdad and Basra. Sulphur came from the Lake of Lut and the eastern parts of Anatolia. The production of gunpowder took place in several powder mills (*Baruthane*) in İstanbul. For the casting of cannons the Arsenal depended on the Imperial Arsenal of Ordnance and Artillery (*Tophane-i Amire*), which produced various types of cannons for the different ships in the Ottoman navy.

The Ottomans financed the acquisition of the materials used in the construction of ships through a variety of taxes. During the sixteenth century the procurement of all the materials was provided for by the *tımars*, or fiefs. Sometimes the cost of the materials was met from poll-tax (*cizya*) revenues raised in the region where the purchase was made. From the late sixteenth century onwards, sources of finance became more diversified. The state purchased some of its materials from merchants at market rates with revenues obtained from the tax farms. A government order in 1606 stated that the cost of the material to be used in the construction of a galley and a horse ship in the Süzebolu *iskele* was to be drawn from the tax farms in the seaside towns of Ahyolu and Midye.[46] But the principal method of extracting a wide range of construction materials from the designated locations was via the direct taxation in kind of the local population through the *avarız* system with which the Ottomans had been experimenting since the early years of the sixteenth century. The latter required the taxpayers of a given area to provide officials with an amount of timber or some other material at the point of production. The state usually defined the tax obligation of the subject populations in monetary terms. In the mid-seventeenth century, for example, the construction of a galley or galleon required roughly 7000-10,000 units of timber costing between 56,000 and 86,000 *akçe*s. In the seventeenth century, in addition to the *avarız* taxes, which were used mainly for the supply of material for ship construction, arbitrary fees were levied on the subject populations of certain *sancak*s to meet the cost of timber for ship construction.[47] When the state failed to procure the required amount of raw material through the *avarız* system, it purchased the remainder at market prices from merchants. The evidence suggests that the dis-

---

[46]*Ibid.*, Cevdet/Belediye (CB) 8729, 26 S. 1015, 3 July 1606.

[47]BOA, MD 83/96, 20 L. 1037, 23 June 1628; and MD 83/99, 21 L. 1037, 24 June 1628.

crepancy between the two prices was one-fifth in favour of the latter. The latter practice encouraged local populations to cooperate with the merchants, who offered better prices for these materials. The registers of important affairs are full of records concerning the prohibition of sales by the subject populations to the merchants. Although such incidents were not uncommon in the sixteenth century, they begin to appear more often in official documents in the seventeenth and early eighteenth century.

In the eighteenth century, problems associated with the procurement of timber, iron, pitch, tar, resin, hemp, sails and other shipbuilding materials from the provinces through the provisioning mechanisms caused the state increasingly to procure its needs from merchants at market rates. By the time the reform of the navy was launched, the traditional provisioning mechanisms had already been dismantled, and all the materials used in the construction of ships were purchased from producers via the mediation of merchants.

Labour

The question of maritime-related labour is complex since it involved a multitude of areas. The principal demand for maritime-related labour was not so much on board the ships as in the arsenals in the capital or the provinces. The arsenals employed skilled and unskilled labour. The majority of the skilled labour force comprised craftsmen and shipwrights who were drawn largely from the *devshirme* corps. The craftsmen who worked on a permanent basis included mainly armourers, storekeepers, oar makers, caulkers, pulley-makers and oakum-workers. Gunners and bombardiers on ships also tended to be employed on a permanent basis. The Grand Admiral retained the right to draft additional skilled workers on a temporary basis from various imperial districts in preparation for a major campaign. These included carpenters, caulkers, clinchers, oar makers, sawyers, saw-makers, tailors and ironsmiths.[48] These temporary workers could be drawn from the local populations either as wage labour or in return for a variety of tax exemptions. The government relied on local judges for the recruitment of the necessary labour force for the Imperial Arsenal. When the small arsenals required labour, their administrators asked the *Porte* to intervene on their behalf to summon the judges of various districts to recruit people for their needs. In one such case, all the judges of the districts

---

[48]People employed in the Imperial Arsenal were classified into various professional categories. For a detailed description, see Salih Özbaran, "Galata Tersanesinde Gemi Yapımcıları, 1529-1530" ("Shipbuilders in the Galata Arsenal"), *Güneydoğu Avrupa Araştırmaları Dergisi*, Nos. 8-9 (1980), 97-102.

from Sinop to Trabzon were ordered to register the carpenters in their districts with a view to sending them to work at the arsenal of Sinop.[49]

As for the personnel employed on board ships, Katip Çelebi notes that the number on a regular galley (*kadırga*) was about 330: 196 oarsmen, 100 warriors and thirty-five crew members.[50] These totals increased slightly during the seventeenth century when the Ottomans began to use large galleons. The latter were manned by 300-400 people, depending on the size of the ship. The flagship of the Grand Admiral, known as *Kapudane-i Hümayun*, was manned by as many as 800 (500 oarsmen, 216 warriors and eighty-four various personnel).[51] From the beginning the captains hired experienced seafarers supplemented by inexperienced peasants.[52] The seafarers came largely from Greek communities. The Gallipoli Arsenal, for example, employed local Greeks as shipwrights for wages or in return for their exemption from a number of taxes such as *kharaj*, *ispençe* or *avarız-ı divaniyye*.[53] During the sixteenth century, some Italian travellers observed the presence of Venetian shipwrights – probably renegades or captives – employed in the Imperial Arsenal. The recruitment of *timariot* cavalry and infantry was conducted by the maritime *sancak beys* who acted at the request of the Grand Admiral. In the sixteenth century the *timariot* cavalry serving in the Ottoman fleet brought their own arms and armour and a fixed number of armed retainers depending on the size and income of their holdings. As mentioned above, oarsmen were recruited by the district judges according to the demand coming directly from Istanbul.

From the late sixteenth century onwards, the method of recruitment changed to parallel the mechanisms used in obtaining the necessary materials for the construction of ships in the Imperial Arsenal. The *avarız* registers began to be kept by local judges to record the oarsmen drawn from a given area. Those who registered with the local judge had to offer another person or property as security (*kefil*). Another source of oarsmen was the craftsmen in cities.

---

[49]BOA, MD 5/1213, 20 Şaban 973, 12 March 1566.

[50]Katip Çelebi, *Tuhfetü'l Kibar*, II, 237.

[51]*Ibid.*, II, 236. At 800 people, Çelebi's figure for the manning levels of the largest vessel in the Ottoman fleet is nearly three times the figure of 300 men put forward by Murat Çizakça, "The Ottoman Empire: Recent Research on Shipping and Shipbuilding in the Sixteenth to Nineteenth Centuries," in Frank Broeze (ed.), *Maritime History at the Crossroads: A Critical Review of Recent Historiography* (St. John's, 1995), 220. Similarly, Çizakça's figure of 200 for the *kadirga* is considerably below Çelebi's figure of 330.

[52]Lester Libby, Jr., "Venetian Views of the Ottoman Empire from the Peace of 1503 to the War of Cyprus," *Sixteenth Century Journal*, IX, No. 4 (1978), 116.

[53]İnalcık, "Ottoman State," 94.

The non-Muslim communities of Istanbul were supposed to supplement the supply of oarsmen from the designated crafts of the city (e.g., *meyhaneciler* [tavern keepers], *bozacılar* [makers of *boza*, a beverage made of fermented millet], *peremeciler* [boatmen] and *hamallar* [porters]). There were also people who volunteered to become oarsmen. In addition to prisoners of war, the Ottomans used convicts, who were condemned to the galleys as punishment. The government took certain measures against the possibility of mutiny; Ottoman writers such as Katip Çelebi recommended that the Anatolian Muslims who volunteered or were conscripted as oarsmen should balance the number of convicted criminals who were put on a ship.[54] The maximum number of oarsmen in the Ottoman navy remained stable until the end of the Cretan campaign in 1669. The first organized effort to establish a corps of regular, salaried, disciplined and trained sailors took place during the naval reforms of the late eighteenth century which were aborted by the dethronement of Selim III.

Conclusion

Having clearly established that the Ottoman Empire was a maritime empire, the question remains as to whether it was also a world power in maritime terms. This is an intriguing question because the "world" changed considerably during the span of Ottoman ascendancy. When the Ottomans made their bid against the Venetians and the Spaniards, at least in the eyes of many in the region the Mediterranean was synonymous with the world, even though we know with the benefit of hindsight that its days were numbered. The extended period of naval warfare characteristic of the "long sixteenth century" ended in a draw and divided the Mediterranean into two halves. The Ottomans had become established as the masters of the eastern half. In any case, the Mediterranean was already on the way to becoming but one small part, and an increasingly unimportant one at that, of a far bigger world, within which the Ottoman bid in the Indian Ocean was mostly of symbolic importance and short-lived. In this scenario, the Ottomans acquiesced to remaining a regional maritime power and did not seek to renew their challenge on a larger scale. Even in the nineteenth century, when the Ottomans acquired the third largest navy in the world, it was not intended to sail far beyond the eastern Mediterranean – it existed merely to protect local waters. During the first phase of this bid, they sought to develop a navy comparable in size to those of the leading powers, while during the second phase they assumed a more realistic posture and endeavoured to match the naval strength of neighbouring rivals, especially the Greeks and Russians. As a consequence, they were first and foremost inter-

---

[54]Katip Çelebi, *Tuhfetü'l Kibar*, II, 250. For a discussion of this issue, see Palmira Brummett, "The Ottomans as a World Power: What We Don't Know about Ottoman Sea Power," *Oriente Moderno*, XX, No. 1 (2001), 1-21.

ested in preserving the maritime *status quo* and the concomitant balance of power in the eastern Mediterranean (obviously including the Black Sea).

We have already argued that the fact that its territory bordered a large swathe of the eastern Mediterranean sufficed to qualify the Ottoman Empire as a maritime power. Given their vast territories, the Ottomans were obliged to maintain regular traffic between Egypt, Syria and Istanbul, as well as between Istanbul and the various Black Sea ports, to ensure the adequate day-to-day provisioning of the huge population of the Empire's vast metropolis. In addition, there was coastal traffic and trade with the numerous Aegean islands. Furthermore, there was the riverborne traffic along the Danube and Nile, as well as the traffic on the less navigable Euphrates and Tigris. Last but not least, there were the myriad craft plying the hive of activity that was Istanbul's own harbour, situated on both sides of the Bosporus.

This sketch highlights the importance of navigation for the daily functioning of the Ottoman Empire. When it came to being a naval power, however, this constituted more of a dead weight than a springboard for the following reasons. First, the vessels used for the various tasks were not suitable for Mediterranean warfare. Second, even in situations of dire need, shifting resources from civilian to military use jeopardized the provisioning and daily life of the Empire. As a consequence, the navy had to maintain its own ships and personnel rather than draw upon the resources of the merchant marine. All attempts at naval power were limited by two factors: first, the availability of resources for shipbuilding and the fitting out and rigging of ships, and second, the ability to recruit skilled manpower for both their construction and sailing. In addition, in the course of time, as the technological gap between the Ottomans and European naval powers widened, the acquisition of foreign technology became more difficult and costly. Finally, during the nineteenth century, the Ottomans had to consider buying ships abroad while also maintaining a limited arsenal of their own that they sought to improve.

Conventional histories of Ottoman naval power insist that even during its heyday it was merely imitative of the Venetian navy and as such was doomed to fall behind once the rising Atlantic powers displaced Venice. There is thus a view that the Ottoman navy was somewhat backward to begin with. In our view, however, there is a more accurate alternative perspective on the state of the Ottoman navy during its heyday. The Ottoman navy, given its restricted reliance on the merchant marine, developed an ingeniously "flexible" organization. It incorporated into its structure the regional corsair fleets. These corsairs were not actually the pirates or sea bandits they are often made out to be. What they were allowed to do was well-defined within the customs and traditions of the Ottoman law of the sea. They could inflict damage on the enemy to finance their activities, maintain and renew their fleets and yet serve the Ottoman navy when called upon. In a sense, they were a second-best substitute to what the merchant marine normally did for the navy in countries like the

United Provinces. Only they were better, in the sense that they did not draw upon the resources of the merchant marine, and they kept their crews in a state of readiness for warfare that even regular drilling could not match. The Ottoman's "flexible navy" was a creative response to the realities they confronted. When the Ottomans made peace and extended capitulations to the French that safeguarded the latter's commercial navigation in Ottoman waters, they undermined the very process on which their classical maritime strength had been built. This they could afford to do because they must have foreseen that after the sixteenth century the Mediterranean was no longer to be the major arena for naval warfare. The relative decline of Ottoman naval power in the seventeenth and eighteenth century was largely due to the fact that it confronted no major threat in the Mediterranean. In a similar vein, when the threat reappeared with the arrival on the scene of the Russians, the Ottomans, a *reactive* maritime power, were forced to take up the challenge. At the end of the eighteenth century, the traditional maritime regime of the Mediterranean disintegrated in the wake of the French Revolution. There followed a massive increase in trade in general, and east-west trade in particular, accompanied by a "flourishing" of Greek and Barbary piracy. Yet with the Greek revolt around the corner and the Russians breaking the Ottoman monopoly over the Black Sea, the Ottoman Empire was in no position to harness and incorporate these new forces into the navy as it once had done. It had to search for a radical new solution within the constraints it faced. It needed to obtain new technology, which meant considerable expenditures that drained imperial finances and led to spiralling foreign debt.[55] A navy was needed to protect independence in the first place, yet this was an open invitation to dependency on foreign powers in order to finance it. Sailing out of this *cul-de-sac* in the course of the "long nineteenth century" proved much more difficult than sailing out of the Mediterranean during the "long sixteenth century."

---

[55]Kaori Komatsu, "Financial Problems of the Navy during the Reign of Abdülhamid II," *Oriente Moderno*, XX, No. 1 (2001), 209-219.

Maritime History in Israel

Ruthy Gertwagen

For a country whose entire western border touches the sea, Israel has a poorly developed maritime history. Ten years ago Haifa University established a research centre and department devoted exclusively to maritime studies. In the intervening years, however, it has focussed exclusively on the natural sciences – marine biology, oceanography and earth sciences – and coastal and underwater archaeology. History has been marginalized, and what history there has been for the most part has been limited to the ancient period. Another department in the same university that is concerned with shipping deals solely with the economic and other aspects of the contemporary industry. Nevertheless, there are historians, some of whom are well known in academic circles, who are working on maritime topics. As we shall see below, most of these historians pursue maritime history as part of a wider range of studies or as by-products of them.

In 1978 Zvi Herman, a non-academic but a prolific writer on maritime themes in Hebrew, wrote in the introduction to his popular *The Man and the Sea: From Ancient Caves to the Kingdom of the Sea* (Haifa, 1978) that he hoped the book would arouse interest in the sea and its problems, something that he felt was needed urgently in Israel. It is indicative of the state of Israeli maritime history that the publication of Herman's book did not spur any academic contributions to the field. Herman, however, has contributed a number of articles.[1] Hillel Yarkoni, formerly a captain in the Israeli national shipping company Zim, recently highlighted the lack of "maritime awareness" during the launch of his new book, *Seventy Years of Hebrew Seafaring* (Haifa, 2003, in Hebrew). He has also proposed the establishment of an archive devoted to the history of Israeli shipping that would bring together material held by different institutions.[2] While Yarkoni was referring to modern Israeli shipping, the same sorts of criticisms could also have been made about Jewish history since biblical times. In fact, Jews are not perceived by scholars as a maritime people, a point that was noted at a symposium entitled "Jews on Maritime

---

[1]For a list of Herman's publications, all in Hebrew, see M. Sas, N. Kashtan and S. Arenson, "Israel," in John B. Hattendorf (ed.), *Ubi Sumus: The State of Naval and Maritime History* (Newport, RI, 1994), 170, notes 10-13.

[2]Yarkoni's argument is cited in *Zim*, LXVIII (2003), 6.

Routes: Jews and Shipping throughout History" at Haifa University in 1997. The fact that this was the first, and so far the only, conference of its kind and that it attracted only eight participants summarizes the state of affairs eloquently.[3] The conference concluded that although there were still abundant historical data to be explored, the lacunae were equally apparent.

It is probable that one reason for the lack of maritime awareness in Israel, as well as the current negative scholarly perception of the relationship between Jews and the sea, is that the history of the Jewish nation has been mostly a story of exile since the second century CE, while Eretz-Israel has only existed as an independent state since 1948. But even in Antiquity the Jewish people played a relatively minor role in seafaring. Furthermore, despite the title of the above symposium, there was no Jewish commercial or naval shipping until the twentieth century. This has resulted in a relatively scanty Jewish maritime historiography.

Maritime Historiography and the Jews

Until the founding of Israel in 1948, the land that currently comprises the Jewish state was occupied by foreign political powers and empires except for two periods. The first was the Kingdoms of David and Solomon, and the Kingdom of Judea immediately afterwards, in the eleventh to the seventh centuries BCE. That epoch was marked by joint Phoenician-Israelite maritime ventures in which the actual seafaring was carried out by Phoenicians from Tyre, on the present Syrian-Lebanese coast. These matters are well recorded by the Bible (1 *Kings* 9:26-27, 10:11 and 10:22=2 *Chronicles* 8:18; 2 *Chronicles* 2:15; 1 *Kings* 22:49=2 *Chronicles* 20:36-37; and 2 *Chronicles* 20:15). The other period of independence was during the Maccabean era in the second century BCE when the Hasmonean rulers liberated their land from foreign domination, opened access to the sea and tried their hands at piracy. Maritime affairs also played a considerable role during Herod's time. His construction of Sebastos (*Caesarea Maritima*) during Roman rule, and its transformation into one of the largest ports and bases of the Mediterranean, was the culmination of an epoch.

To my knowledge there is only one scholarly monograph relating to ancient Jewish seafaring. Written by an Israeli-born academic – the late Raphael Patai – it was the first PhD awarded by the University of Jerusalem. After teaching at the same university, he left for the United States. Patai's book, *The Children of Noah, Jewish Seafaring in Ancient Times* (Princeton, 1998), pub-

---

[3]The papers were published as a special issue of the *Mediterranean Historical Review*, XV (2000) under the title, "Seafaring and the Jews." R. Stieglitz and N. Kashtan followed the source that initiated this conception for biblical Israel and the later periods; see, Kashtan, "Introduction," 1; Stieglitz, "Hebrew Seafaring in the Biblical Period," 5-6; and Kashtan, "Seafaring and Jews in Graeco-Roman Palestine: Realistic and Symbolic Dimensions," 10-11.

lished two years after his death, covers the period from Biblical to Talmudic times (700 BCE to 700 CE).[4] It is principally a translation, with minor updating, of the first Hebrew edition of the book that was published in Jerusalem in 1938 as *Jewish Seafaring: A Chapter in Ancient Hebrew Civilization.* The latter had itself been a by-product of Patai's PhD dissertation, which was published in book form in Hebrew as *Water: A Study of the Geography of the Land [of Israel] and of Israeli Folklore in the Biblical and Mishnah Periods* (Tel Aviv, 1936). Yet among the hundreds of articles and thirty-odd books produced by Patai, his two versions of *Jewish Seafaring* were the only ones that dealt with maritime affairs. Another work that relates to Jewish involvement in maritime affairs from the Biblical period until 1948 is by a non-academic: Shmuel Tolkowsky, one of the founding members of the Marine League of Israel. Tolkowsky goes almost straight from the times of the Second Temple to the Age of Discovery.[5] Sas has argued that the endeavour to strengthen the nautical inclination of the Jewish people during the British Mandate period (1918-1948) through the study and revival of old traditions resulted in works like Patai's and Tolkwosky's.[6] Patai's updated 1998 edition includes reference to the discovery of the famous 2000-year-old boat in the Sea of Galilee in the 1980s, but he refers to it merely as an archaeological find without discussing its historic significance for Jewish commerce and seafaring in the Sea of Galilee during the Roman period. Nor does Kashtan do so in his essay "Seafaring and Jews in Greco-Roman Palestine."[7] In fact, only the underwater archaeologist who excavated the boat has sought to link the discovery to Jewish maritime and trade activities in the area, basing his work on historical and archaeological sources, although he does this in a popular manner as part of a discussion of the excavation methods used and his own personal experiences and feelings during the excavation.[8]

---

[4]See review by R. Gertwagen, *The Northern Mariner/Le Marin du Nord*, IX, No. 3 (1999), 69-70.

[5]Shmuel Tolkowsky, *They Took to the Sea* (New York, 1964). Its Hebrew version was published in Tel Aviv in 1970.

[6]Sas, Kashtan and Arenson, "Israel," 170.

[7]In Kashtan (ed.), *Seafaring and the Jews*, 16-28.

[8]Shelley Wachsmann, *The Sea of Galilee Boat. An Extraordinary 2000 Year Old Discovery* (New York, 1995). Although written as a popular book it contains valuable information for scholars, mainly regarding archaeology but also on the history of the area in the Roman period. See the reviews by R. Gertwagen, *The Northern Mariner/Le Marin du Nord*, V, No. 2 (1995), 89-90; and R.J.O. Millar, *International Journal of Maritime History*, XII, No. 2 (December 2002), 31-33.

The Haifa "Jews and the Sea" symposium produced fresh information based on newly-acquired or reinterpreted historical data; updated Patai's and Tolkwosky's works; and filled, as we shall see later, some of the considerable gaps between the Roman era and the modern period. It is ironic, though, that the contribution on the biblical period was written by a Jewish scholar from the United States. At the conference two Israeli scholars discussed the Hellenic and Roman periods. One was Kashtan, a maritime historian of the ancient period who, in his essay, "Seafaring and Jews in Greco-Roman Palestine," argued that historic circumstances in those periods increased maritime activities, inspired by the Maccabeans, and more interestingly, by Herod.[9] Kashtan presumed, without putting forward any solid evidence, that Jewish families in the port towns along the coast of Roman *Palestina* were involved in fishing, port and naval works, local commerce and long-distance maritime trade. This explained their acquaintance with ship construction techniques and sea routes, although there is scant evidence of Jewish operators and shipowners. Kashtan felt that the maritime symbolism in Jewish writings and Jewish iconographic images of ships did not necessarily stand for real seafaring but represented, in an allusive manner, the deep cultural assimilation of maritime perceptions into Judaism. He argued that there was a decline in seafaring in the Mediterranean in the late Roman period and that both Romans and Jews began to perceive it negatively. This negative attitude towards maritime activity remained in the collective memory of later Judaism and was formalized in the Talmud. There is, however, a contrary view, argued by Zeev Safrai, a specialist in the social and economic life of Roman Palestine. Using Jewish evidence, he claimed that in the Roman period non-Jews controlled most international commerce in the large towns along the Palestinian coast.[10] In 1988 Daniel Sperber, an expert on the Talmud, published an important work that collected and interrelated all Palestinian and Rabbinic data pertaining to nautical matters not dealt with by Patai, and correlated them with contemporary literary, archaeological and

---

[9]Kashtan is the former director of the National Maritime Museum in Haifa. His publications include "Akko Ptolemais: A Maritime Metropolis in Hellenistic and Early Roman Times, 332 BCE-70 CE, as Seen through the Literary Sources," in I. Malkin and R.L. Hohlfelder (eds.), *Mediterranean Cities: Historical Perspectives* (London, 1986), 37-53; and (ed.), *The Maritime Holy Land, Mediterranean Civilizations in Ancient Israel from the Bronze Age to the Crusades/La Terra Santa e il Mare. Le Civiltà mediterranea nell'Antica Terra d'Israele dall'Eta del Bronzo alle Crociate* (Genoa, 1992).

[10]Z. Safrai, "Commerce in Eretz-Israel in the Roman Period," in B.Z. Kedar, Trude Dothan and Shmuel Safrai (eds.), *Commerce in Palestine throughout the Ages: Studies* (Jerusalem, 1990), 120-121 and 137-138 (in Hebrew).

other evidence.[11] Sperber claimed that during Roman rule the Talmud considered seafaring to be one of the lower and more dubious professions while trade was also perceived negatively.[12] In the framework of the 1997 symposium Sperber, who focused on the first four centuries of the Common Era, claimed he had come to realize in the decade after his *Nautica Talmudica* that the rabbinical sources gave a one-sided picture because the fragments of nautical information that had come down in the literature reflected a wider involvement than had hitherto been imagined.[13] The Jewish rebellion against Rome and the destruction of the Temple (69-70 CE) resulted in the devastation of agriculture and exile for most of the Jews; as a consequence, resistance to trade became an anachronism. In fact, the Mishnah and the Talmud of the third to fourth centuries CE testify to the existence of both Jewish shipowners' guilds and insurance.[14]

By the second century CE, the Jewish diaspora had spread throughout the Mediterranean coastal and port towns. A pioneering attempt to outline a longitudinal survey of Jewish involvement in international maritime trade, shipping, seafaring and ship ownership from the early Middle Ages to the Age of Discovery in the Atlantic and the Indian Ocean was published in 2000 by Sara Arenson. Her conclusions, based as they were on sparse published information, lack foundation and demonstrate that maritime history cannot be detached from other aspects of history, including the relationship between Jews and the host societies within which they lived. These have to be studied using a wide range of archives and in collaboration with experts in various fields. Her ideas regarding Jewish involvement in maritime affairs from the early Medieval period to the tenth century CE, based on Byzantine and Western documents, are essentially guesses and speculation. More informative, albeit referring to two converted Jews, is an essay by the late Yaron Dan, "Two Jewish Merchants in the Seventh Century," *Zion*, XXXVI (1971), 26-31 (in Hebrew). Furthermore, Arenson did not distinguish clearly between Jewish-owned ship-

---

[11]Daniel Sperber, *Nautica Talmudica* (Leiden, 1986).

[12]For the negative attitude to trade in general and particularly to maritime trade, see Z. Safrai, "Regarding the Question of the Integration of the Jewish Nation in the Roman Economy," in A. Kashar, G. Fuks and U. Rappaport (eds.), *Greece and Rome in Eretz-Israel: Collected Essays* (Jerusalem, 1989, in Hebrew), 143-173.

[13]D. Sperber, "*Nautica* in Talmudic Palestine," in Kashtan (ed.), *Seafaring and the Jews*, 29-32.

[14]Sperber, *Nautica Talmudica*, 103-104.

ping and Jewish participation in maritime trade.[15] Using the same documents
that Arenson employed, while adding others and considering additional factors,
Kenneth Stow, a prominent expert on medieval European Jewish studies, has
argued that conclusions in favour of an important "European" Jewish role in
international trade in Western Europe and in seafaring in Southern Europe in
the ninth and tenth centuries are unwarranted.[16] Benjamin Arbel has argued
convincingly that in spite of Jewish involvement in international trade, their
subordinate status within the Medieval societies that tolerated their presence
prohibited them from owning ships or serving as captains. In other words,
there were social, political, religious and economic factors which combined to
exclude Jews from these occupations.[17]

The study of Jewish involvement in maritime affairs in the early Medieval Muslim world and in the Mediterranean in the late Middle Ages was
initiated in Israel by a distinguished and world famous scholar of the Hebrew
University of Jerusalem, the late Eliyahu Ashtor, as part of his research on the
socio-economic conditions, culture and internal organization of the Jews in the
Muslim and Christian worlds. Such studies fit within his larger research
agenda on international trade in both basins of the Mediterranean throughout
the entire Middle Ages. He used Arabic and European sources as well as Hebrew and Judeo-Arabic documents from the Cairo Geniza.[18] Regarding the
early Medieval Muslim world Ashtor, as well as Moshe Gil, dealt with the
Râdhânite Jews, or *radhaniyya*, first mentioned in the famous description made

---

[15]S. Arenson, "Medieval Jewish Seafaring," in Kashtan (ed.), *Seafaring and
the Jews*, 26-46.

[16]Kenneth R. Stow, "By Land or By Sea: The Passage of the Kalonymides to
the Rhineland in the Tenth Century," in S. Menache (ed.), *Communication in the Jewish Diaspora* (Leiden, 1996), 59-72.

[17]Benjamin Arbel, *Trading Nations, Jews and Venetians in the Early Modern
Eastern Mediterranean* (Leiden, 1995), 169-175, dedicated a chapter to this subject in a
book that relates to a later period. He referred to this again in "Shipping and Tolera-
tion: The Emergence of Jewish Ship Owners in the Early Modern Period," in Kashtan
(ed.), *Seafaring and the Jews* 56-60. I shall return to Arbel's two publications later.

[18]A detailed list of Ashtor's publication from 1933 to 1988 is available in
B.Z. Kedar and A.L. Udovitch (eds.), *The Medieval Levant: Studies in Memory of
Eliyahu Ashtor (1914-1984)*, a special issue of *Asian and African Studies*, XXII,
(1988), 11-33. The wide range of topics on the medieval period that Ashtor was involved with are discussed by Benjamin Z. Kedar, "In Memoriam: Eliyahu Ashtor,
1914-1984," *Asian and African Studies*, XIX (1985), 119-121.

by the Abbasid postmaster Ibn Khordadhbeh at the end of the ninth century.[19] These Jews traded between the Mediterranean, Red Sea and Indian Ocean. Ashtor also contributed to the controversies regarding the origin of the Râdhânite Jews and their itineraries and importance for the refutation of the Pirenne thesis regarding the beginning of the Dark Ages. Yet as Arenson rightly noted, neither Ashtor nor Gil distinguished between commercial activities and seafaring when referring to the Râdhânite Jews. Nevertheless, Arenson's assertion that these people possessed ships in both the Indian Ocean and the Mediterranean remains a speculation without documentary evidence to support it.[20] Still, one can safely argue that in contrast to early feudal Europe, the Jews in the Muslim world played a central role in international trade in the early Middle Ages and later.

The discovery in the late nineteenth century in a synagogue in Fustat, near Cairo, of the important corpus of Jewish documentation known as the Geniza Letters has shed light on various aspects of Jewish life in the Muslim world from the late tenth to the late thirteenth century. There is an abundance of documentation regarding Jewish involvement in a prosperous international commerce that involved maritime trade and shipping. But in contrast to the Indian Ocean, Jews in the Mediterranean were seldom sailors or shipowners.[21] Only a small part of the archive is in Israel, with most of it spread throughout Europe, Russia and the United States. Only two Israeli scholars, Moshe Gil and Menahem Ben-Sasson, have worked on the Geniza Letters, collecting, editing and translating a great portion into Hebrew. The emphasis, however, is on economic, communal and cultural life, and the juridical status of Jews in the Islamic world, and less on maritime affairs and seaborne trade. The same could be said about Gil's two introductions to the edited and translated documents. The contributions by Gil and Ben Sasson were entitled *Palestine during the First Muslim Period*, *The Jews of Sicily 825-1068* and *In the Kingdom of Ishmael*, respectively.[22] Although published in Hebrew, these volumes, as well

---

[19]M. Gil, "The Râdhânite merchants and the Land of Râdhân," *Asian and African Studies*, XVII (1974), 299-328; and Gil, *In the Kingdom of Ismael* (4 vols., Tel Aviv, 1997, in Hebrew).

[20]Arenson, "Medieval Jewish Seafaring," 36.

[21]S.D. Goiten, *A Mediterranean Society: The Jewish Community of the Arab World as Portrayed in the Documents of the Cairo Geniza* (5 vols., Berkeley, 1967-1988), I, 11-12 and 17-21, provides a general discussion of the Geniza records, including Jewish maritime affairs; regarding the rarity of Jewish ownership, see I, 311.

[22]M. Gil, *Palestine during the First Muslim Period (634-1099)* (3 vols., Tel Aviv, 1983, in Hebrew); M. Ben Sasson, *The Jews of Sicily 825-1068: Documents and Sources* (Jerusalem, 1991, in Hebrew); and Gil, *In the Kingdom of Ishmael*.

as other Geniza documents, have rarely been used by Israeli scholars to produce general studies on Medieval maritime affairs. Ruthy Gertwagen has used
them to shed new light on the trade routes between Egypt and Sicily in the
eleventh and twelfth centuries.[23] Hassan Khalilieh, whose expertise is in early
Medieval Islamic maritime legal history, has used the Geniza Letters to study
the legal rulings by Muslim jurists on salvage in the same time period and has
compared them to the Rhodian Sea Law and the maritime laws of Roman
Europe.[24]

The exploitation of the Geniza archive by Israeli scholars with specific
reference to the Jewish relationship with the sea is also relatively scant. Ashtor
pointed to the extensive involvement of Jews in seaborne trade between Sicily
and Egypt but noted that there were no Jewish shipowners. Instead, the owners
came from the Muslim ruling class – emirs, sheiks, cadis and their consorts.[25]
Gil's essay on the Jews in Sicily deals with their legal position and their economic and mercantile activity, including maritime trade along the Sicily-North
Africa-Egypt axis.[26] The continuous exploitation of the Geniza Letters has produced fresh evidence to further support the above-mentioned arguments. Uda
Zabiah, who has studied the Geniza correspondence of Abraham Ibn Farah
(1053-1057), claims that there were no Jews among the twenty-seven shipowners mentioned. Instead, they used ships belonging to Muslims and Christians.
Uda also argues that Jews were not acquainted with seamanship.[27] Nadia
Zeldes and Miriam Frenkel, who used Geniza Letters and the Halachic Re-
sponsa of Maimonides from the eleventh to the thirteenth centuries to study
Jewish maritime trade between Sicily, Egypt and North Africa, claim that the
names of the captains and shipowners they have encountered sailing along

---

[23]R. Gertwagen, "Geniza Letters: Maritime Difficulties along the Alexandria-
Palermo Route," in Menache (ed.), *Communication*, 73-92.

[24]Hassan S. Khalilieh, "Salvage in the Eleventh and Twelfth-Century Mediterranean: Geniza Evidence and its Legal Implications," in Kashtan (ed.), *Seafaring
and the Jews*, 47-55.

[25]E. Ashtor, "Gli Ebrei nel commercio mediterraneo nell'alto medioevo," in
Ashton, *The Jews and the Mediterranean Economy* (London, 1983).

[26]Moshe Gil, "The Jews in Sicily under Muslim Rule, in the Light of the
Geniza Documents," *Italia Judaica* (1981), 87-112.

[27]U. Zabiah, "A Lexicon of the Ships and of the Ships Owners in Abraham
Ibn Farah's archive in the Cairo Geniza," in E. Fleischer, M.A. Friedman and J.L.
Kraemer (eds.), *Masaat Moshe. Essays on the Culture of Israel and the Arav Dedicated
to Moshe Gil* (Jerusalem, 1998), 286-296 (in Hebrew). A different argument is put
forward by Arenson, "Medieval Jewish Seafaring," 45 and notes 51-52, who used
Goitein incorrectly and ignored Zabiah.

these routes were without exception Muslims or people native to Muslim countries, including Christians. The Jews merely travelled as passengers. Furthermore, both scholars argue convincingly that the activity of Jewish merchants never ceased completely, even in the later Middle Ages, and that they maintained regular connections between Sicily, Egypt and North Africa. This evidence refutes the hitherto accepted notion that Jewish trade ended as a consequence of political upheavals in the eastern Mediterranean and the rise of the Italian maritime republics from the late tenth century.[28]

The evidence put forward by Zeldes and Frenkel supports Ashtor's conclusions along the same lines concerning the fifteenth century.[29] Ashtor, however, used Christian notarial deeds and other documents in the archives of Sicily, the Italian mainland – including Venice, Crete and the Near East – to show that during that period Jewish traders had a considerable share of the seaborne trade in both basins of the Mediterranean and in its central part between Sicily, Malta and North Africa. The documents prove that in these years there was no maritime route on which Jewish traders were inactive. Ashtor further emphasized that these Jews were not descendents of families native to Egypt or Syria, such as those encountered in the Geniza Letters, but rather Jews from Christian countries such as Crete, Italy and Catalonia. They participated actively or made commercial loans to merchants going abroad. The Jews from Sicily and Apulia had more opportunities than those from Venice, which did not allow its Jews to participate in the luxury trade in spices from the Levantine ports. In 1474, the Jewish community of Trapani in western Sicily, which was active on all routes of the town's seaborne commerce, obtained from the king confirmation of its right to engage in these trades and to move freely on the sea. For their trade they chartered entire ships or parts of them.[30]

---

[28]Nadia Zeldes and Miriam Frenkel, "The Sicilian Trade. Jewish Merchants in the Mediterranean in the Twelfth and Thirteenth Centuries," in *Michael: A Collection for the History of the Jews in the Diaspora*, XIV (1997), 88-137 (in Hebrew). The English version of the article, without the attached documents, was published in Nicolò Bucaria (ed.), *Gli Ebrei in Sicilia dal tardoantico al medioevo. Studi in onore di Mons. Benedetto Rocco, a cura di Nicolò Bucaria* (Palermo, 1998), 243-256; Many of Zeldes's and Frenkel's arguments contradict Arenson's, who neglected their essay: Arenson, "Medieval Jewish Seafaring," 38-40, 45 and notes 49-53. Both Zeldes and Frenkel dealt with this subject as part of their participation in the "Oriens Judaicus" project at the Insititute of Yad Izhac Ben-Zvi in Jerusalem. Both were research assistants in the compilation of Ben-Sasson, *Jews of Sicily*.

[29]Ashtor, "The Jews in the Mediterranean Trade in the Fifteenth Century," in Ashtor, *Jews and the Mediterranean Economy*, 441.

[30]*Ibid.*, 441-454; Ashtor, "New Data for the History of Levantine Jewries in the Fifteenth Century," in *ibid.*; and Ashtor, "The Jews of Trapani in the Later Middle Ages," *Studi Medievali*, XXV (1984), 1-30.

Another distinguished scholar who has worked on the Medieval Mediterranean, with particular reference to its eastern basin and the Jewish relationship with maritime trade in the later Middle Ages, is David Jacoby of the Hebrew University of Jerusalem. Although retired, Jacoby is still a prolific writer. While he has not dedicated a specific study to the relationship of the Jews with the sea, he has referred to it when dealing with the socio-economic status of Jews in Byzantine Constantinople prior to the Fourth Crusade, as well as in Venice and its colonies. Regarding the Jews of Venice, Jacoby added to the information already supplied by Ashtor. The status of the Jews in Venice's Aegean colonies and in the outposts in Crusader Levant and Constantinople was much higher than in Venice itself, where they were barred from legal residence until the early sixteenth century, although a number already lived in Venice permanently from the fifteenth century. From the late fourteenth century onwards, Jews in the Venetian colonies and the outposts of the eastern Mediterranean were not allowed to ship their wares or capital on state galleys; consequently, their participation in the trade in precious goods, especially spices, the most lucrative branch of long-distance maritime commerce, was severely reduced. This reinforced the Jews' orientation towards money lending, which to some extent stimulated economic activity, including manufacturing – hides, silk and furs – and commerce. Their condition was best in Venetian Crete where they were able to participate in maritime trade via loans to non-Jewish merchants. Together they bought small boats to trade with the Greek mainland or the Aegean islands, although the Jewish shares in the boats were quite modest. Furthermore, the Jews had their own typical commercial products, such as *kasher* cheese and wine and barrels, which they exported to all the Jewish communities in the eastern Mediterranean, Venice and the *Terra Ferma*. As Jacoby has shown, further research based on published, but particularly unpublished, sources, including Jewish documents, may enable us to some degree to fill in the substantial chronological and geographic gaps in our present knowledge.[31]

Jewish involvement in various aspects of maritime trade in the early modern period has been tackled by three Israeli scholars. Minna Rozen has discussed it within the context of Jewish economic life in the Mediterranean from their expulsion from Spain in 1492 until the end of the eighteenth century. She has also dealt with the participation of the Jews of Salonica in Medi-

---

[31]David Jacoby, "Venice and the Venetian Jews in the Eastern Mediterranean," in Jacoby, *Studies on the Crusader States and on Venetian Expansion* (Northampton, 1989). Many of Jacoby's essays dealing with Jews can be found in a volume of his collected studies entitled *Recherche sur la Méditerranée orientals du XIIe au XIVe siècle* (London, 1979). See also Jacoby, "Les quartiers juifs de Constantinople à l'époque Byzantine," *Byzantion*, XXXVII (1967), 189-216; and Jacoby, "On the Status of the Jews in the Venetian Colonies in the Middle Ages," *Zion*, XXVIII (1963), 59-64 (in Hebrew).

terranean maritime commerce during the first half of the eighteenth century.[32] The aforementioned Benjamin Arbel, whose expertise centres on the early modern Venetian maritime empire, especially Cyprus, has discussed the involvement of Venetian Jews in sixteenth-century international trade in *Trading Nations: Jews and Venetians in the Early Modern Eastern Mediterranean*, which was based largely on the Venetian archives.[33] Like Rozen, Arbel pointed to the centrality of Jews in international trade in this period. Important evidence for their improved status after the Middle Ages was demonstrated by the opening of a central sphere of economic activity – the ownership of vessels. Arbel, who had already discussed this subject in his book, subsequently gave it a more exhaustive treatment in a separate essay which broadened the spatial limits of his study from the Mediterranean to various parts of Europe and the New World and extended the chronological parameters to the centuries between the Renaissance and the French Revolution. Discussing the meaning of ownership and its implications, Arbel argued that a radical change in this sphere occurred from the Middle Ages onward as part of a shift in the legal status of Jews in the societies in which they lived that began in the eastern Mediterranean and the Ottoman Empire in the 1520s and reached Venice in the seventeenth century. Arbel also claimed that one of the prerequisites for this shift had been a change in the attitude of Jewish entrepreneurs who began to regard shipping as a legitimate economic activity. The spread of this phenomenon to the Western Hemisphere during the early modern period indicates the relative tolerance which characterized the countries concerned, as well as a process of secularization among the Jews engaged in this field of endeavour.[34] Arbel's essay showed that rich opportunities in this field still await exploration. But the Jewish shipping activity that took place in the diaspora did not mean the establishment of commercial fleets.

Another aspect of maritime trade is piracy. A. Bashan has discussed this as part of his general study on *Captivity and Ransom in Jewish Society in*

---

[32]M. Rozen, "La vie économique des Juifs du basin Méditeranéen de l'expulsion d'Espagne (1492) à la fin du XVIII siècle," in S. Trigano (ed.), *La société juive à travers l'histoire. Vol. 3 : Le passage d'Israel* (Paris, 1993); and Rozen, "Contest and Rivalry in Mediterranean Maritime Commerce in the First Half of the Eighteenth Century: The Jews of Salonika and the European Presence," *Revue des Etudes Juives*, CXLVII (1988); On Rozen's main fields of activity, which are not necessarily maritime, see Kashtan (ed.), *Seafaring and the Jews*, 103.

[33]Benjamin Arbel, *Cyprus, the Franks and Venice, 13th-16th Centuries: Collected Studies* (Aldershot, 2000). Only one of the essays, however, deals with maritime affairs.

[34]Arbel, *Trading Nations*, 169-184; and Arbel, "Emergence of Jewish Shipowners," 60-67.

Mediterranean Countries (1391-1830) (Ramat Gan, 1980, in Hebrew). Jews became captives because of either piracy at sea or piratical raids on the coasts. Bashan also discussed the involvement of Jews in trade with the pirates and in the redemption of Jewish and, less frequently, Christian captives. Whenever Jews took an active part in piracy it was after they had became Moslems, and they acted mainly against the Christians.

Fishing is another calling associated with the sea. Minna Rozen has discussed Jewish involvement in this field, as well as in short-haul shipping in Istanbul as reflected in newly unearthed Ottoman documents from Mahmut II's reign and the registers of the rabbinical court of Istanbul from 1833 to 1923. These documents contain information about the Jewish centres of activity, the organization of guilds of boatmen and fishermen, the social welfare system, family life, places of residence and social and economic status.[35]

In the twentieth century up to the founding of the state of Israel in 1948 there was some activity by a Jewish merchant navy in Eretz-Israel, or Palestine, as it was then called under the British Mandate. This activity was initiated in the 1930s by Jewish seamen who had emigrated from Germany in 1933. It included the founding of independent shipping companies and culminated in the establishment of Zim, the national shipping company which replaced them in 1947. This period was the subject of the paper given by Daniela Ran at the "Jews on Maritime Routes" conference entitled "The Contribution of German Jewish Immigrants to Maritime Development in Israel," and published in Kashtan (ed.), *Seafaring and the Jews*, 94-101. This period is also covered in the book by Yarkoni, which looks at a seventy-year period, including the fifty-five years since the establishment of Israel. The creation of an Israeli navy and its role in the War of Independence, when the newly-created state was struggling for its survival, has yet to be recounted in detail.[36]

The Historiography on Maritime Activity in Palestine

Little attention has been given to the maritime aspects of the land of Israel and its coast prior to the establishment of the Israeli state. Maritime activity along its coast is almost completely ignored, while its role in Mediterranean commerce suffers from vast lacunae. This is evident in a volume dedicated to *Commerce in Palestine throughout the Ages: Studies*, edited by B.Z. Kedar, Trude Dothan and Shmuel Safrai (Jerusalem, 1990, in Hebrew). The book, which covered the period from the early Bronze Age (late fourth millennium BCE) until the nineteenth century CE, contained eighteen essays, sixteen of

---

[35] Rozen, "Boatmen and Fishermen's Guilds in Nineteenth-Century Istanbul," in Kashtan (ed.), *Seafaring and the Jews*, 72-89.

[36] What exists is very limited; Sas, Kashtan and Arenson, "Israel," 170 and note 6.

which were written by Israeli scholars. Reference to the role of Palestine and its ports and harbours in the Mediterranean trade system was quite marginal in most of the essays dealing with the period prior to the late Middle Ages. In his essay "Economic Life in Eretz-Israel in the Byzantine Period (the Fifth to the Seventh Century)" (181-195), Yaron Dan made almost no reference to maritime trade.[37] The essays in the collection which deal with the Hellenistic and Roman periods that refer to archaeological objects as proof of the presence of international commerce ignore the excavations carried out in the port towns along the coast. Indeed, there is just one essay that relates specifically to harbours along the Israeli coastline: R. Kark, "The Change in the Status of the Coast Towns in the Nineteenth Century" (324-335). In her essay Kark, who is an historical geographer, dealt with the effects of geopolitical and commercial factors in the eastern Mediterranean on the demography, economy and urban layout of these towns. One would have expected, however, that Amnon Cohen's article, "The Commerce of Eretz-Israel in the Ottoman Period" (300-308), would have dealt with the consequences of the coming of steam as a consideration in the foundation of Haifa as a harbour for Acre.

The Crusader period was deliberately not included in this volume due to the existence of a number of publications which at that time were considered to be exhaustive in their treatment of the subject. One such scholar was the late Joshua Prawer, who wrote *The Crusaders: A Profile of a Colonial Society* (Jerusalem, 1975), 460-493 (in Hebrew); and "The Italians in the Latin Kingdom," in Prawer, *Crusader Institutions* (Oxford, 1980), 217-249. Both of Prawer's publications referred to the socio-economic, religious and military aspects of the Crusader conquest of Palestine and to the kingdom they established there in the twelfth and thirteenth centuries. A second scholar in this category is Eliyahu Ashtor, especially in his "The Crusader Kingdom and the Levant Trade," in B.Z. Kedar (ed.), *The Crusaders in Their Kingdom, 1099-1291* (Jerusalem, 1987), 30-54 (in Hebrew). The same author has an essay in the above-mentioned *Commerce in Palestine throughout the Ages* entitled "European Trade in Eretz-Israel in the Late Middle Ages," 280-209 (originally published in German in 1982). At that time Palestine formed part of Mameluke Egypt. Medieval Palestine's involvement in international trade during that period was also treated in his other essays dealing with the whole of the Medieval Levant, collected in two volumes. One is *Studies on the Levantine Trade in the Middle Ages* (London, 1978), while the other was edited after Ashtor's death by B.Z. Kedar and published under the title *East West Trade in the Medieval Mediterranean* (London, 1986). Ashtor's pioneering work related to various aspects of international trade in both the Christian and the Muslim

---

[37] Yet in his book *The City in Eretz-Israel during the Late Roman and Byzantine Periods* (Jerusalem, 1984), 184-199 (in Hebrew), Dan did make reference to seaborne commerce.

parts of the Mediterranean, based on Western European archives and Muslim documents. The studies culminated in his important work, *Levant Trade in the Later Middle Ages* (Princeton, 1983).

Another scholar who has studied Crusader Palestine's involvement in international commerce is David Jacoby, to whom reference was made earlier. Using Venetian archives and focussing on the Crusader period, he has published "A Venetian Manual of Commercial Practice from Crusader Acre," in Gabriella Airaldi and B.Z. Kedar (eds.), *I Comuni italiani nel regno crociato di Gerusalemme* (Genoa, 1986), 403-428; "The Venetian Privileges in the Latin Kingdom of Jerusalem: Twelfth and Thirteenth-Century Interpretations and Implementation," in B.Z. Kedar, J. Riley-Smith and R. Hiestand (eds.), *Montjoie. Studies in Crusader History in Honour of Hans Eberhard Mayer* (Aldershot, 1997), 155-175. Jacoby, who dealt with the role of the Medieval port town of Acre in maritime commerce as well as the urban layout of the Crusader town and its port, was a pioneer in the study of the history of ports using both history and archaeology.[38]

In Israel the study of ports and harbours up to the Middle Ages is considered to be the domain of archaeologists. More often than not, there is little communication between historians and archaeologists. The latter study the sites in isolation and use historic documentation only to support their findings. Indeed, they often consider their finds as *the* historic reality, even if their interpretation does not correspond to historical evidence. Due to the politics of fundraising and the need to justify continuing their research, archaeologists sometimes invent ports in places where they simply did not exist, while appearing unwilling to admit previous errors. Nevertheless, historians like Jacoby seem all too willing to rely on the often questionable data provided by archaeologists. Lacking the technical skills to verify the information, historians tend to interpret documents in a manner that concurs with the archaeological data.[39] Jacoby was followed by Gertwagen, who used a multi-disciplinary approach which involved history, archaeology, oceanography and marine engineering, and displayed a more accurate picture of the medieval port of Acre in "The Crusader Port of Acre: Layout and Problems of Maintenance," in M. Balard (ed.), *Autour de la Première Croisade* (Paris, 1966), 553-582. Despite

---

[38]David Jacoby, "Crusader Acre in the Thirteenth Century: Urban Layout," *Studi Medievali,* Third series, XX (1979), 1-45; Jacoby, "Venetian Anchors for Crusader Acre," *Mariner's Mirror*, VII (1985), 5-12; and Jacoby, "The Trade of Crusader Acre in the Levantine Context: An Overview," *Archivio Storico del Sannio*, New series, III (1998), 103-120.

[39]R. Gertwagen, "The Concept of Ports in the Medieval Eastern Mediterranean: Construction and Maintenance on Crete to the End of the Fifteenth Century," *International Journal of Maritime History*, XII, No. 1 (June 2000), 179-180. The reference is to Medieval ports, but it is also applicable to the earlier period.

its title, the essay deals with the early Muslim period as well. Employing identical methodology, Gertwagen also dealt with *Caesarea* in "Crusader *Caesarea* from a Port Town to A Coastal Town," in Bella S. Gallil and Y. Mart (eds.), *The Mediterranean Continental Margin of Israel* (Haifa, 1991), 8-14, and with the entire Israeli coastline in "The Israeli Shoreline during the Medieval Period (6th to 13th Centuries) – A Coast without Ports," *Revue Méditerranée* (2004, in press). There is an important and comprehensive essay on the Palestinian coast in the early Muslim period by Amikam Elad, entitled "The Coastal Towns of Eretz-Israel in the Arabic Period (640-1099 CE) according to Arabic Documents," *Kathedra*, V (1982), 156-178 (in Hebrew). Elad has also published essays on two coastal towns in the same period: "Arsuf in the Early Arabic Period," in I. Roll and E. Ayalon (eds.), *Appolonia and the Southern Sharon. A Model of a Coastal Town and Its Hinterland* (Tel Aviv, 1989), 289-301 (in Hebrew); and "Comments on Haifa in the Arabic Period," in B. Oded (ed.), *Studies on the History of Israel-Nation and on Eretz Israel* (Haifa, 1990), 189-203 (in Hebrew). Such studies would be a desideratum for the later periods.[40]

Scholarly Publications on General Themes in Maritime History

In contrast to the limited number of studies on the relationship of Jews with the sea and about the Palestinian coastline, there are a considerable number of works on maritime aspects of other countries or on general maritime subjects by Israeli scholars, although these centre mostly on the Medieval and early modern periods. In addition to Ashtor, Jacoby has also been at the forefront in this field, dealing with the whole eastern Mediterranean from the tenth to the fifteenth century CE. His many important studies relating to various aspects involving seafaring have been collected in a number of volumes. In addition to the one mentioned above, there are two others: *Trade, Commodities and Shipping in the Medieval Mediterranean* (Aldershot, 1997), and *Byzantium, Latin Romania and the Mediterranean* (Aldershot, 2001); Regarding maritime powers, there are two publications by Benjamin Z. Kedar: *Merchants in Crisis: Genoese and Venetian Men of Affairs and the Fourteenth-Century Depression* (New Haven, CT, 1977); and "Mercanti genovesi in Allessandria d'Egitto negli anni sessanta del secolo XI," in Kedar, *The Franks in the Levant, 11th to 14th Centuries* (Aldershot, 1992). Sara Arenson has published an essay on Venice and its colonies entitled "Food for a Maritime Empire: Venice and Its Bases in the Middle Ages," in K. Friedland (ed.), *Maritime Food Transport*

---

[40]There only two studies relating to Jaffa. See R. Kark, *Jaffa: A City in Evolution, 1799-1917* (Jerusalem, 1990); and Kark, "The Development of the Cities of Jerusalem and Jaffa from 1840 up to the First World War. A Study in Geographic History" (Unpublished PhD thesis, Jerusalem, 1976, in Hebrew).

(Cologne, 1994), 177-185. Ruth Gertwagen has also published two essays on Venice and its colonies: "The Port of Modon in the Venetian Commercial System of Foodstuff, 1358-1500," in the Friedland volume cited above, 187-198; and "The Venetian Colonies in the Ionian and Aegean Seas in Venetian Defence Policy in the Fifteenth Century," *Journal of Mediterranean Studies*, XII, No. 2 (2002), 351-384. Arbel has written on "Creta nel commercio mediterraneao del cinquecento," in G. Ortalli (ed.), *Venezia e Creta* (Venice, 1998), 245-260; Another important scholar who has dealt with Muslim navies is Yaacov Lev, whose output includes "Fatimid Navy, Byzantium and the Mediterranean Sea C.E. 909-1036/297-427," *Byzantion*, LIV (1984), 220-252; "The Fatimid Army and Navy, and the Crusades," in Lev, *State and Society in Fatimid Egypt* (Leiden, 1991), 93-121; and "The Navy," in Lev, *Saladin in Egypt* (Leiden, 1999), 161-175.

General themes that have been studied include the history of maritime law in the early Muslim period compared to the Byzantine in Hassan S. Khalilieh, *Islamic Maritime Law: An Introduction* (Leiden, 1998), and *"Testimonium*: The Legal Opinion of Maliki Jurists Regarding Andalusian Muslim Pilgrims Travelling by Sea during the Eleventh and Twelfth Centuries CE," *Mediterranean Historical Review*, XIV, No. 1 (1999), 59-73.[41] Sara Arenson has published *The Encircled Sea* (London, 1990), a companion volume to the ten-part television series aired on Channel Four in the UK. The book deals with the culture and civilizations on the shores of the Mediterranean that have shaped the history of mankind from prehistoric times. The author employs a multi-disciplinary approach using the most recent publications available at the time in history, marine sciences, archaeology, social anthropology, marine engineering and geophysics to demonstrate the unique contribution the Mediterranean has made to modern civilization. Arenson has also published a popular essay on navigation based on previously published studies called "Navigation and Exploration in the Medieval World," in E.E. Rice (ed.), *The Sea and History* (Stroud, 1996), 97-110, while B. Arbel has written on "Life on Board Venetian Ships according to Renaissance Travel Accounts and Diaries," *Graeco Arabica*, VIII (2004, in press).

Another theme is ports and port towns. Arbel has published on the urban layout of Cypriot port towns from the twelfth to the sixteenth centuries and on travellers' literature about Levantine port towns in the sixteenth century.[42] Gertwagen's publications on this subject are of a more "technical" nature, including urban architecture and marine engineering, and are based on archive material; they also relate to other Mediterranean ports. Of particular

---

[41]See the review of the former by R. Pennel, *International Journal of Maritime History*, XII, No. 2 (December 2002), 240-242.

[42]Reprinted in Arbel, *Cyprus, the Franks and Venice*.

relevance are "The Venetian Port of Candia, Crete (1299-1363); Construction and Maintenance," in I. Malkin and R.L. Hohlfelder (eds.), *Mediterranean Cities: Historical Perspectives* (London, 1988), 141-158; and "The Venetian Sea Bases at the Western End of the Silk Routes – Technical Aspects (14th-16th Centuries CE)," in L. de Albourquerque and M. de Ruvio (eds.), *Portas Maritimas e Redes Associadeas* (*Maritime Routes and Associated Networks*), (Lisbon, 1992), 1-18. Other essays by Gertwagen are wider in scope and also refer to maritime trade, naval activities and navigational routes; these include "Maritime Activity Concerning the Ports and Harbours of Cyprus from the 12th to the Late 16th Centuries," in N. Coureas and J. Riley-Smith (eds.), *Cyprus and the Crusades* (Nicosia, 1995), 511-538; "L' isola di Creta e i suoi porti (dalla fine del XII secolo alla fine del XV secolo)," in Ortalli (ed.), *Creta e Venezia*, 337-365; "Venetian Modon and its Port (1358-1500)," in A. Cowan (ed.), *The Mediterranean Urban Culture* (Exeter, 2000), 125-148 and 248-254; "The Concept of Medieval Ports," *International Journal of Maritime History*, XII, No. 1 (June 2000), 63-133 (this also includes a methodological introduction to the topic); "Does Naval Activity – Military and Commercial – Need Artificial Ports? The Case of Venetian Harbours and Ports in the Ionian and Aegean until 1500," *Graeco-Arabica*, IX (2004, in press); and "Harbours, Ports and Facilities along the Sea Lanes to the Holy Land," in J. Pryor (ed.), *How they Made War in the Age of the Crusades* (2004, in press).

Another subject dealt with by Israeli scholars is piracy. These works include A. Levinson, "The Barbary Pirates and the First American Navy," *Keshet*, IV (1976), 157-167 (in Hebrew); N. Zeldes "*Testimonium Ad Pirati-cum Exercendum*: Two 'Piratical' Contracts from Early Sixteenth-Century Sicily," *Mediterranean Historical Review*, XV, No. 2 (2000), 111-116; Zeldes, "A Trap on the High Seas: Sicily and the Depredation of *Converso* Jews on Their Way from the Iberian Peninsula to the Ottoman Empire in the Fifteenth and Sixteenth Centuries," in Levinson, *The Jews of the Ottoman Empire: Culture and Society, Collected Essays* (Bar-Ilan, 2004, in press, in Hebrew); and R. Gertwagen and A. Zemer (eds.), *Pirates, The Skull and Crossbones* (Haifa, 2002), which includes essays by Gertwagen on "Piracy in the Middle Ages (7th-16th Centuries)," 25-29 (in Hebrew) and 234-238 (in English); "Pirate and Regular Vessels in the Mediterranean – Characteristics, Weaponry and Battle Tactics (8th Century BCE-16th Century CE)," 69-80 (in Hebrew) and 160-176 (in English), which includes the evolution of ships and weapons; "Life among the Pirates," 91-98 (in Hebrew) and 154-158 (in English); and "Pirates – Facts and Fiction," 99-103 (in Hebrew) and 148-152 (in English, with E. Blechman and S. Nudel). Gertwagen also wrote an essay on Medieval ships entitled "Characteristics of Mediterranean Ships in the Late Medival Period (13th-15th Centuries CE)," in Xavier Barral i Altet and Joan Alemany (eds.), *Splendour of the Medieval Mediterranean. Culture, Politics, Navigation and Commerce in the Mediterranean Maritime Cities (13th-15th*

Centuries) (Barcelona, 2004), 543-561. Finally, Shavit Yaacov has recently published *A Mediterranean Anthology* (Tel Aviv, 2004, in Hebrew) using historic and geographic texts, *belles lettres*, travellers' accounts and the cultural and philosophical ideas of philosophers and writers since the late eighteenth century that have defined the Meditteranean as a geo-cultural unit distinct from other areas. The texts also demonstrate the unified character of the Mediterranean and its human cultures over thousands of years.

Conclusion

Historians in Israel who have written on various aspects of maritime history have dealt mainly with non-Jewish and non-Palestinian topics and have operated outside the frontiers of their nation-state and the boundaries of a national history by using European archives. Even dealing with typical Jewish documents, like the Geniza Letters, often requires visits to archives in Europe, Russia and the United States. Furthermore, more often than not the publications are in English and other European languages. It is a picture that is quite different from the image of traditional maritime history based on rich local archives, depicted by the late Frank Broeze in his "Introduction" to Broeze (ed.), *Maritime History at the Crossroads: A Critical Review of Recent Historiography* (St. John's, 1995), ix-xxi.

Nevertheless, notwithstanding the list of publications mentioned in this essay that refer to various maritime aspects, only four scholars identify themselves as maritime historians in Israel: Arenson, Gertwagen, Kashtan and Khalilieh. The last three practice maritime history at the university level, where Gertwagen and Khalilieh combine it with general history. Arenson, who left the University of Haifa in the 1980s, went on to found the Association of Man and Sea, which is concerned with educational programmes for young people and the wider public. The reason for this small number of maritime historians is the mistaken belief in Israeli academic circles that maritime history is too specialized and occupied merely with naval history, ships and underwater archaeology, whereas all the publications mentioned in this essay demonstrate clearly that maritime history cannot be divorced from general history. Topics like navigation, sea routes, naval architecture or ports and harbours are directly connected to maritime trade and naval activity. Moreover, they all also require expertise in other fields since, as some of the publications have shown, scholars deprived of this broader knowledge may come to erroneous conclusions, not unlike maritime historians who regard maritime subjects as detached from general history. In addition, many of the scholars mentioned above deal with maritime topics as by-products of their general research or as secondary elements within it. This may perhaps explain why it has been impossible thus far to create an Israeli Commission of Maritime History.

Printed and bound by CPI Group (UK) Ltd, Croydon, CR0 4YY

16/04/2025

14658576-0001